W.A.Harbinson was bo[illegible] nineteen years of age, h[illegible] Royal Australian Air Force (RAAF), serving in Australia, Thailand and Malaysia. Returning to London six years later, he became the editor of a variety of men's magazines and then began his long career as a freelance writer. His published works include a Number One US bestselling biography, *The Illustrated Elvis* (1975); two bestselling novels, *Genesis* (1980) and *Revelation* (1982); and a British bestseller biography, *Evita: Saint or Sinner* (1996). He is the author of the epic 'Projekt Saucer' series of novels, which remained in print for most of the 1990's. The five novels in the series are: *Inception*, *Phoenix* (nominated for the Arthur C. Clarke Award, 1995), *Genesis*, *Millennium* and *Resurrection*. Harbinson's early Australian novel, *The Running Man* (1967), was turned into a feature film, *The City's Edge*. He has also written for radio and adopted various film scripts into book form. His most recent works are the autobiographical *The Writing Game:Recollections of an Occasional Bestselling Author*, available only through the Internet at www.amazon.com; and *All at Sea on the Ghost Ship*, also available from www.amazon.com. W.A. Harbinson, when not travelling, which he does a lot, divides his time between an apartment in Paris, France, and a renovated farmhouse in West Cork, Ireland.

Projekt UFO

The Case for Man-Made Flying Saucers

W.A.Harbinson

BookSurge Publishing

ISBN 1-4196-7638-5

Designed in the Isle of Wight, Great Britain, by www.inkdigital.org

To order additional copies, please contact us.
BookSurge Publishing
www.booksurge.com
1-886-308-6235

Contents

Introduction i

Acknowledgements 1

Foreword 2

Chapter 1 7
Biblical and Other Historical UFO Sightings

Unidentified flying objects in ancient records - Aerial phenomena interpreted in the Bible as religious apparitions or visions - The planet Venus; mock suns and moon dogs; meteors; lenticular and noctilucent clouds; temperature inversions; plasmoids, corona discharges and ball lightning - Ancient astronaut proponents - The fantasy world of Erich von Däniken - The Book of Ezekiel - Ancient reports and paintings explained in the light of modern atmospheric and astrological knowledge.

Chapter 2 31
The Great Airship Scare of 1896-7

First recorded use of the word 'saucer' in relation to UFOs- The wave of mystery airship sightings of 1897 - Newspaper speculation, misidentifications, hysterical imaginings and hoaxes - First contact with airship passengers - Photographs - Reported crashes - Final sighting - European development of similar airships -

United States patents and drawings - Technology of the period in support of advanced airship designs - The Massachussetts Institute of Technology (MIT) and Sibley College, Cornell University, Ithica, New York - The greatest period in the history of Aviation - The mysterious Mr. Wilson - The airship of Edward Joel Pennington.

Chapter 3 53
Technology and Sightings of World War II

The 'foo' fighters of World War II - UFOs over Western Europe and Scandinavia - Great aviation achievements - The Russian and American rocket geniuses, Tsiolokovski and Goddard - The German Amateur Rocket Society - Rocket development at Kummersdorf - Captain Walter Dornberger, Werner von Braun, and the German Rocket Research Institute - Rocket development at Peenemünde - The boundary layer: a new branch of aerodynamics - Vertical-rising aircraft - The first jet-propulsion aircraft – The 'all wing' aircraft of Germany's Walter and Riemer Horten - Suction airfoils, porous metals, and the concept of circular, remote-controlled aircraft - German secret weapons and military technology - the disk-shaped Feuerball.

Navy Commander R. B. McLaughlin - Three positive cases cited by Captain Edward J. Ruppelt - Confirmation that UFOs are intelligently controlled vehicles - UFOs finally accepted as genuine phenomenon.

Chapter 6 113
The UFO Invasion

Cinetheodolite camera stations of the White Sands Proving Range -UFO photos and films - The Lubbock lights - The Fort Monmouth Sightings - Air Technical Intelligence Centre (ATIC) investigates - The Pentagon is informed - The UFO 'invasion' of Washington D.C. - The White House is surrounded - Ruppelt is frustrated - Retractions and disinformation - Operation Mainbrace - A growing belief in US flying saucers.

Chapter 7 129
The Man-Made Flying Saucers

US concern that the flying saucers are of Russian origin - the flying saucer of Jonathan E. Caldwell - UFOs seen most often over top-secret military areas - First mention of flying saucer project at A.V. Roe, Canada - Russians planning to build Horten 'flying wing' aircraft – From flying wings to flying saucers -The US Navy's Flying Flapjack - The US News and World Report *speculates - Similarities between Flying Flapjack and UFO sightings over the White Sands Proving Range - Flying Flapjack project dropped and prototype stored with Smithsonian Institution - New flying saucer project at AVRO Canada, Malton, Ontario - The photograph of Jack Judges - The Avrocar is unveiled -* The Royal Air Force Flying Review *confirms - Canadian Minister of Defence announces the termination of the project - US Air Force Secretary announces new flying saucer project - The Frost flying disk - Reporters allowed to view the Frost saucer - The flying saucer described - Comparison between Frost saucer and Lubbock sightings - Canadian and US government announce end of saucer projects - Possibility of Soviet, Canadian and US flying saucers based on World War II German designs.*

Chapter 8 147
UFO Landings and UFOnauts

Dr J. Allen Hynek - Four kinds of UFO contact - The dubious claims of Frank Scully - Crashed saucers and frozen alien corpses - The mysterious Hangar 18 - Senator Barry M. Goldwater and astronaut Gordon Cooper - A collection of UFO landings - More landings at Holloman AFB - The Roswell incident analyzed - Investigations of Roswell incident by William Moore and Stanton Friedman - Roswell recollections of W.W. Brazel - The crash at Magdalena - The Socorro incident analyzed - Examination of the Socorro landing site - Investigations of the Socorro incident by Ray Stanford - The UFO insignia - The possibility of a man-made craft from the White Sands Proving Range.

Chapter 9 179
UFOnauts and Close Encounters

The Freedom of Information Act - From World War II technology to the modern UFO - The White Sands Proving Ground - The case advanced for man-made, disk-shaped aircraft - CE-IV, or Close Encounters of the Fourth Kind - The fantasy of George Adamski - Some other farfetched abductee stories - The New Hampshire case -The Pascagoula case - Dr James A. Harder's automata - The CE-IV at Alamogordo - Hypnotism, paralysis and psychosomatic illnesses - Other famous contactee cases and their UFOnauts - Explanations within the present technology - Mental and physical mind control - Floating contactees and UFOnauts - A reason for amnesia - Dr Walter Hess and electrode implantation - The robotizing of the human being - Experiments behind closed door - Computer-controlled implanted humans - Artificial organs and synthetic skin - Myoelectric prosthetics and other surgical nightmares - The most extreme operation known to surgical science - David Fishlock's Man Modified - *Vance Packard's* The People Shapers - *Human guinea pigs - Harvesting the living dead - Head transplants and two-headed dogs - The lack of legal, ethical and religious restraint - Man-machine interaction, including phantoms, CAMS, and exoskeletons - Thought control of man-machine manipulators and advanced prosthetics - Ethics in medical progress - The case for the cyborg.*

Chapter 11 239
Speculations on Terrestrial UFO Bases

Unidentified Submarine Objects, or USOs - The case for and against the Bermuda Triangle - Charles Berlitz's Without A Trace - *Connections with the Devil's Sea - Magnetic aberrations - Dr Manson Valentine's theory of dematerialization - Undersea laboratories and USO bases - Back on dry land - Renato Vesco's theory of Canadian origin of the flying saucers - The 'hollow Earth' Theory - The Essa-7 satellite photographs - Ray Palmer's theory of holes at the Poles - The exploitation of Rear-Admiral Richard E. Byrd - The Land Beyond the Pole and Rainbow City - What Byrd actually said - The 'hollow Earth' theory disproved - Ice-free areas in Antarctica - Antarctic exploration and territorial claims - Mysticism in Nazi Germany - The 'World Ice' theory of Hans Hörbiger - The lost civilisation of Thule - Nordic man and the Master Race - Heredity research, anthropological experiments, and human breeding colonies - Nazi secret weapons and underground spaces - The Antarctic voyage of Captain Alfred Rischter - Neu Schwabenland is created and protected by German gunboats - Submarine U-977 - An Argentinean connection - The International Geophysical Year (IGY) OF 1957-58.*

'I have never seen what I would personally consider to be a flying saucer. I've spoken to thousands of people who have. I spent fourteen years in industry as a nuclear physicist, chasing neutrons and gamma rays, radiation shielding. I have never seen a neutron or a gamma ray; I think they're real too. I've never even seen Australia, but it's there'

-Stanton T. Friedman

For Adam Webb

Introduction

After all these years...

'**In 1945** Allied pilots submitted reports which described mysterious "fireballs" that tailed their aircraft during night missions over Germany. **In 1950** a now-declassified CIA document revealed the agency's concern that "a far advanced German science" was the origin of the many flying saucers sighted since the end of the war. **In 1952** a secret US Air Force Memorandum for the Record stated: "Discussions with astronomers have produced an argument which seems to exclude non-terrestrial origin of the saucers." **In 1953** a now-declassified CIA report revealed that Air Force engineers at the A.V. Roe Company were engaged in the construction of a flying saucer prototype based on World War II German designs. **By 1960** many people were claiming, even under hypnosis, that they had been abducted by "aliens" in flying saucers and submitted to unusual painful surgical examinations. ***By 1970*** eminent surgeons and biotechnicians were openly discussing experimentation with microelectric control of the brain, surgical mutation to produce cyborgs for work in outer space, and other forms of nightmarish science. **In 1990** an award-winning American reporter revealed that the US government had formed a top-secret UFO Working Group whose members met regularly in the Pentagon. Finally, **in 1995**, after a decade of research, bestselling author W.A.Harbinson has produced *Projekt UFO: The Case for Man-Made Flying Saucers* – arguably the definitive UFO book.'

So said the dust-jacket of the hardcover edition of this book, originally published in 1995 by Boxtree, London. It was a fairly accurate description of the contents. Alas, when the paperback edition was published a year later, an enterprising editor had written a shorter description, most likely without reading the book. In this new cover-text it was claimed that 'Harbinson offers proof that UFOs come not from outer space but are the result of a secret ex-Soviet project…' By adding, 'Furthermore, the Soviets lifted most of their technology from the Nazis,' the editor managed to emphasize even more that the book was about secret *Soviet* flying saucer construction projects. The US and Canada, clearly shown in the book to be the major perpetrators, weren't even given a mention.

Alas, I was not shown a copy of the cover until the paperback had been printed and bound, by which time it was too late to correct the misrepresentation. As readers of the first edition of this book will know – and as readers of this new edition are about to find out – *Projekt UFO* is actually about joint US-Canadian flying saucer construction projects, with the Soviets playing only a minor role.

Of course, to even mention such misrepresentation is to invite UFO conspiracy theorists to insist that it was a clandestine attempt, possibly engineered by British, Canadian or US Intelligence, to shift attention away from the true source of the man-made flying saucers. This is not too much different from what happened when I, then a fledgling writer, naïvely gave the original publishers of my novel *Genesis* my only copy of the German magazine, *Brisant*, instead of a photocopy. Naturally, they lost it. In this instance 'lost' almost certainly means 'lost', but for years after the publication of the novel I was to read articles (mostly on the Internet) claiming either that *Brisant* had never existed in the first place or that my copy, a true rarity, had been 'stolen' from the publisher's offices. To this was added the novel theory that I had been tasked to write *Genesis*, the subsequent 'Projekt Saucer' series of novels based upon it, and, one must suppose, this non-fiction work, in order to deflect attention from the *true* source of the flying saucers. I had been tasked to do this either by the National Security Agency (NSA), which sought to deflect attention from their real 'black' technology projects (research programs so highly classified that they cannot be identified publicly), or by the extraterrestrials themselves, who, having 'brain-implanted' me without my knowledge, were using me, as an author of *man-made* UFO books, to deflect attention from their regular incursions into Earth's atmosphere in their own flying saucers.

Paranoia stalks the world of the UFOlogist. Naturally, I cannot prove that I am neither a NSA agent nor the victim of an extraterrestrial brain-implant, but can only use this space to insist that I am neither. In defence of my normality, I will even confess that I have never seen what I personally would consider to be a flying saucer. But, like physicist Stanton T. Friedman, quoted at the front of *Projekt Saucer*, defending his own admitted lack of UFO sightings: 'I've never even seen Australia, but it's there.' So while not sharing the paranoia of my fellow UFO conspiracy theorists, I would simply like to say that while I myself have doubts about certain theories put forward in this book, the technology described in it, much of it black technology, is still ongoing behind closed doors and cannot be stopped.

An update on such technology and other related UFO matters has been added as an Afterword to this new edition.

W.A.Harbinson

Acknowledgements

When planning this book, I decided from the onset to avoid the prejudices and misinformation of those with vested interests. This I did by taking the unprecedented step of researching without recourse to the major UFO organisations or individual UFOlogists, even where reportedly reliable. Instead, I focused on the literature, tried separating the wheat from the chaff influenced by nothing other than my own judgement, and otherwise relied only on the following, none of whom, to the best of my knowledge, belong to UFO groups or are blinded by an obsession with the subject.

My thanks to: Adam Webb, writer, researcher and computer wizard for his generous supply of video-and-cassette tapes, an introduction to cyberspace, and written information on a variety of UFO-related subjects. Bob Turner, Fleet Street librarian, writer and researcher, for valuable articles. Perrott Phillips, writer and editor, also for valuable articles. Ken Welsh, photographer and writer, for photographic assistance, great trips and moral support. Paul Grzybowski, for vintage newspaper accounts of the Great Airship Scare in general and the mysterious Mr Wilson in particular. Ruediger and Hannelore Vogt for assistance with German research and illustrations.

Thanks, also, to my former wife, Ursula Mayer, for the German translations; to her late brother, Willi Mayer, for giving me the information that kicked off the whole project; and last but not least to the late Alan Earney, an editor who liked writers and had faith in this project when it began as a novel, *Genesis*, many years ago.

W.A. Harbinson

Foreword

In May, 1978, at Stand 111 in a scientific exhibition in the Hanover Messe Hall, some gentlemen were giving away what at first sight appeared to be an orthodox scientific newspaper called *Brisant*. The paper contained two seemingly unrelated articles: one on the scientific and ecological value of the Antarctic, the other about a German World War II flying saucer construction program named 'Project Saucer' (*Projekt Untertasse*).

The first article, written from a neo-Nazi standpoint, included an assertion that West Germany should claim back their right to Queen Maud Land in the Antarctic, which the Nazis stole from the Norwegians during World War II and renamed Neu Schwabenland. The second article, which asserted that the German scientists were the first, but not the only ones, to construct highly advanced saucer-shaped aircraft, was accompanied by reproductions of technical drawings of a World War II flying saucer.

The unnamed author failed to name the designer of the flying saucer and claimed that the drawings had been altered by the West German government to render them 'safe' for publication. Adding weight to his claim, he also pointed out that during the Second World War, all such inventions, whether civilian or military, would have been submitted to the nearest patent office where, under paragraphs 30a and 99 of the *Patent-und Strafgezetsbuch*, they would have been routinely classified as secret, confiscated, and passed on to one of Himmler's many SS research establishments... and at the end of the war some of those patents disappeared into secret Soviet files, others disappeared into equally secret British and American files, and the remainder disappeared with 'missing' German scientists and SS troops.

The rest of the article was just as intriguing. It claimed that throughout the course of World War II the Germans sent ships and planes to Queen Maud Land, or Neu Schwabenland, in the Antarctic with equipment for massive underground complexes, similar to those they had constructed in Thuringia and the Harz Mountains, in Germany; that at the end of the war, some of the scientists and engineers who had worked on Project Saucer escaped from Germany by submarine and ended up in an underground base in the Antarctic, where they continued to construct even more advanced flying saucers; and that the Americans and Soviets, upon learning about this, then used their captured German scientists and technical papers for the secret construction of their own flying saucers.

This theory would explain why, even before glasnost, all the nations of the world, even the Soviets and the Americans, had cooperated with one-another only in the Antarctic.

In short, the flying saucers seen by so many people since World War II, are not extraterrestrial spacecraft, but are, in fact, extraordinarily advanced, top-secret, man-made machines.

They come from right here on Earth.

An unlikely scenario or a frightening truth?

Intrigued by this material, but uncertain of its veracity, I decided to turn it into a work of fiction. During my two years of intensive research, I uncovered written and photographic material which proved beyond doubt that Nazi Germany had in fact initiated a research program for the development of saucer-shaped aircraft; that at the close of the war seasoned Allied pilots were submitting official reports about harassment by 'balls of fire' that tailed them and made their aircraft and radar malfunction; that one of the leading members of Germany's Project Saucer development team disappeared into the Soviet Union and another went to work with German rocket expert, Werner von Braun, for NASA, in the United States; that most of the known post-war 'tailless' aircraft and 'flying wings' were constructed in the wilds of Canada; that the Canadian AVRO flying saucer, the existence of which was officially denied until it was photographed illicitly by an American journalist, was later handed over to the US, all too publicly proclaimed to have been a failure, then placed on display in the US Air Force Museum in Fort Eustis, Virginia; and, finally, that articles about man-made flying saucers, including the German *Kugelblitz* and the Canadian AVRO-Car prototype, had been published not only by the 'lunatic' fringe but by highly respected aeronautical magazines such as *Luftfahrt International*, the *Royal Air Force Flying Review*, and the *US News & World Report*.

So flying saucers, whether primitive or highly advanced, were certainly constructed in Nazi Germany and post-war Canada, in the latter case with the aid of the United States.

In 1980, my 615-page novel, *Genesis*, based on a mass of research material, including that mentioned above, was published. It became a bestseller on both sides of the Atlantic, eventually dropped off the bestseller lists, but then became a 'cult' book, and now, ten years after its publication, it remains in print.

Reviewing the novel on its publication in the US, *Publishers Weekly* said: 'Harbinson has drawn so heavily on factual material and integrated it so well into the text that the book begins to read like non-fiction...' This conclusion was drawn by other reviewers and over the years I received many letters from readers who obviously thought the same and asked me to tell them which parts of the book were fact and which were fiction.

Since responding individually to those many requests would have been an exhausting endeavour, I naturally avoided doing so. However, a continuing fascination with the subject, encouraged by the new, often startling data that continued to come my way via readers, UFO organisations and my own researches, eventually encouraged me to expand the original novel into a five-book series, *Projekt Saucer*, which would include much of this new material. It also convinced me that there was enough material for a non-fiction book on this unique, intriguing and often frightening subject.

The following pages are an attempt to separate fact from fiction regarding whether or not UFOs, or, more accurately, flying saucers, originate right here on Earth and have been designed and constructed, possibly in secret cooperation, by European, Soviet, Canadian and American scientists.

If the facts contained herein point to man-made flying saucers, then what we are faced with is an unprecedented, international cover-up... and the most nightmarish official secret of our times.

The facts are as follows..

Chapter 1

Biblical and Other Historical UFO Sightings

Ancient monuments, artifacts, paintings and written records bear eloquent witness to the history of man's visions and rationalizations for the unknown, showing gods, devils, angels, ghosts, sundry monsters, winged chariots, flying ships and shields, and other magical manifestations in an eternal struggle between good and evil, which changes, with the passing of time, only in its externals.

The gap between flying carpets and flying saucers is not all that large. Both may be serving a purpose for different ages and cultures: to explain the inexplicable, make sense of the unknown, reduce mysteries to comprehensible terms, make real what seems unreal. Only in the light of modern atmospheric and astrological knowledge have we come to learn about comets, meteors, lenticular and noctilucent clouds, dust and ice crystals, temperature inversions, corona discharges, plasmoids, ball-lightning, parhelia and paraselenae, or mock suns and sundogs, mock moons and moondogs. In ancient times such phenomenon were viewed as mystical visions or visitations by the gods of the sea or sky. In modern times they are mistaken for UFOs.

The term 'flying saucers' was coined only in 1947, but UFOs, or Unidentified Flying Objects, go back to the dawn of time.

What appear to be unusual flying objects, often disk-or cigar-shaped, have been found in prehistoric cave drawings. The earliest written record of a strange object in the sky is by the Egyptian Pharaoh Thutmose III, circa 1504-1450 B.C. Aristotle, the fourth century B.C. Greek philosopher, made references to 'heavenly disks' and claimed to have seen a meteorite fall at Aegospotami, rise up in the wind, and descend elsewhere. The first century B.C. Roman historian, Livy, recorded phantom ships gleaming in the sky, an 'altar' surrounded by men in white clothes which was seen in the sky at Hadria in 214 B.C., and approximately thirty other celestial phenomena, some of which have since been interpreted as descriptions of UFOs. Also of great interest to modern UFOlogosts are the references by the first century Roman historian, Cicero, to nine celestial phenomena, the most notable of which is his statement that on one occasion the sun was seen *at night*, accompanied by loud noises in the sky, which seemed to split open, revealing strange spheres. During the reign of Alexander the Great, two 'UFO' reports were recorded: in 329 B.C., two shining 'silver shields' dived repeatedly on Alexander's army while the men were attempting to cross the Jaxartes River into India; and in 322 B.C., during Alexander's siege of Tyre, a triangular formation of five round 'shields' circled over Tyre and destroyed its walls and towers with beams of light, thus enabling Alexander's legions to conquer the city. According to Pliny, in 66 B.C. a spark fell from a star, descended towards Earth until it was the size of a moon, then stopped and remained hovering in the sky for a while, diffusing cloudy light. It took the shape of a blazing torch when it returned to the sky.

If a trained, twentieth-century pilot can mistake natural atmospheric phenomena for a flying saucer, what must our distant ancestors have thought about the sky's more magical offerings? UFOlogists of the 'ancient astronauts' ilk repeatedly remind us that many of the IFO (Identified Flying Objects) such as aircraft, weather balloons, rockets and satellites, which are mistaken for UFOs (Unidentified Flying Objects), did not exist in ancient times; but even then, natural atmospheric phenomena offered plenty to confuse the eye and ear - more so given what was then a relatively limited knowledge of the atmosphere.

For instance, it was not then known that the planet Venus, when viewed under certain atmospheric conditions, will appear as a glowing orb that moves in the most extraordinary patterns. Nor was it known that comets, meteors, clouds, plasmoids, corona discharges, parhelia and paraselenae, the sun and moon and stars, even lightning and birds, can all look like bright, solid objects moving at high speed.

Mock suns, or sundogs, are caused by the sun's light, which can reflect an eerie image of the sun onto shifting clouds. Similarly, when the moon is close to the horizon, or when it enters cloud, it can take on strange shapes and colours, giving the illusion that it is in flight or magically hovering - a mock moon, or moondog (paraselenae). Other UFOs are caused when the light of the moon shines on ice particles contained in drifting clouds, making the particles seem like shining, round-shaped objects in flight, in the phenomenon known as parhelia.

Stars offer many illusions, notably the phenomenon known as 'atokinesis' in which a given star will appear to move in the dark sky, sometimes darting about erratically just like a glowing flying saucer. In this context, a cloud obscuring a star can do so in a manner that makes the star appear to streak away at tremendous speed or even 'go out like a light bulb' - again, as many UFOs appear to do.

Meteors are minute pieces of rock which flare up as they enter the Earth's atmosphere and are heated to incandescence by the friction. Mostly white in colour, they often appear as a spectacular streak of light in the sky - and meteor showers, which are common, can look to the untrained eye like a whole formation of UFOs in flight. Larger meteors, which take longer to burn up and seem to move more slowly across the sky in near horizontal trajectories, are known as 'fireballs' or 'bolides' and are often a spectacular orange or greenish-blue in colour.

Lenticular clouds are formed in circular, dome-shaped layers and, appearing singly or in groups, are often mistaken for domed, disk-shaped UFOs. Even more spectacular are noctilucent clouds, formed miles high in the atmosphere by ice particles and debris, and visible only at night. Given their tremendously high altitude, the sun can reflect off them, even at night, thus causing an eerie crimson luminescent mass, again shaped like a UFO, or flying saucer, that is visibly moving (as the cloud is moving).

A similar phenomenon is caused by temperature inversions: various layers of air, all at different temperatures, which bend and twist and generally distort rays of light to create what is best termed a mirage. Indeed, a temperature inversion can pick out a boat at sea and project it as a vivid mirage in the sky, with its shape often distorted enough to make it resemble a strange flying object. Similarly, given the proper temperature inversion, lights glowing up from the dark earth at night can be bent and sent traveling, then bounce off another temperature inversion many miles away and appear to the observer of the second inversion as a mass of glowing, darting objects.

The highly reflective underbellies of certain birds have often been mistaken for UFOs, as have bioluminescent clouds of insects, various kinds of windblown, light-reflecting debris, and even the natural gases given off from marshlands.

Various forms of lightning can also be mistaken for UFOs. While 'forked' lightning is recognizable to even the most untrained eye, 'sheet' lightning, which flashes only briefly, can be misinterpreted as a speeding UFO. As for plasmoids, corona discharges and 'ball lightning', they are basically formed by electrified gas that when burning brightly oscillates, vibrates, wobbles, flies horizontally, climbs vertically, glows in blue and red colours, and can look like a sphere or disk or a gigantic torpedo. They also hum and make other strange sounds and can be very frightening.

The skies, then as now, were filled with enough bizarre atmospheric phenomena to make those mentioned above believe they were either having mystical visions or witnessing visitations from the gods or other extraterrestrial creatures. But why, in the light of modern knowledge, do so many persist in believing that those ancient monuments, artifacts, paintings and writings were primitive reproductions of UFOs and their occupants?

The widespread, contemporary belief that descriptions of UFOs in general or flying saucers in particular can be found in numerous biblical and other historical writings was first stirred by a string of popularizing 'factual' books published during the UFO craze caused by the Kenneth Arnold sightings of 1947 and continuing into the 1960s. The first of these, published in the United States in 1956, was *UFO and the Bible*, written by astrophysicist Morris K. Jessup, who proposed that many of the Bible's improbable events would seem more probable if read as descriptions of the intervention of alien superintelligences brought to Earth by UFOs. This was followed by the British publication in 1960 of *The Sky People*, in which UFOlogist Brinsley Le Poer Trench, actually the Earl of Clancarty and former editor of *Flying Saucer Review*, paraded a wide-ranging, largely unsubstantiated range of opinions on the theme of extraterrestrials: notably that they had come from the region of the Great Bear, the Little Bear and Sirius, had seeded the human race to create *Homo sapiens*, were still returning periodically to review human progress, and may even have underground bases on Earth for their flying saucers. *The Morning of the Magicians*, by Louis Pauwels and Jacques Bergier, first published in France in 1960, and *One Hundred Thousand Years of Man's Unknown History* by another Frenchman, Robert Charroux, published in France in 1963, were bestselling books that covered a much broader spectrum of esoteric subjects, including the Ark of the Covenant, the Great Pyramid, the lines on the plain of Nazca, the statues of Easter Island, the Gate of the Sun at

Tiahuanaco, the drawings in the caves of Tassili, the Piri Re'is map, and the destruction of Sodom and Gomorrah - all of which, according to the authors, were evidence for Earth's visitation by alien spacecraft and their occupants.

The theories of these authors were later regurgitated and exploited with extraordinary success by the Swedish author, Erich von Däniken, who, more than any other individual, created an almost fanatical, worldwide belief in extraterrestrial intervention in human affairs.

Erich Von Däniken wrote *Chariots of the Gods?* in 1966, the same year that the 'God is dead' movement got under way and *Intelligent Life in the Universe*, a serious work, co-authored by astronomers I.S. Shklovskii of the USSR and Carl Sagan of the US, was published. *Intelligent Life in the Universe* is an attempt between a noted Russian astronomer and a leading American space scientist to speculate on 'the origins of the universe, the evolution of stars and planets, the beginnings of life on Earth, and the development of intelligence and technical civilizations among galactic communities' based firmly on the scientific knowledge of that time. As such, it certainly lent legitimacy to the idea that extraterrestrial life was a distinct possibility. However, ignoring the scientifically based, speculative approach of Shklovskii and Sagan in favour of startling, dogmatic theories based on a combination of selective facts, misinterpretations, outright invention, and the unreliable works of his abovenamed predecessors, Erich von Däniken managed to create, in a series of bestselling books, an immensely popular fantasy of cosmic proportions.

As Ronald Story shows in greater detail in his definitive exposé, *The Space Gods Revealed* (1978), consistency is not one of von Däniken's strong points. In *Chariots of the Gods?* his basic thesis is that alien visitors discovered Earth accidentally, observed that it had the necessary conditions for the development of intelligent life, began breeding experiments on its apelike creatures, artificially fertilized some of the females, and have returned throughout the ages (in flying saucers) to check on the progress of *Homo sapiens* and weed out those likely to hold back the march to civilization. In an era in which skepticism about God and religion was commonplace, even fashionable, von Däniken's view of evolution presented a novel replacement for lost faith. However, in his second book, *The Gold of the Gods*, he offers a completely different theory.

In this scenario, the extraterrestrials landed on Earth after losing in a cosmic war and fleeing from their enemies in a spaceship. Since Earth's atmosphere was not suited to them, they built a series of underground tunnels in which they hid from their pursuers, and after using various fantastic methods to get rid of their enemies, returned to the surface of the earth, wearing helmets, gas masks and other breathing equipment to help them adjust to Earth's atmosphere (which explains the 'astronaut' drawings found in many prehistoric cave drawings, such as the one in Tassili, in the Sahara Desert). Naturally, once back on Earth's surface, the extraterrestrials manipulated the genes of monkeys to create intelligent human beings in their own image, exterminated those who didn't shape up quickly enough… and so on and so forth.

Von Däniken spiced this rich stew with many of the equally wild theories of Pauwels, Bergier and Charroux. By doing so, he managed to sell millions of copies of his books and spread the belief that man was not created by God or cosmic accident, but by vastly superior, extraterrestrial beings.

Unlikely as it seems, support for von Däniken's theories came from Josef F. Blumrich, member of the American Institute of Aeronautics and Astronautics, the American Association for the Advancement of Science and the American Astronautical Society and, at the time of his retirement in 1974, Chief of the Advanced Structural Development Branch of the National Aeronautics and Space Administration (NASA) and winner of NASA's Exceptional Service Medal.

In a bid to *disprove* von Däniken's claim that the Biblical prophet Ezekiel had witnessed the landing and departure of an alien spacecraft, Blumrich ended up doing the opposite by attempting to design a spacecraft based on Ezekiel's descriptions, then publishing his findings in *The Spaceships of Ezekiel* (1974). With technical drawings, dense scientific prose and, in the words of Ronald Story, 'an extreme form of rationalization', Blumrich attempts to prove that Ezekiel was describing a spacecraft or, at least, some kind of highly advanced helicopter.

As Blumrich's scientific respectability has lent such credence to von Däniken's contradictory ramblings, it may be worthwhile to compare what Ezekiel actually said with what von Däniken and his supporters deduced from it.

In the Book of Ezekiel, Chapter 1, Ezekiel describes how 'a whirlwind came out of the north, a great cloud, and a fire unfolding itself, and a brightness *was* about it...' Out of the amber-coloured cloud and fire of this materialization, or supposed spacecraft, emerged four living creatures which had 'the likeness of a man'. However, while resembling normal men in certain ways, each creature had 'the sole of a calf's foot' and 'the face of a lion' on the right side, 'the face of an ox' on the left side, as well as 'the face of an eagle'. Each creature also had four wings, which were 'on their four sides' and were joined one to another. 'And their wings were stretched upward; two wings of every one were joined one to another, and two covered their bodies.' Thus joined together by their wings, which revealed human hands beneath, the creatures 'turned not when they went; they went every one straight forward.'

Ezekiel goes on to say: 'Their appearance was like burning coals of fire, and like the appearance of lamps; it went up and down among the living creatures; and the fire was bright, and out of the fire went forth lightning... And the living creatures ran and returned as the appearance of a flash of lightning.'

Proponents of the ancient astronauts hypothesis, including von Däniken and Blumrich, insist that the 'brightness' within a 'great cloud' and 'fire' is a perfect description of a landing UFO; the creatures with the combined features of lion, ox, eagle and calf were astronauts in bulky spacesuits and oxygen masks; the 'wings' which revealed human hands beneath were actually the rotor-blades of some kind of mechanical device being controlled by the astronauts; and the 'lightning' and 'appearance of lamps' from which the creatures emerged and to which they returned are further indications that they were observed leaving and entering a UFO with brightly lit portholes.

In verse 15, Ezekiel states that in the fire and lightning near these creatures he beheld 'a wheel upon the earth.' In the following verse, the singular has become plural: 'The appearance of the wheels and their work was like unto the colour of a beryl... and their appearance and their work was as it were a wheel in the middle of a wheel... When they went, they went upon their four sides; and they turned not when they went.'

By verse 18, this wheel within a wheel has become more machine-like: 'As for their rings, they were so high that they were dreadful; and their rings were full of eyes round about them four...' The four living creatures are now picked up in the fire and lightning, but more importantly: 'And when the living creatures went, the wheels went by them: and when the living creatures were lifted up from the earth, the wheels were lifted up' and 'the spirit of the living creatures was *in* the wheels...'

Ignoring the religious symbolism and insignia in such descriptions and instead interpreting them as primitive descriptions of advanced technology, the proponents of the ancient astronauts hypothesis insist that the 'wheel in the middle of a wheel' and the 'rings full of eyes' are perfect descriptions of a flying saucer, with its ring-disks revolving around its domed centre and illuminated portholes.

Likewise viewing Ezekiel's words as primitive attempts to describe highly advanced technology, Blumrich interpreted Ezekiel's 'wings' as rotary blades which made a loud noise while moving ('And when they went, I heard the noise of their wings, like the noise of great waters, as the voice of the Almighty': Ezekiel 1: 24) and which folded like wings when not in use ('When they stood, they let down their wings...'). Basing his experimental work on such assumptions, he then attempted to design Ezekiel's spacecraft and came up with 'a capsule on a main body supported by four helicopter units with telescopic legs, retractable wheels and mechanical arms.'

According to Margaret Sachs, in *The UFO Encyclopedia*, Blumrich 'believes that the robot-like appearance of the helicopter units may have led Ezekiel to describe them as living creatures. And even though Ezekiel later refers to the creatures as cherubim, Blumrich insists that this was because 'he had realized they were not ordinary men.'

Other UFOlogists are just as insistent on this extraterrestrial interpretation of Ezekiel's visions. For instance, by Chapter 1:19, the creatures, still joined together each by two of their four wings, are ascending toward the sky inside the wheel-like craft. According to Ezekiel, 'the likeness of the firmament upon the heads of the living creatures was as the colour of the terrible crystal, stretched forth over their heads above... And above the firmament that was over their heads was the likeness of a throne, as the appearance of a sapphire stone...'

What is actually being described here?

Ezekiel makes it perfectly clear in the first verse of this chapter that he is not describing a real event, but a religious vision, or, in his own words, 'visions of God'. It is therefore evident that the creatures he describes are cherubim - a cherub being a winged figure with a human head and animal body. Such mythical creatures are of early astrological significance and can be found in various cultures in the shape of the sphinx and winged bulls and lions. Indeed, since Ezekiel describes his creatures as having the combined features of a 'lion', an 'ox', and an 'eagle,' as well as 'the sole of a calf's foot', it is worth noting that in early astronomy and cosmology, the Lion represents the summer solstice, the Bull the vernal equinox, the Eagle the winter, and the Babylonian 'Scorpion-man' the autumnal equinox.

As we have seen, various atmospheric phenomena look like shining disks or flying 'wheels' and would certainly have been part of the mystical consciousness of the time. As astronomer and astrophysicist Donald Menzel has noted, a common form of parhelia takes the form of a ring of light around the sun, or 'a wheel in the middle of a wheel'. In this particular optical illusion 'a vertical and a horizontal streak of light may cross both rings like the spokes of a wheel'. The wheel is also symbolic of the Sun and the Moon; and in ancient times the wheels of chariots often had the likeness of various creatures carved into them. Thus 'wheel' shapes are common as symbols or insignia in numerous ancient records, as well as in paintings and on artifacts.

In order to interpret 'the likeness of the firmament' that was above the living creatures as something that was solid and had 'the colour of the terrible crystal', the 'likeness of a throne', and the 'appearance of a sapphire stone' - in other words, a second, larger flying saucer, or mother ship - the UFOlogists ignore Ezekiel's earlier statement that he is describing 'visions of God', not real phenomenon. More tellingly, they also ignore the rest of the chapter, which states that 'upon the likeness of the throne' was the likeness of a man from whose loins poured 'the appearance of fire' and who was surrounded by 'the bow that is in the cloud in the day of rain.'

We can assume, then, that this is not a description of another astronaut in a flying saucer, or the mother ship. Rather, as Ezekiel states categorically in the final verse of Chapter 1: 'This *was* the appearance of the likeness of the glory of the LORD.'

In short, a religious vision of God and his cherubim, which made Ezekiel fall to his knees and pray.

As Erich von Däniken and other proponents of the ancient astronaut hypothesis have pillaged most of the Bible for supposed references to ancient astronauts and their flying saucers, to refute them all would require the whole of this book. It will, however, be instructive to deal with a few of the most often used, or abused, subjects.

According to proponents of the ancient astronaut hypothesis, the Ark of the Covenant was actually an electric condenser or radio transmitter; the Great Pyramid could only have been built by, or with the aid of, extraterrestrials of superior technical knowledge; the lines on the plain of Nazca, Peru, were either runways or landing sites for alien spacecraft; the gigantic statues of Easter Island and the mighty temples of Tiahuanaco could only have been constructed by a highly advanced, therefore extraterrestrial, technology; the drawings in the caves of Tassili, in the Sahara Desert, circa 6000 B.C., are of an extraterrestrial astronaut; the Piri Re'is map, drawn in 1513 by a Turkish general of that name, could only have been completed with knowledge gained from an aerial survey of Earth, therefore by extraterrestrials; and the destruction of Sodom and Gomorrah can only be explained as the result of an atomic or nuclear blast.

What truth is there in these theories?

According to the Book of Exodus, the Ark of the Covenant was a chest built by Moses, under instructions from God, to be used as a repository for sacred objects and carried only by divinely appointed persons. In the Book of Numbers it is stated that a person touching any holy objects in the Ark will die; and in the Second Book of Samuel, a man named Uzzah is struck dead upon attempting to steady the Ark with his hand.

While there is no mention anywhere in the Bible of the Ark being surrounded by sparks, von Däniken claims that it was, that its bearers were instructed to wear special protective shoes and clothing, and that Uzzah was killed by electrocution. However, writer Clifford Wilson argues that since no two pieces of gold on the Ark were separated by an insulator, there was no possibility of there being a negative and a positive plate; that if the ark *had* been charged, it would have short-circuited; and that if Uzzah had truly been killed by electrocution, then so too would have been the bearers of the Ark. Wilson also points out that as God had communicated with Moses before the Ark was built, he had no need of the radio transmitter for the reasons suggested by von Däniken.

The pyramids of Egypt are the oldest of the Seven Wonders of the World and the most famous are the three pyramids at Giza. Of these, the largest is known as the Great Pyramid and was built by Pharaoh Khufu, or Cheops.

According to von Däniken and others, the pyramids could not have been built without the superior knowledge and tools of extraterrestrials. In support of his claims, von Däniken insists that the ancient Egyptians could not have moved the massive blocks of the Great Pyramid with rollers and ropes, as suggested by scholars and archaeologists, since they had no rope or wood at that time. This is nonsense, as the many drawings of these items in Egyptian illustrations clearly demonstrate, as do the dated samples of rope and wood which have been found in the vicinity of the pyramids. Von Däniken also insists that the Egyptians would not have had the capability of levelling the ground for the pyramid so accurately; but various scholars have proven that they could, while a television documentary produced by the British Broadcasting company showed the method most likely used. Von Däniken states that the pyramid's stone blocks were joined together to a thousandth-of-an-inch, which was beyond the capability of the Egyptians; when in fact they are joined together to about two-hundredths-of-an-inch, which certainly *was* within the capability of the ancient Egyptians. Von Däniken claims that it would have taken human workers, unaided by extraterrestrial technology, approximately 664 years to complete the construction; but the archaeological evidence indicates that the Great Pyramid, and others, were built within one century by ordinary human beings - and the study of Egyptian funerary edifices shows a logical, chronological development from small tombs to the true pyramids within the space of two centuries.

No evidence for extraterrestrial intervention in the

construction of the Great Pyramid or others has ever been found.

In claiming that the lines on the plain of Nazca, Peru, were runways for alien spacecraft, Von Däniken ignores the fact that contemporary spacecraft, let alone flying saucers or other craft of extremely advanced technology, do not need runways. He also ignores the fact that the surface of the Nacza Plain is not rigid enough to serve as a runway (automobiles and trucks that accidentally run off the man-made roads get stuck in the sandy soil and loose gravel) and the supposed 'runway' is less than one metre wide. Likewise, he ignores the fact that many religious groups throughout history have placed their gods in the skies and created figures and symbolic shapes that can only be seen from the air (even the 'cross' shape of Christian churches can be seen only from the air). Last but not least, in asserting that the Nazca lines could only have been formed with the help of airborne extraterrestrials, he ignores the fact that small-scale models have been found alongside some of the designs, thus suggesting that the immense figures were merely created from the models by human hands. In fact, when viewed from the air, the lines on the plain of Nacza form the very clear outlines of various totemic birds and animals.

Easter Island, located in the South Pacific, is famous for its hundreds of immense stone statues. As they have done regarding the stones of the Great Pyramid, von Däniken and his followers insist that the enormous weight of the Easter Island statues excludes the possibility of their having been transported and erected by the local people. To this argument von Däniken adds the fiction that the island did not have the wood required to make the rollers necessary for the human transportation of the statues (just as, according to von Däniken, the Egyptians did not have the rope and wood required for the construction of the Great Pyramid), and that the volcanic rock from which the statues are carved is too hard to have been cut with primitive tools.

In fact, although most of Easter Island's trees were destroyed by fire or cleared for agriculture, they once covered the whole island; and in 1955 the famous Norwegian explorer, Thor Heyerdahl, personally witnessed the local natives carve, transport and erect a typical Easter Island statue with primitive tools. According to Heyerdahl (*Aku-Aku - The Secret of Easter Island*, 1958), the outline of the statue became visible after only three days of cutting with primitive tools. Based on this observation, Heyerdalh estimated that even the largest statue on the island could have been completed in under a year. Heyerdalh also bore witness to the fact that 180 men were able to drag the completed statue over the ground to its chosen site with relative ease. Using wooden legs as levers and rocks as supports, twelve men were able to erect a twenty-five ton statue in a period of eighteen days.

So much for extraterrestrial intervention on Easter Island.

Regarding the mysterious civilization of Tiahuanaco, Bolivia, which constructed the great Gate of the Sun, von Däniken claims that a calendar which gives 'the equinoxes, the astronomical seasons, the positions of the moon for every hour and also the movements of the earth' was found in 'the dry mud of Tiahuanaco' and that the beings who 'produced, devised and used the calendar had a higher culture than ours.' This would be fascinating were it true... however, in the words of Donald Story, 'If this calendar exists, its whereabouts seem to be unknown'.

Von Däniken claims that the rock painting found in a cave in Tassili, in the Sahara, circa 6000 B.C., is of an extraterrestrial astronaut wearing a spacesuit and oxygen mask. In making this claim, however, von Däniken ignores the fact that many similar frescos are to be found in the same area, that they belong to an artistic period known as the 'Period of the Round Heads', and that the work of that period was based mainly on representations of the natives of the area who, in neolithic times, when the rock paintings were done, often wore masks for their religious rituals. The so-called 'spaceman', named by his French discoverer, the archaeologist Henri Lhote, as Jabbaren, or *le grand dieu martien*, is actually a neolithic, ritually masked celebrant - not the 'great god Mars', as suggested by von Däniken.

The Piri Re'is map? Drawn in 1513 by a Turkish general of that name and found in the Topkapi Palace in Istanbul in 1929, the map was based on many earlier charts, including Greek maps dating back to the time of Alexander the Great and one chart used by Christopher Columbus. The Pire Re'is map was considered of particular interest because it appeared to depict the coastlines of the Americas and Antarctica as they could not have been known at the time - particularly since the Antarctic was not discovered until Captain Cook reached it in 1773... 260 years after the map was drawn.

According to von Däniken, this and other ancient maps could only have been drawn by extraterrestrial spacemen from 'space stations in orbit'. To support his claim, he states that the Pire Re'is map is 'absolutely accurate', that 'the contours of the Antarctic were also precisely delineated' on it, and that Professor Charles H. Hapgood had suggested in his *Maps of the Ancient Sea Kings* that the map could only have been made from the air. In fact, as Hapgood's book makes abundantly clear, the Piri Re'is map is notoriously inaccurate, mistaking Cuba for *Espaniola* (now Haiti and the Dominican Republic), omitting almost a thousand miles of the South American coastline, duplicating the Amazon River in two different locations, and showing Antarctica as a landmass joined directly to South America.

Von Däniken claims originality for even this nonsensical theory, but he was actually beaten to it by almost a decade by Louis Pauwels' and Jacques Bergier's The Morning of the Magicians, Donald Keyhoe's *Flying Saucers: Top Secret*, and Robert Charroux's *One Hundred Thousand Years of Ma''s Unknown History*, none of which are to be recommended for their accuracy. While the Piri Re'is map is one of several that were found in the Topkapi Place, Istanbul, in 1929, Pauwel and Bergier claim that it was found in the middle of the nineteenth century, when Piri Re'is personally presented it to the Library of Congress; Charroux claims that it was found in 1957; Keyhoe claims that a Turkish naval officer submitted a copy of the map, plus the original Christopher Columbus map, to the US Navy Hydrographic Office in 1933, though he carefully omits to name the naval officer in question; and von Däniken, coming desperately late in the game but trying to take credit for it, claims in *Chariots of the Gods?*

that the map was discovered in the eighteenth century - though he amends this to the proper date in his later book, *In Search of Ancient Gods*.

As for the destruction of Sodom and Gomorrah, von Däniken plumbs new depths of irrationality by suggesting that the angel's urgency in making Lot and his wife flee from the impending catastrophe indicates that a 'countdown' was in progress and that the biblical account describes a nuclear explosion. The Bible gives not the slightest indication that a 'countdown' was taking place, but it certainly indicates, in Genesis, 19: 24, that 'the LORD rained upon Sodom and Gomorrah brimstone and fire from the LORD out of heaven' and, in verse 28, that 'lo, the smoke of the country went up as the smoke of a furnace'.

The ancient cities of Sodom and Gomorrah were located in the Great Rift Valley, an area that extends from approximately one hundred miles north of Palestine to the southern shore of the Dead Sea and has been subject to earthquakes since time immemorial. Geological and archaeological evidence indicates that the cataclysm described in the Book of Genesis did take place approximately 2000 B.C. in the form of an earthquake accompanied by explosions of a natural gas formed by the large quantities of oil, asphalt and sulphur, or brimstone, in the area.

It can reasonably be assumed from this that Sodom and Gomorrah were destroyed by a dreadful, but otherwise natural, earthquake and that extraterrestrial intervention had nothing to do with it.

Proponents of the ancient astronauts hypothesis are quick to grab at anything that lends legitimacy to their fanciful, unsubstantiated theories. Thus, Erich von Däniken is eager to point out that an 'outstanding technician' (Josef Blumrich) has taken his proposals seriously; just as countless numbers of UFOlogosts are deeply impressed by the fact that Brinsley Le Poer Trench is actually the Earl of Clancarty and a member of the House of Lords in London, England.

It may be *because* he is a member of the House of Lords, with all the power and prestige that goes with it, which accounts for the fact that the Earl of Clancarty, formerly of the Nautical College of Pangbourne, the Standard Bank of South Africa, the Royal Artillery, and the *RAF Flying Review* and *Practical Gardening*, managed in his lifetime to become Editor of *The Flying Saucer Review*; President of the worldwide UFO organization, Contact International; Vice President of the British UFO Research Association (BUFORA); an Honourary Life Member of the Ancient Astronaut Society; and head of a House of Lords All-Party UFO Study Group; as well as the author of numerous books about UFOs and their occupants. Certainly it was not due to the quality of his research or writing.

What von Däniken, Clancarty, and the others mentioned above, share is a naked desire to read ancient astronauts and flying saucers into biblical descriptions of earthquakes, volcanic eruptions, dust storms, lightning, other atmospheric phenomena, and visions filled with the religious symbols or insignia of the period. What they also share is a talent for misinterpretation, selective omission, wilful distortion, and even outright invention when it comes to analyzing the facts and figures of ancient history.

Perhaps the most notorious example of this is Erich von Däniken's 'blacked out' reproduction and accompanying explanation for the drawing on the lid of a Mayan sarcophagus, or coffin, found in the Temple of Inscriptions in Palenque, Mexico, in 1952. By deliberately blacking out various traditional Mayan elements in the painting reproduced in his book, von Däniken hopes to persuade us that the resulting work is a depiction of an ancient astronaut piloting a rocket. In fact, in the original, drawn from the incised stone by Agustin Villagra, the traditional Mayan elements show it to be a representation of the Mayan ruler, Pascal, suspended between the worlds of the living and the dead, with a quetzal bird (blacked out in von Däniken's reproduction) symbolizing the dawn, or the rising of the Sun God, perched on top of a cross, which is made of stylized corn plants, symbolizing fertility. The skull-like monster below Pascal's chair, when not partially blacked out by von Däniken, clearly represents the world of the living, or Earth.

As Colin Wilson says in *The Directory of Possibilities*, most of the evidence for ancient astronauts 'collapses on close examination'. Wilson also reminds us that the ancient-astronaut theory depends heavily upon the assumption that our ancestors were primitive and unsophisticated creatures, only one degree more intelligent than gorillas, whereas an increasing body of evidence suggests quite the opposite: that Neanderthal and Cro-Magnon Man were more civilized and inventive than suggested by von Däniken, Clancarty and Co.; that they carved stones into spheres and disks (which suggests Sun worship, rather than UFOs), and painted the Moon on their cave walls; and that they would not have needed the assistance of a superior intelligence from outer space to invent the wheel or build their megalithic monuments.

To conclude: UFOs, or Unidentified Flying Objects, were commonplace in the past; flying saucers and extraterrestrials were not.

Chapter 2

The Great Airship Scare of 1896-7

The term ‘flying saucer’ was coined in 1947 with the Kenneth Arnold sightings, as mentioned in Chapter One. However, the first known use of the word ‘saucer’ in relation to an unidentified flying object was actually made in the *Denison Daily News* of Denison, Texas, on 25 January 1878, when it recorded that farmer John Martin, of Dallas, had reportedly seen a large, orange object in the sky, which was ‘the size of a large saucer and evidently at great height’.

This isolated incident was followed nearly two decades later by the first truly contemporary UFO flap: the Great Airship Scare of 1896-1897. The two best reports of this extraordinary event are to be found in *The UFO Controversy in America* by David Michael Jacobs and *UFO Exist!* by Paris Flammonde. We can summarize the major events from these excellent works.

According to Flammonde, the prelude to the major UFO, or mystery airship, flap began modestly enough in late October 1896, when a Miss Hegstron caught sight of a glowing light in the sky near her home in San Francisco. However, the real flap began on 1 November when a mountainman and hunter named Brown related to a newspaper reporter that he had seen an ‘airship’ in the morning sky over Bolinas Ridge, near the city. Brown was adamant that what he had seen was not a light at night, but an 'airship' in broad daylight, albeit slightly obscured by the morning mist. This was followed by a brilliant white light that was witnessed by hundreds of people as it moved across the sky on the evening of 17 November. One witness, while unable to verify that what he saw was an actual craft of some kind, was adamant that the light had been moving *against* the wind at an altitude of three or four hundred feet. Another witness confirmed that the object was moving into the wind and added that while it was too far away for its specific shape to be distinguished, it carried 'controlled illumination' and moved like 'a seagoing craft ploughing rough water'. Countless other witnesses saw the traveling light and many stated that it was being manipulated to sweep both land and sea as if to avoid collision with high buildings or mountains. All of those who reported seeing the actual craft from which the light was beaming described it as being a large oblong shape with flattened ends, or an ovoid; though opinions differed as to whether its small passenger cockpit was located above the main body or was dangling underneath. Some witnesses insisted that they had seen members of the craft's crew; others swore that they had heard voices drifting down from the object.

As to be expected, that sighting led to an outbreak of wild newspaper speculation, misidentifications, hysterical imaginings, and hoaxes; but based on the more reliable sightings, the great airship was moving southwards and eventually, on the evening of 20 November, was observed by thousands of people as it glided across the sky over Oakland, California. One witness noted that apart from its large lamp, it had 'wings or winglike propellers' and was heading across the bay. This appears to be true, as the light beaming from the craft was later witnessed by inhabitants of the Mission area as it moved across Twin Peaks. Other sightings were made the next day and the following night, and all reported that the 'light' or 'enormous flying device' was heading southwards.

While an inflamed public imagination led to many fantastical, Jules Verne styled newspaper and magazine reports, individual witnesses were surprisingly consistent in what they described: an egg, cigar or ovoid shape; an up-and-down or 'wavy' flight pattern (like 'a seagoing craft ploughing rough water'); an upper cockpit or suspended gondola; and a light, often compared to an arc lamp, that swept to and fro, surveying the hills or township below. There was also general agreement that the craft was intelligently controlled.

The 'hoax' element raised its ugly head again when a lawyer from Alameda, George D. Collins, claimed that he was the personal representative of the 'inventor of the remarkable airship'; but after causing a nationwide press sensation with his claim, Collins recanted and the man named as the inventor, a dentist named E.H. Benjamin, insisted that he had nothing to do with airships or any other kind of aeronautical craft. Within twenty-four hours of this disclaimer, W.H.H. Hart, former attorney general of the State of California, announced that he was in charge of the 'destiny' of the airship, that this had come about because of Collins' 'inability to exercise discretion in his relationship with the press', that the real inventor of the airship was a Dr Catlin, and that the dentist, E.H. Benjamin, despite his denials, had been Catlin's assistant. Finally, even though the United States was not then at war with Cuba, Hart announced that the airship, with only two or three men, could be used to destroy the city of Havana within forty-eight hours. Not satisfied with this, the former attorney general then announced that the airship's inventor was 'the cousin of the electrician of General Antonio Marco, commander of the patriotic forces in Cuba.'

The use of Cuba is interesting in the light of later events (see below), but what remains most fascinating about Hart's highly voluble involvement in the Great Airship Scare is that it confused serious enquiry, opened the door to spurious 'official' pronouncements on the nature and purpose of the unidentified flying object, and made it more difficult to discover the truth - in other words, an early example of 'disinformation' with regard to UFOs.

Nevertheless, the great airship, or airships, continued to fly, with the sightings ranging from Tacoma, Washington, to southern California. The first actual 'contact' with the occupants of an airship was reportedly made in the morning of 2 December on the beach near Pacific Grove, a village north of San Francisco. According to the witnesses, there were three occupants and the airship was about twenty yards long, cigar-shaped, and had wings that could be folded against the fuselage of the craft. Many discounted this sighting when the witnesses reported that the three occupants had managed to lift the airship and carry it away from the beach, into hiding. The report of an airship crashing near Twin Peaks, San Francisco, during the following night was likewise treated with some skepticism and was almost certainly a newspaper invention.

A lull in the sightings between late 1896 and the first

months of 1897 was followed in April by an even greater number of truly startling sightings, now spreading out from California to sweep across the whole country. With what some thought was exquisite timing, the great airship suddenly appeared over Kansas City, Missouri, at approximately eight o'clock in the evening of April Fools Day 1897. For over an hour the craft's lamp swept the streets, rooftops and bluffs upon which the public, including the governor and other officials and professional people, gathered to observe the phenomenon. From these and other witnesses it was apparent that what was observed, apart from the sweeping light, was a large dark mass that could perform manoeuvres or hang motionless in the air. In the words of the New York *Sun* of 3 April 1897: 'the powerful lights on board were reflected on the cloud[s] and the outlines of a ship about thirty feet long apparently were clearly distinguished'. The mystery craft remained above Kansas City for ninety minutes, then ascended and moved off, eventually disappearing in the northwest. Shortly after, there were reports from the town of Everest, sixty miles away in the neighbouring state of Kansas, that an unidentified light had passed overhead.

The next night, the phenomenon appeared over Omaha, Nebraska, and was 'broadly recognized as a very real airship'. By the following evening it had reached Topeka, where it reappeared on several consecutive evenings, before disappearing and turning up again over Omaha, where, according to the New York *World* of 7 April 1897, 'it was the first time the outline of the vessel could be clearly seen'. Many brothers of the local Ak Sar Ben organization saw it and one of them described it as having 'a steel body, the length of which could only be estimated at thirty feet'.

As we shall see later, the 'steel' body could in fact have been thin aluminium, but certainly, whatever the craft was made of, by 7 April it had travelled a good distance eastward to appear over Sioux City, Iowa, where one witness described it as 'a big cigar-shaped balloon... about thirty-five feet long, ten or twelve thick...underneath it was a car... it had a row of windows along the side and the light shone through them.'

As Flammonde points out, by this time 'the growing catalogue of sightings makes it extremely difficult to attribute all of them to a single craft. The "high speeds" described were relative and not impressive by contemporary standards...' Therefore 'the large number of communities reporting UFOs at the same time makes the conclusion of more than one vessel reasonable.'

Whether one or many, by this time the mystery craft had been observed by thousands of people and there was increasing consistency about the descriptions of its major features. According to the majority of reports, it was some kind of balloon, approximately thirty or forty feet long, with folding wings along its side, a passenger gondola, a directable searchlight, and smaller green, red and white lamps. The majority of the witnesses were in agreement that the airship carried three crew members (at least two reports contradicted this by stating six crew members). The majority of witnesses also described the balloon as making 'hissing' noises and swore that the airship was under control and could manoeuvre or hover in the air. Practically every report confirmed that the directable searchlight was used to survey the terrain or townships below.

The craft kept traveling. On 10 April a newsstand dealer, Walter McCann, managed to take two photographs when an airship flew over Rogers Park in Illinois - an event which was witnessed by three other men and which was lent further credibility by the fact that numerous other people in the vicinity reported seeing such a craft at approximately the same time. Those photographs were reproduced in a couple of newspapers - the *Chicago Times-Herald* and the *New York Times*. While the former reproduced a pen-and-ink etching of the photograph and claimed that the etcher's 'expert' analysis had concluded that the photograph was genuine, its rival, the *Chicago Tribune*, after also reportedly having the photograph examined by an expert, claimed it was a fake. Nevertheless, true or false, the photographs showed a vessel shaped like an elongated ovoid which, according to Flammonde, had ‘the appearance of a large silk envelope, below which was a cabin of light construction, giving the appearance of white metal’.

Shortly after this sighting, there were newspaper reports that a mystery airship had crashed near Kalamazoo, Michigan. Reportedly, the crash was witnessed by ‘two old soldiers’ and corroborated by a local, Mrs Wallace, who claimed that her family had heard the noise of the crash, or explosion. It was also reported that parts of the machine had been found scattered over the area, some as much as two miles apart. Whether this was true or not, the reported ‘crash’ was followed by more mystery airship sightings from other parts of Michigan, as well as Oklahoma, Kansas, Illinois and Indiana. By 15 April another airship appeared over Chicago where, according to one account, it descended to approximately six hundred feet above the earth. Quoted in the New York *Herald* of 15 April 1897, witness G.A. Overocker stated: 'The lower portion of the airship was thin, and made of some light white metal, like aluminium. The upper portion was dark and long, like a big cigar, pointed in front and with some kind of arrangement in the rear to which cables were attached [see description of the 'Pennington' airship, below]. The pilot pulled these and steered the course from south to northeast... I can swear that I saw an airship.'

Daytime sightings were rare, but there was a remarkable one on 16 April when citizens of Linn Grove, Iowa, watched an airship pass slowly overhead, then land briefly a few miles outside town. Viewed by other citizens from a distance estimated at about two-thousand feet, the airship was described as having 'a twin pair of huge wings'. Even more mysteriously, when it took off again, it discharged 'two large boulders of unknown composition' - an incident that would be repeated during the famous Maury Island UFO sighting of 1947.

Meanwhile, mystery airships were being seen elsewhere, with further sightings over the San Francisco bay area. More importantly, a fisherman on Lake Erie, Cleveland, Ohio, got a close look at a forty-foot craft. He mistook this for another boat until 'an enormous, elaborately decorated, cylindrical balloon, approximately fifty feet in length, inflated' and 'swept the boat and its occupants at least two hundred yards into the sky, where it circled several times'. According to the witness, the airship's occupants were a young man, a woman, and a boy, one of whom threw out a large swordfish as the craft ascended.

At roughly the same time there were sightings as far apart as Missouri, Iowa, Tennessee, Kentucky, and several towns in Texas - which certainly suggests that more than one airship was crossing the country. A report of a daytime landing in Iowa led to press descriptions of a vessel 'forty feet long, constructed of varnished canvas stretched over a cigar-shaped frame and surmounted by a cockpit. It had wings, some kind of rudder, and a tail pipe exuding steam.' On 18 April a craft was sighted over Sisterville, West Virginia; viewed through binoculars, it matched other descriptions by being cone-shaped and having fins (or wings), and with brilliant red, green and white lights at one end.

The following day, an estimated three thousand people at Cripple Creek, Kansas, saw an unidentified object shining in the sunlight, hovering about a mile high in the sky. According to Flammonde: 'inspection through a telescope revealed a large, slowly moving, conical object'.

More reports, some of which were obviously hoaxes, poured in over the next few days until, on 30 April, the last airship was sighted by three people in the early hours of the morning over Yonkers, New York. According to witnesses, this final airship flew over Yonkers at approximately 3am, heading north toward the sea, before being swallowed up by the darkness.

The Great Airship Scare of 1896-1897 formally came to an end with that eerie sighting.

While the reaction of a largely hostile scientific community was to dismiss the sightings as optical illusions caused by atmospheric phenomena or hoaxes, their claims hold little water in view of the actual nature of the sightings. The Great Airship Scare of 1896-97 was not one in which people reported strange 'lights', 'ghost ships' or 'flying saucers', but one in which most reports had remarkable consistency in their details and were based on lengthy, close sightings. As Paris Flmmonde points out regarding the unidentified object observed over Omaha, Nebraska, on 5 April 1897: 'A hundred of the city's most prominent citizens were prepared to testify that they had monitored more than a mere light, however brilliant and fanciful in its flight. They had seen an *airship.* Likewise, when on 10 April the same, or another, airship hovered over Chicago, it was clearly observed by many people from the top of a skyscraper in the Loop.

These sightings, therefore, were definitely of a manned, motor-driven airship of the kind still in its infancy even in Europe, but not known to have been constructed in America.

Could such a craft have been designed and built, in secret, in America by 1896?

Contrary to popular belief, it was certainly possible.

The scientific community's reluctance to accept the reality of the Great AirShip Scare was based on the fact that though airships existed in 1896, most of them were constructed and flown in Europe, not America, and even those could do little other than hover helplessly in the air or fly slowly for very short distances.

The first European airship was built in 1852 by Henry

Giffard of France. Powered by a 350-pound engine, it was successfully flown over the Paris Hippodrome at a speed of six miles an hour. An internal-combustion engine fuelled by hydrogen from the airship's bag was then used by the German, Paul Haenlein, for his even more successful flight of 1872. Albert and Gaston Tissandier of France successfully powered an airship with an electric motor in 1883; and the following year, Charles Renard and A.C. Krebs made a short return flight at about thirteen miles per hour in a nonrigid dirigible powered by an electric motor. The first rigid airship, with an aluminium-sheeting hull and powered by a gasoline-fired engine, was built by David Schwartz in Germany in 1897. The first dirigible with an internal-combustion engine was built by another two Germans, Wolfert and Baumgarten, though it exploded before its trial flight. The first truly successful nonrigid, controllable airship, using two internal-combustion engines, was designed and constructed in France by Alberto Santos-Dumont, who subsequently thrilled the whole of France by flying from St. Cloud to the Eiffel Tower and back, a distance of seven miles, in thirty minutes. Finally, in June 1900, Count von Zeppelin's first airship flew across Lake Constance; and the Germans subsequently used a number of large Zeppelin airships to bomb Paris and London throughout the Great War of 1914-1918.

(Ironically, the first *successful* dirigible, Thomas Baldwin's *California Arrow*, was constructed and flown in Oakland, California, in 1904, months after the Wright brothers made the first sustained, powered and controlled flights in history at Kitty Hawk, North Carolina, in their biplane, the *Flyer*.)

Though the European airships were the ones most widely known, it is possible that some were constructed, possibly in secret, in the United States during that same period. Certainly, though the Great Airship Scare took place five years *before* the first historic experiments of Orville Wright and his brother, Wilbur, there were, by that time, various airship designs on the drawing boards or in the Patent Office. For instance on 11 August 1896, three months before the beginning of the Great Airship Scare, patent number 565805 was given to Charles Abbot Smith of San Francisco for an airship he intended having ready by the following year. Another patent, number 580941, was issued to Henry Heintz of Elkton, South Dakota, on 20 April 1897, a few weeks before the airship flap ended. It should be noted, however, that while many of the UFOs sighted were shaped roughly like the patented designs, there is no record of those airships having been built.

Which doesn't necessarily mean that *no* airships were built.

Was the state of scientific knowledge in the United States at that time up to the task?

The short answer is 'Yes.'

It is a widely held misconception that those were early days for advanced technology, but they were in fact the most productive days in the history of science. By 1895 Rontgen had discovered X-rays, Marconi had invented wireless telegraphy, Auguste and Louis Lumiere had invented the cinematograph, the first main railway was electrified, and Ramsay had detected, by spectroscope, helium from a terrestrial source. By 1896 we had Rutherford's magnetic detection of electrical waves, the construction of an electrical submarine in France, and the first successful flights of S.P. Langley's flying machines. By 1897 numerous patents for flying machines had been registered, and J.J. Thomson's work on cathode rays had led to the evaluation of the electron.

Regarding aeronautical knowledge in particular, American interest in the possibilities of flight was intense, a lot of research work was under way, and the experimental work of the period was certainly more advanced than is generally believed.

In 1896, perhaps the most renowned seat of aeronautical teaching was the Massachussetts Institute of Technology, more widely known as MIT. Although there were no formal aeronautical courses at MIT in the late 1800s, there were plenty of informal courses on propulsion and the behaviour of fluids - two subjects necessary to aeronautical experimentation and which rocket inventor, Robert H. Goddard, an MIT pupil, later made his own.

The first degree in aeronautics was conferred by MIT in 1892; by 1896, instructors and students there had built a wind tunnel and were experimenting with it to get practical knowledge of aerodynamics. The tunnel was a rectangular duct leading from the forced ventilating system in the basement of the old engineering building, 'Eng.A', on Trinity Place in Boston (diagonally across from the old Boston Art Museum; a site now occupied by the Sheraton Plaza Hotel) and the tests included measurements of lift and drag, airspeed determination by a vane anemometer, and the action of wind pressure on various surfaces, or wings.

The second most important seat of learning was Sibley College, Cornell University, in Ithica, New York, where by the mid-1890s it was possible to obtain a Bachelor of Sciences in Aeronautics. Courses at Sibley College included mechanical and electrical engineering, and machine design and construction. At Sibley College the experimental engineering courses were conducted by professors Rolla Clinton Carpenter, George Burton Preston, Aldred Henry Eldredge, Charles Edwin Houghton, and Oliver Shantz - some of the greatest aeronautical thinkers of their day. Also lecturing occasionally at Sibley was Octave Chanute, the world-famous engineer who wrote *Progress in Flying Machines* (1894); and, in 1896, emulated the successful manned hang-glider experiments of the German, Otto Lilienthal, at an aerial experiment station on the Lake Michigan sand dunes near Miller, Indiana.

Specific aeronautical texts of the time were surprisingly advanced and would have included the Smithsonian Institution's *Experiments in Aerodynamics*, published in 1891; the Lawrence Hargraves experiment reports of 1890 to 1894; the 1893 reports on Sir Hiram Maxim's experiments on engines, propellers, aeroplanes and flying machines; and the *Aeronautical Annual* of 1895, 1896, and 1897, which contained original contributions from most of the leading aeronautical scientists.

Therefore, assuming that experiments with airships were being funded in secret, the knowledge and talent would certainly have been available, and airships of advanced design could have been constructed in the United

States by the time of the Great Airship Scare.

As for doing so in secret, this also would have been possible, since it was a time when financiers were in fierce competition with one-another to sink money into experimental aeronautical projects - and most of those projects were wrapped in the strictest secrecy. Given this situation, a talented aeronautical engineer or inventor could have worked in almost total anonymity with the full support, even encouragement, of his financial backers. Also, the US government was known to have quietly financed more than one aeronautical project; while the US Army Air Force occasionally took over civilian aeronautical projects and either ran them in strict secrecy or, for one reason or another, quietly aborted them.

Thus it is possible that an airship of the capabilities described by thousands of witnesses during the Great Airship Scare could have been constructed in secret in the United States during that period.

But by whom?

In the mid-1890s, in the US, the general belief was that aerial navigation would be solved through an airship, rather than a heavier-than-air flying machine - so most of the earlier designs looked like dirigibles with a passenger car on the bottom. What stands out in the 1896-97 sightings is that the unidentified flying objects were mostly cigar-shaped, that they frequently landed, and that their occupants often talked to the witnesses, usually asking for water for their machines. The most intriguing of the numerous contactee stories involved a man who called himself 'Wilson'.

The first incident occurred in Beaumont, Texas, on 19 April 1897, when one J.B. Ligon, the local agent for Magnolia Brewery, and his son Charles, noticed lights in a pasture a few hundred yards away and went to investigate. They came upon four men standing beside a large, dark object which neither of the witnesses could see clearly. One of those men asked Ligon for a bucket of water. As Ligon fetched the water, the man introduced himself as 'Mr Wilson'. He then told Ligon that he and his friends were traveling in a flying machine, that they had taken a trip out to the gulf (presumably the Gulf of Galveston, though no name was given) and that they were returning to the quiet Iowa town where the airship and four others like it had been constructed. When asked, Wilson explained that electricity powered the propellers and wings of his airship - then he and his buddies got back into the airship and Ligon watched it ascending.

The next day, April 20, Sheriff H.W. Bayer of Uvalde, also in Texas, went to investigate a strange light and voices in back of his house. He encountered an airship and three men - and one of the men introduced himself as Wilson, from Goshen, New York. Wilson then enquired about one C.C. Akers, former sheriff of Zavalia County, saying he had met him in Fort Worth in 1877 and now wanted to see him again. Sheriff Baylor, surprised, replied that Captain Akers was now at Eagle Pass, and Wilson, apparently disappointed, asked to be remembered to him the next time Sheriff Baylor visited him. Baylor reported that the men from the airship wanted water and that Wilson requested that their visit be kept secret from the townspeople; then he and the other men climbed back into the airship and: 'its great wings and fans were set in motion and it sped away northward in the direction of San Angelo'. The county clerk also saw the airship as it left the area.

Two days later, in Josserand, Texas, a whirring sound awoke farmer Frank Nichols, who looked out from his window and saw brilliant lights streaming from what he described as 'a ponderous vessel of strange proportions' floating over his cornfield. Nichols went outside to investigate, but before he reached the large vessel, two men walked up to him and asked if they could have water from his well. Nichols agreed to this request - as farmers in those days mostly did - and the men then invited him to visit their airship, where he noticed that there were six or seven crew members. One of those men told him that the ship's motive power was highly condensed electricity and that it was one of five that had been constructed in a small town in Iowa with the backing of a large stock company in New York.

The next day, on April 23, witnesses described in the Houston *Post* as two 'responsible men' reported that an airship had descended where they lived in Kountze, Texas, and that two of the occupants had given their names as Jackson and... Wilson.

Four days after that incident, on April 27, the Galveston *Daily News* printed a letter from the aforementioned C.C. Akers, in which he claimed that he had indeed known a man in Fort Worth, Texas, named Wilson; that Wilson was from New York; that he was in his middle twenties; and that he was of a mechanical turn of mind and was then working on aerial navigation and something that would astonish the world.

Finally, early in the evening of April 30, in Deadwood,

Texas, a farmer named H.C. Lagrone heard his horses bucking as if in stampede. Going outside, he saw a bright white light circling around the fields nearby and illuminating the entire area before descending and landing in one of the fields. Walking to the landing spot, Lagrone found a crew of five men, three of whom engaged him in conversation while the others collected water in rubber bags. The men informed Lagrone that their airship was one of five that had been flying around the country recently; that theirs was in fact the same one that had landed in Beaumont a few days before; that all the airships had been constructed in an interior town in Illinois - which borders Iowa - and that they were reluctant to say anything else because they hadn't yet taken out any patents. By May that same year, the wave of sightings ended - and the mysterious Mr Wilson wasn't heard from again.

While I have used the mysterious 'Wilson' as a major protagonist in my five *Projekt Saucer* novels, creating what I believe is a plausible explanation for him, it has to be conceded that no proof for his existence, other than that mentioned above, has ever surfaced and he has not been heard from since the end of the Great Airship Scare in 1897. Nevertheless, even given that the letter from C.C. Akers printed in the Galveston *Daily News* on 27 April 27 1897 could have come from a hoaxer after he had read the original story about Akers' friendship with Wilson, we are still left with a surprising consistency in the various reports, as well as in the recollection of the name 'Wilson' from witnesses in widely scattered areas who would not have had access to news stories from other states.

That Wilson existed as 'Wilson' or was someone else

using a pseudonym is a matter of relative unimportance. The major question raised by the 'Wilson' mystery is whether or not a person, or persons, constructed an advanced airship, or airships, in secret and flew it, or them, across the United States from November 1896 to May the following year.

UFO historian Lionel Beer is of the opinion that a manned airship was responsible for the Great Airship Scare. Beer also points out that Dr Geoffrey Doel, former president of The British Unidentified Flying Object Research Association (BUFORA), had made a convincing case for this, suggesting that the man responsible was Edward Joel Pennington, of Racine, Wisconsin.

In 1890 Pennington started a company called The Mount Carmel Aerial Navigation Company and filed patents for a four-cylinder radial engine for the propulsion of an aerial vessel. In 1891 he exhibited a thirty-foot airship powered through its tethering cable by an electrically turned airscrew; and by 1895, after announcing that he intended to open an airship passenger service between Chicago and New York, he deposited patents with the American Patents Office for a full-sized airship.

Regarding this, it is worth noting that the average length of the craft sighted during the Great Airship Scare of 1896-97 was thirty feet and that many were reported as having 'cables' and electrically powered airscrews.

According to Lionel Beer, the two photographs of the mystery airship taken by Walter McCann in 1897 showed a 'distant object' closely resembling Pennington's design. In *The UFO Controversy in America* David Michael Jacobs says that it 'remarkably resembled' the mystery airships sighted by so many in 1896 and 1897, and had 'a cigar-shaped gas bag with wings attached to the sides, a large railroad-like car hanging from the bottom of the bag, and storage batteries to light the car'.

On 15 April 1897, shortly after newspapers reported that an airship had crashed, farmers Jeremiah Collier and William York claimed that they had come across a grounded airship on Wood Patch Hill, Brown County, Indiana. According to these gentlemen, the craft had been damaged and the crew, who were carrying out repairs, claimed that it belonged to E.J. Pennington. When interviewed about this on April 19, Pennington admitted that the damaged airship was his, that reports about the machine blowing up (New York *Herald*, 14 April 1897) had been exaggerations, and that 'owing to the roof of our machine springing a leak, one of our electrical circuits became grounded and the dynamo burned out'. He also claimed that he had three machines in the air, presently over the central states, and that while one would be turning up at the Tennessee exposition, he would be flying another to Cuba, to 'join the patriots in their struggle for liberty'.

While no motor-powered airship materialized at the Tennessee exposition of May that year, a bicycle-powered airship was demonstrated, flying successfully for short distances. (As far as the history books are concerned, the first motor-driven airship was built and flown in the United States in 1900 by A. Leo Stevens.) As for Pennington's reference to Cuba (which echoes the remarks of W.H.H. Hart), on the evening of April 14, in Springfield, Illinois, farmworker John Halley and another resident, Adolf

Wenke, witnessed the descent of an airship on a field just outside town and were informed by the pilot, before the airship took off again, that his craft would be 'used in Cuba' as soon as 'Congress recognized Cuban belligerency'.

Pennington neither flew his airship to Cuba nor opened his planned airship passenger service; and as far as can be ascertained, he stopped constructing airships and dropped out of sight shortly after the Great Airship Scare ended. While David Michael Jacobs states that this was because Pennington 'could not raise the necessary funds to actually build the ship', Beer says that 'it is not known for sure' why he failed to complete his project and suggests that he was possibly 'shrewd enough to realize that aeronautical designers in France and Germany were well ahead of him and that the Zeppelins would not be long in coming'.

Nevertheless, the fact remains that during the Great Airship Scare thousands of people across the United States saw what was clearly a manned, motor-driven airship. The true identity of the genius who built it may never be known.

Chapter 3

Technology and Sightings of World War II

Before writing the *Genesis* book in the *Projekt Saucer* series, while researching a World War Two novel, I obtained through the Imperial War Museum, London, two short articles which attracted my attention. One was a routine war report by Marshall Yarrow, then the Reuters special correspondent to Supreme Headquarters in liberated Paris. The particular cutting I had was from the *South Wales Argus* of 13 December 1944 and it stated: 'The Germans have produced a "secret" weapon in keeping with the Christmas season. The new device, which is apparently an air defence weapon, resembles the glass balls which adorn Christmas trees. They have been seen hanging in the air over German territory, sometimes singly, sometimes in clusters. They are coloured silver and are apparently transparent. The second article, an Associated Press release published in the New York *Herald Tribune* of 2 January 1945, illuminated the subject even more. It said:

> Now, it seems, the Nazis have thrown something new into the night skies over Germany. It is the weird, mysterious 'Foo fighter' balls which race alongside the wings of Beaufighters flying intruder missions over Germany. Pilots have been encountering this eerie weapon for more than a month in their

> night flights. No-one apparently knows what this sky weapon is. The 'balls of fire' appear suddenly and accompany the planes for miles. They seem to be radio-controlled from the ground, so official intelligence reports reveal.

Either because of the famous line from the popular Smokey Stover comic strip, 'Where there's foo, there's fire', or simply because the French word for 'fire' is *feu*, these 'eerie' weapons soon became widely known as 'foo fighters'.

Official 'foo fighter' reports were submitted by pilots Henry Giblin and Walter Cleary, who stated that on the night of 27 September 1944 they had been harassed in the vicinity of Speyer by 'an enormous burning light' that was flying above their aircraft at about 250 mph; then by Lieutenant Edward Schluter, a fighter-pilot of the US 415th Night-Fighter Squadron based at Dijon, France, who, on the night of 23 November 1944, was harassed over the Rhine by 'ten small reddish balls of fire' flying in formation at immense speed. Further sightings were made by members of the same squadron on 27 November, 22 December and 24 December.

In a report published in the New York *Times* of 2 January 1945, US Air Force Lieutenant, Donald Meiers, claimed that there were three kinds of foo fighter: red balls of fire that appeared off the aircraft's wingtips, other balls of fire that flew in front of them, and 'lights which appear off in the distance - like a Christmas tree in the air - and flicker on and off'. Meiers also confirmed that the foo fighters climbed, descended or turned when the aircraft did so. The foo fighters were witnessed both at night and by day, yet even when pacing the Allied aircraft they did not show up on the radar screens.

A classified project had actually been established in England in 1943 under the direction of Lieutenant General Massey, to examine a spate of reports of unidentified flying objects submitted by British, French and American pilots flying bombing missions over occupied France and Nazi Germany. While no official designation of the foo fighters was offered, most reports indicated that they were ‘balls of fire’ that flew in parallel formation with the Allied aircraft, often pacing them for great distances, at speeds exceeding 300 mph, frequently causing their engines to malfunction by cutting in and out. While a few reports of crashing Allied aircraft suggest that foo fighters caused the crashes by making the aircraft’s engines cut out completely, most reports indicate that this was unlikely and that the foo fighters merely tailed the planes and caused psychological harm, rather than physical damage. They also flew away when fired upon.

At first it was assumed that the ‘balls of fire’ were static electricity charges, but the mounting body of evidence made it clear that they were under some kind of control and were certainly not natural phenomena. Indeed, according to a London *Daily Telegraph* report of 2 January 1945, RAF pilots were describing them as ‘strange orange lights which follow their planes, sometimes flying in formation with them, and eventually *peeling off and climbing* (author's emphasis)’. This soon led to speculation that they were German secret weapons, radio-controlled from the ground, and designed either to foul the ignition systems of the bombers or act as 'psychological' weapons that confused and unnerved the Allied pilots. Finally, unable to solve the mystery, both the RAF and the US Eighth Army Air Force concluded that they were the products of 'mass hallucination' and subsequently did no more about them.

Sightings of the foo fighters tailed off and ceased completely a few weeks before the end of the war.

The next wave of UFO sightings occurred in Western Europe and Scandinavia, where from 1946 to 1947 many people, including airline pilots and radar operatives, reported seeing strange cigar- or disk-shaped objects in the skies. On 21 June 1947, Harold Dahl reported seeing saucer-shaped objects flying toward the Canadian border. Three days later, Kenneth Arnold made his more famous sightings of saucer-shaped objects over the Cascades, also heading for the Canadian border.

These and subsequent sightings led to speculation that both the Soviets and the Americans, utilizing the men and material captured in the secret research plants of Nazi Germany, including those at Peenemünde and Nordhausen, were developing advanced saucer-shaped aircraft.

In the words of Captain Edward J. Ruppelt, then head of the US Air Force's Project Blue Book: 'When World War II ended, the Germans had several radical types of new aircraft and guided missiles under development. The majority of these projects were in the most preliminary stages, but they were the only known craft that could even approach the performance of the objects reported by UFO observers.'

Were such speculations based on facts?

It would certainly seem so.

The late 1800s and early 1900s produced some of the greatest advances in the history of aviation. The first successful flights of S.P. Langley's flying machines were made in 1896 - the first year of the Great Airship Scare - and by 1900 numerous patents for airships had been registered. In 1900 Count von Zeppelin's dirigible balloon, powered by an internal combustion engine and propellers, became the first real directed flight by man; and by 1901, in Paris, France, Santos Dumont had flown an airship from S. Cloud to the Eiffel Tower and back in under thirty minutes to win the French Aero Club prize; two years later, at Kitty Hawk, North Carolina, the Wright Brothers made the first successful heavier-than-air manned flight; on the last day of December 1908, Wilbur Smith flew 77 miles in two hours and thirty minutes; seven months later, the French aviator, Louis Blériot, flew across the English channel, from Calais to Dover; and throughout the Great War of 1914-18 the Germans successfully used advanced Zeppelin airships to bomb London and Paris.

However, while these great aeronautical achievements were enthralling the world, even more radical theories and experiments were taking place quietly elsewhere. In 1895, a year before the Great Airship Scare, the renowned Russian physicist, Konstantin Tsiolkovsky, was theorizing about the possibilities of space flight in his essays. By 1898 he had understood and written about the necessity for liquid-fuelled rocket engines. His later reputation as the 'father' of space flight rests on a series of articles he wrote on the theory of rocketry, and by the 1920s he was suggesting some of the devices that the American rocket genius, Robert H. Goddard, was to develop so brilliantly.

Goddard was always well ahead of his time. Born in Worcester, Massachusetts, in 1882, he graduated from the Worcester Polytechnic in 1908, received his Ph.D. in physics at Clark University in Worcester in 1911, taught at Princetown, but returned to Clark in 1914, the same year in which he obtained his first two patents for rocket apparatus. Five years later, he published his book, *A Method of Reaching Extreme Altitudes* (1919), and by 1923 he was already testing the first of his rocket engines using gasoline and liquid oxygen - the first advance over solid-fuel rockets. In 1926 he sent his first rocket soaring successfully skyward, and a larger one, financed by the Smithsonian Institution, went up three years later as the first instrument-carrying rocket. In 1930, with further help from the Smithsonian Institution, the philanthropist Daniel Guggenheim and famed aviator Charles Lindbergh, he set up an experimental station in a desolate area near Roswell, New Mexico, where he built larger rockets and introduced many of the ideas that are now standard in rocketry, including appropriate combustion chambers, the burning of gasoline with oxygen in such a way that the rapid combustion could be used to cool the chamber walls, various revolutionary rocket steering systems, including rudder-like deflectors and gyroscopes, and the basics for the first multistage rocket. From 1930 to 1935, in the seclusion of his testing grounds near Roswell, New Mexico, Goddard launched rockets that attained speeds of up to 350 mph and heights of a mile and a half.

Even more remarkable than Goddard's achievements

was the fact that they were, at least until the advent of World War II, ignored by the United States Government - though certainly they were not ignored in Germany.

The German amateur rocket society, the *Verein für Raumschiffart*, or VfR, also known as the Spaceship Travel Club, had come into being in 1927 when a group of brilliant space-travel enthusiasts took over an abandoned three-hundred acre arsenal, which they called their *Raketenflugplataz*, or Rocket Flight Place, in the Berlin suburb of Reindickerdorf. From there they actually shot some crude, liquid-fuelled rockets skywards.

By 1930 the VfR included most of the rocket experts of the day, including Rudolf Nebel, Hermann Oberth, Willy Ley, Max Valier, Klaus Riedel and the then 18-year old Werner von Braun, who would end up in America, heading the moon program for the National Aeronautics and Space Administration (NASA).

In April 1930, the Ordnance Branch of the German Army's Ballistics and Weapons Office, headed by General Becker, appointed Captain Walter Dornberger to work on rocket development at the army's Kummersdorf firing range, approximately fifteen miles south of Berlin. Two years later, after many experiments to find the most promising method of propulsion and the most stable means of flight, the VfR demonstrated one of their liquid-fuelled rockets to Dornberger and other officers at Kummersdorf.
In 1933, when Hitler came to power, the VfR was taken over by the Nazis and become part of the Kummersdorf program.

Many of the German engineers, including the up-and-coming Werner von Braun, revered Goddard and were known to have based their work on his ideas. While in the United States, Goddard's theories were still being received with indifference and even contempt, Hitler's Germany was spending fortunes on rocket research that was, by and large, based on Goddard's work.

As early as December 1934, two highly advanced A-2 rockets, constructed at Kummersdorf, gyroscopically controlled, and powered by oxygen-and-alcohol fuelled motors, were launched from the island of Borkum in the North Sea and reached an altitude of one-and-a-half miles. Those stabilised, liquid-fuelled rockets were, at the time, the only known, serious challengers to the rockets of Robert H. Goddard.

Nor did it end there. Shortly after Hitler's infamous advance across the Hohenzollern Bridge on 7 March 1936, Captain Walter Dornberger, the head of the Rocket Research Institute, his assistant, Werner von Braun, and their team of 150 technicians, demonstrated some more motors at Kummersdorf, including one with an unprecedented 3,500 pounds of thrust. Those demonstrations so impressed the German Commander-in-Chief, General Fritsch, that permission was given for Dornberger and von Braun to build an independent rocket establishment in a suitably remote part of Germany, where research and test firings could be carried out in the strictest secrecy. The chosen site was near the village of Peenemünde, on the island of Usedom, off the Baltic Coast.

The rest is now history. After numerous experiments in the Zeppelin subsonic wind tunnel at Friedrichshafen and the University of Aachen's supersonic wind tunnel, and with the completion of a remarkably reliable gyroscopic control system by the electrical specialists, Siemens, radio-controlled A-5 rockets were soon being dropped from heights of up to 20,000 ft and speeds exceeding Mach 1, or the speed of sound. By late 1944, numerous V-1 and V-2 rockets were falling on London.

What is not so well known is that when the V-2 rockets were inspected by Allied scientists in the captured Nordhausen Central Works at the close of the war, it was discovered that the most notable features of the propulsion unit were the shutter-type valves in the fixed grill, the fuel injection orifices incorporated in the same grill, the combustion chamber, spark plugs and nozzle - all of which were to be found in a Robert H. Goddard patent, issued 13 November 1934 and reproduced in full in the German aviation magazine, *Flugsport*, in January 1939.

There were other striking similarities between the V-2 and Goddard's original rocket. Both rockets had the same motor-cooling system; the same pump drive; the same layout front to rear; the same stabilizer; and the same guidance and fuel injection systems. Indeed the only notable difference between the two was that Goddard's rocket motors used gasoline and oxygen, whereas the V-2 used hydrogen and peroxide; Goddard's rocket fuel was liquid oxygen and gasoline, whereas the V-2 used liquid oxygen and alcohol; and, finally, Goddard's original rocket was a lot *smaller* than the V-2.

The V-2 rockets had a thrust of 55,000 pounds, attained a velocity of 6,400 ft per second, and could soar to an altitude of 68 miles. What this meant, in effect, is that the Germans had taken designs shamefully neglected by the American Government and used them as the basis for a radical, highly advanced, supersonic technology. They had also learned through Goddard of the necessity for gyroscopic control and thus potential control of the boundary layer.

What is the boundary layer?

While being four or five thousand times less viscous than oil, air *is* still viscous. Because of this, the air sweeping in on the solid body of an aircraft forms imperceptible stratifications of resistance and consequently decreases the speed of the body in flight. These layers of air are therefore known as the 'boundary layer' - and the boundary layer increases its resistance in direct proportion to the increasing speed of the flying object, thus imposing severe limitations on its speed and manoeuvrability.

Though the boundary layer affects all forms of flight, the major problem regarding ultra-high speed flight is to somehow move this negative air as far to the rear of the aircraft as possible, thus minimizing the expenditure of energy required to propel the aircraft through the sky. Moreover, it is possible that a revolutionary type of aircraft could - by not only *completely* removing the boundary layer, but by somehow *re-routing* it and utilizing it as an added propulsive force - fly through the skies using little other than the expelled air itself. Should this be accomplished, we would have an aircraft capable of remarkable speeds while using only the bare minimum of conventional fuel.

The Germans were working on all aspects of the boundary layer even before the beginning of the Great War of 1914-18.

Physicist Dr Eduard Ludwig worked with the famous aircraft designer Hugo Junkers at his factory in Dessau where, in 1910, they produced one of the earliest 'flying wing' designs. According to Ludwig, the first physicist to consider 'this new branch of aerodynamics' was Professor Jubowski, of Moscow. Before the First World War, Jubowski worked with Dr Kutta, of the Technical High School of Stuttgart, Germany, on the development of the theory of aeroplane-wingbeam and succeeded in establishing the differential equation of the boundary layer, which for the first time threw light on why 'a plane-wing can bear a load while moving forward through the air'. Since then, according to Ludwig, the Kutte-Jabowski Theory of Aeroplane wingbeam has been the foundation of all aerodynamics.

However, even earlier than that, in 1904, at the Aerodynamic Experimental Institute of the Göttengen University, Professor Ludwig Prandtl, the great physicist now known as 'the father of aerodynamics', discovered the boundary layer, which in turn led to the understanding of the way in which 'streamlining' would reduce the drag of aeroplane wings and other moving bodies. Prandtl's work soon became the basic material of aerodynamics, and he went on to make pioneering discoveries in subsonic airflow, advanced wind tunnel design, and other aerodynamic equipment design. He also devised a 'soap film analogy' for the analysis of torsion forces of structures, and produced invaluable studies on the 'theory of plasticity'.

By 1915, another member of the Technical High School of Stuttgart, Professor H.C. Bauman, utilizing the theories of the abovenamed, received a patent for a Splitwing 'through which the artificial interruption of the course of the current, the tearing of the boundary layer, and the consequent braking and diminishing of the landing speed would be attained'.

Meanwhile, Anton Flettner, the German director of an aeronautical and hydrodynamic research institute in Amersdam, had invented the rotor-ship, a vessel propelled by revolving cylinders mounted vertically on the deck. In 1926 he established an aircraft factory in Berlin, where he used what became known as the 'Flettner-Rotor' for the production of Flettner F1 282 and other helicopters. Soon, at the behest of Professor Junkers, the Flettner-Rotor ('a cylinder turning at great speed') was being utilized by professors Prandtl, Ludwig, and others, as a means of investigating 'to what extent the uplift of a wing could be increased'.

The experiments were fraught with difficulty and cost the lives of at least four test pilots. This was due to 'inexplicable vibrations and axle breakages', leading the scientists to the conclusion that 'only a gas-turbine could produce the required uplift of the cylinder'. This led in turn to the building of a wind tunnel in which many invaluable experiments on the relationship between supersonic speeds and the boundary-layer were conducted, culminating in the first successful flight of a jet aircraft in 1939, as well as the launching of the V-1 and V-2 rockets during the closing stages of World War II.

The German scientists and engineers believed that the perfect flying machine would be one that required no runway, since it would take off vertically, would be able to hover in mid-air, and would not be limited in manoeuvrability or speed by the boundary layer. As the build-up of the boundary layer is dramatically increased by the many surface protuberances of a normal aircraft - wings, tails, rudders, rotors, cockpits - it was felt that by getting rid of them completely, by somehow wrapping them together as part and parcel of the one, circular, smooth-surfaced flying wing, the first step in the conquest of the boundary layer would be achieved.

Germany was the country with most interest in such developments and certainly the most advanced at that time. A disk or saucer-shaped aircraft, without any surface protuberances, powered by ultra-high speed engines, is what they were after and many designs of the time were based on that conception. It is therefore no accident that as early as 1935 a German, Hans von Ohain, had applied for a patent for a jet engine. Nor was it an accident that the first flight of a jet-powered aircraft was made by a Heinkel He 178 at Rostock, Germany, on 27 August 1939.

Regarding vertical-rising aircraft, the Focke-Achgelis Company had already announced in 1939 that it had almost completed its FW 61 helicopter, which would be the first fully operational helicopter in existence. That the Germans produced the first successful helicopter, yet were not known to have used such craft during World War II, may be due to the fact that already they were more concerned with tailless aircraft or 'flying wings', devoid of vertical stabilizing or control surfaces. This would lead them to the search for a jet-propelled, disk-shaped aircraft, or flying saucer.

By 1932 the Horten brothers of Bonn had produced some successful prototypes for the German Air Ministry at their factory in Bonn. The Horten 1 was an 'all wing' aircraft, which in prototype form was a wooden-framed glider. It had a span of 40.7 feet, a wing area of 226 square feet, and a wing-loading of 2 pounds per square foot. It had a flying weight of 440 pounds, a gliding angle of 21 degrees, and a flying life of approximately seven hours. As the Horten brothers were convinced that the most important form of aircraft would be the all-wing type, there were no vertical stabilizing or control surfaces on the Horten 1. It was virtually flat and crescent-shaped, like a boomerang, with the pilot placed in a prone position, to reduce cockpit size. This so-called 'flying wing' certainly flew for seven hours, but it could never have been the basis of a flying saucer for one very good reason: it was still faced with the problem that had repeatedly foiled other German aeronautical engineers - the limitations imposed by the boundary layer.

A more advanced model, the Horten II, D-11-167, was built in 1934 and test-flown at Rangsdorf, Germany, on 17 November 1938. According to the report of Hanna Rasche (the popular female pilot who also demonstrated the Focke-Achgelis helicopter the same year), this test flight turned out to be highly unsatisfactory. The so-called tailless aircraft possessed great static-longitudinal stability and complete safety in relation to the spin, but its control surfaces were so heavy that measurements of manoeuvring stability could not be carried out. The unsatisfactory arrangement of its undercarriage necessitated too long a takeoff; the relation between its longitudinal, lateral and directional controls was unsatisfactory; its turning flight and manoeuvrability were fraught with difficulty, and side-slipping could not be carried out.

Nevertheless, the Horten designs were the first on the road to a disk-shaped aircraft and, as we shall see, would cause great concern amongst Allied scientists and intelligence officers involved in post-war investigations into the possibility of German, or German-based, Russian flying saucers.

While experiments with 'flying wings' and spherical aircraft were being conducted by the likes of the Horten brothers, many other German scientists, including Betz, Flettner, and Junkers, were experimenting with specially equipped airwings in attempts to reduce the boundary layer. Most of these experiments were based on the 'suction' method, in which the negative air is sucked into the wing itself, through tiny holes or slots, then expelled by means of a pump located in the fuselage.

While this was a step in the right direction, the resulting aircraft still required heavy, obstructive engines (also the main problem with the Horten brothers' envisaged flying wing jet-fighter), but the belief remained that in order to get rid of the boundary layer completely - and in order to make use of the 'dead' air not only for acceleration, but for manoeuvring as well - the requirement was for an aircraft devoid of *all* obstructing protuberances, such as wings, rudders and even normal air-intakes, and one not requiring a large, heavy engine. In other words, this revolutionary new aircraft should be the perfect 'flying wing' that offers the least possible resistance, sucks in the 'dead' air of the boundary layer, and then uses that same air, expelling it at great force, to increase its own momentum. It would therefore have to be a circular 'wing' that is, in a sense, wrapped around its suction pump, with the pump being part and parcel of the engine: a machine shaped like a saucer.

Further: if such a craft could be built with a 'porous' metal that would act like a sponge and remove the need for air-intakes altogether, it would result in 'frictionless air-flow' during flight.

Speaking at the 34th Wilbur Wright Memorial Lecture held on 30 May 1946, at the Royal Aeronautical Society in London, the well known British aerodynamics expert Professor E. F. Relf stated that 'a further system of regulating the boundary layer by means of suction through minute holes heavily distributed over the surface' had recently been undertaken by the National Physical Laboratory. Discussing similar possibilities at a conference held in December the same year on the future of British aeronautics, Sir Ben Lockspeiser said that such a plane would 'slip through the air in the same way as a piece of wet soap slips through the fingers'.

The speed and manoeuvring capabilities of such a craft would be virtually limitless.

While the idea of 'porous' metal sounds like something from science fiction, it was in fact being developed in Nazi Germany, as well as in Britain. Among the many other advanced experiments being run in the wind tunnel in the Zeppelin works at Friedrichshafen were those concerning the different 'porous' metals, or 'aeropermeable surfaces', that were being created by the scientists of Göttingen, Aachen, and Volkenrode - various compounds of magnesium and aluminium, sinterized and permeated with microscopic holes. It was called *Luftschwamm*, or 'aero-sponge'.

Other top-secret experiments relating to supersonic flight were taking place all over Nazi Germany and its captured territories.

In the densely forested areas of the Schwarzwald, German scientists were experimenting with a liquid gas that would, when blown with considerable force over an aircraft, catch fire from the aircraft's exhaust and cause that aircraft to explode. The existence of this gas was confirmed by a German organic chemist, Dr Rosenstein, who, when interrogated in Paris in 1944 by members of the American ALSOS mission (created to locate and assess the fruits of Nazi Germany's scientific research), stated that the Germans had succeeded in perfecting a new gas whose use would have caused 'strong vibrations and even breakages in aircraft engines' by encouraging immediate and repeated self-ignition. The captured papers also revealed that in July 1944, Dr Hans Friedrich Gold, a chemical engineer working in the rocket division of the R-Laboratory in Volkenrode, discovered that by mixing a certain percentage of myrol with air, internal combustion engines would immediately begin detonating irregularly or, depending upon the mixture, stop completely.

Further to this, it should be noted that according to Major Rudolph Lusar's *German Secret Weapons of World War II*, in April 1945, on the outskirts of the Hillersleben testing grounds west of Berlin, members of the Intelligence

Technical Branch of the 12th Army Group found the rusty remains of an odd item called the *Windkanone* - a cannon that shot gas instead of shells - and another item called the *Wirbelringkanone*, or 'whirlwind annular vortex cannon', which was designed to shoot, then ignite, a gas ring that would spin rapidly on its own axis and form a fierce 'ball of fire'.

By 1945 the Oberbayerische Forschunsanstalt, or O.B.F., a Luftwaffe experimental centre at Oberammergau, in Bavaria, had completed its research into an apparatus capable of short-circuiting the ignition system of another aircraft engine from a distance of about one hundred feet by producing an intense electrical field.

Even remote-controlled flying devices were being developed. As far back as 1939 Dr Fernseh of Berlin, in collaboration with Professor Herbert Wagner of the Henschel-Rax Works at Wiener Neustadt, was working on the development of a television component that would enable pilots to control bombs and rocket bombs *after* they had been launched, as well as a micro-television camera that would be installed in the nose of an anti-aircraft rocket and guide it precisely to its target. As the Allies also discovered at the end of the war, through the investigations of ASLOS, the British Intelligence Objectives Sub-Committee, and other scientific intelligence groups, the German scientists had been developing radio-controlled interceptor weapons and aeroplanes, such as Messerschmitt's radio-controlled interceptor planes, the *Krache* and the *Donner*, as well as electromagnetic, electroacoustical and photoelectric fuses and even more advanced warheads which were sensitive to the natural electrostatic fields that surround aircraft in flight.

Also found in the records of the experimental centre at Göttingen were details of the test-flight of a light-winged aircraft that had a slot running along the entire length of its wing span and an extra propeller in the fuselage to suck in the boundary layer and increase the lift of the original airfoil by eight times.

Last but not least, a research complex at Berlin Britz had designed the *Kreiselgerät*: the prototype of a new mechanism that had managed to reduce the oscillations of a violently shaking body to under one-tenth of a degree, thus paving the way for the conquest of the boundary layer.

The theoretical work of the German scientists, particularly those at Göttingen and Aachen, was put to practical application at the laboratories of the Deutsche Versuchsanstalt für Luftfahrt (DVL) at Adlershof and the rocket research station at Peenemünde. In this context it is worth noting that according to Philip Henshall in *Hitler's Rocket Sites*, the wind tunnel at Peenemünde was then the most advanced in the world, containing its own research department, instrumentation laboratory, workshops and design office. It is also of considerable interest that at Guidonia, the great research centre near Rome, Italy, the Germans were conducting extensive research in supersonic aerodynamics.

It therefore seems possible that the results of the oscillation tests in Göttengen, which had proved that the boundary layer could be conquered, combined with the practical applications at Adlershof, Peenemünde and Guidonia, could have produced between them a revolutionary new structural design that would be devoid of all obstructing protuberances, such as wings and rudders, devoid even of the normal air intakes, and powered by a highly advanced turbine or jet engine. In other words, a technologically advanced, tailless aircraft, or 'flying wing', that could be radio-controlled from the moment of take-off, then automatically track enemy aircraft and make their engines malfunction without firing upon them or otherwise touching them.

In essence, a small flying saucer with 'invisible' weapons.

Renato Vesco was an aircraft engineer specialising in aerospace and ramjet developments. Educated before World War II at the University of Rome, he then studied aeronautical engineering at the German Institute for Aerial Development. During the war, he was sent to work with the Germans at Fiat's immense underground installations at Lake Garda, near Limone in northern Italy, where he helped in the production of aeronautical devices that were tested at the Hermann Goering Institute of Riva del Garda. After the war, in the 1960's, Vesco worked for the Italian Air Ministry of Defense as an undercover technical agent, investigating the UFO phenomenon.

In 1971 Vesco published a book, *Intercettateli Senza Sparare*, which was the first detailed examination of the possible technology behind the flying saucers. Vesco's work was also the first to examine UFOs in the light of contemporary technology, as well as the only one to trace their origins back to Nazi Germany and credit their continuance to postwar developments by the former Allies and, possibly, the Soviet Union.

According to Vesco, captured German papers indicated that by 1945 the L.F.A. at Volkenrode and the Guidonia research centre were working on a revolutionary new type of aircraft that was devoid of all surface protuberances, such as wings and rudders, devoid even of normal air intakes, and powered by a highly advanced turbine engine. This was the so-called foo fighter - actually the German *Feuerball*, or Fireball, which had evolved from the research work done at Volkenrode and Guidonia, but was constructed at an aeronautical establishment at Wiener Neustadt (probably the Henschel-Rax Works) with the help of the Flugfunk Forschungsanstalt of Oberpfaffenhoffen (F.F.O.), located south of Munich and specialising in research into high frequency guided missiles, infrared radiation, radar, and general electronics. The *Feuerball* was an armoured, disk-shaped, flying machine, powered by a special turbojet engine. It was radio-controlled at the moment of take-off, but then, attracted by the enemy aircraft's exhaust fumes, it automatically followed that aircraft, automatically avoided colliding with it, and automatically short-circuited the aircraft's radar and ignition systems. During the day, this device looked exactly like 'a shining disk spinning on its axis' - which may account for the first Allied newspaper reports of 'silver balls' observed in the sky over Nazi Germany - and by night it looked like a 'burning globe'.

In Vesco's words:

> The fiery halo around its perimeter - caused by a very rich fuel mixture - and the chemical additives that interrupted the flow of electricity

> by over-ionizing the atmosphere in the vicinity of the plane, generally around the wing tips or tail surfaces, subjected the H2S radar on the plane to the action of powerful electrostatic fields and electromagnetic influences.

Under the armoured plating of the *Feuerball* was a thin sheet of aluminium that acted as a defensive 'switch': a bullet piercing the armoured plating would automatically establish contact with the switch, trip a maximum acceleration device, and cause the *Feuerball* to fly vertically out of range of further enemy gunfire.

In a very real sense, then, the *Feuerball* took the form of a circular 'wing' that was wrapped around the suction pump, which in turn was part and parcel of the engine. In other words: the *Feuerball* was a symmetrical disk devoid of all surface protuberances.

Vesco also claims that the basic principles of the *Feuerball* were later applied to a much larger 'symmetrical circular aircraft', the *Kugelblitz*, or Ball Lightning Fighter, which was the first example of the vertical-rising, 'jet lift' aircraft.

Could the technology described above and demonstrated in the shape of the V-2 rockets and foo fighters have led to a larger, piloted, flying saucer? The immediate post-war years would produce some startling revelations regarding this possibility.

Chapter 4

Division of the Scientific Spoils of War

At the end of World War II, Germany's scientific papers had been hidden, and were eventually found, in tunnels, caves, dry wells, ploughed fields, river beds and even cess pits. Also found across the length and breadth of Nazi Germany and its occupied territories were the well known V-1 flying bombs and V-2 rockets, as well as lesser known, but equally formidable, heat-guided ground-to-air missiles, sonic-guidance torpedoes, the highly advanced U-XX1 and U-XXIII electrical submarines, ME-262 jet-fighters, rocket planes that flew even faster than the Messerschmitts, the prototypes for other, vertical-rising jet aircraft, the beginnings of an Atom Bomb project, and even, in the immense underground Riva del Garda complex, where Renato Vesco had worked, the manufacturing process for a metallic material which could withstand temperatures of about 1000°C.

Because of this, there was a race between the Allies and the Russians to capture as many of the rocket scientists and engineers as possible, as well as the invaluable technical documentation. Deals were thus struck between the conquerors and their former enemies, particularly with regard to those involved in rocketry and other advanced weaponry.

Along with 150 of their best men, General Dornberger, Walther Riedel, and Werner von Braun went to the United

States, the first to work for the Bell Aircraft Company, the second to become director of rocket engine research for North American Aviation Corporation, and the third to achieve fame through his Apollo moon program under the auspices of the National Space Administration for Astronautics, or NASA. However, the Russians also gained a wealth of documentation and material, including the V-2 rockets, buzz bombs, ocean-spanning surface-to-surface and surface-to air missiles found in Peenemünde; about 70 per cent of the 12,000 tons of technical equipment stranded on the docks at Lübeck and Magdeburg; and the Gotha plant (where the Horten Brothers' Go-8-229 and Go-P-60 night fighters were being constructed at great speed); as well as 6,000 German technical specialists, including Dr Bock, Director of the German Institute of Airways Research; Dr Helmut Gröttrup, the electronics and guided-missile expert; and an aeronautical engineer, Klaus Habermohl.

It was therefore no accident that the great achievements of NASA and their Soviet equivalents can be traced back to the V-2s shipped from Germany to New Mexico in 1945. The launch of American V-2s commenced at the White Sands Proving Ground in March the following year, under the direction of Werner von Braun; and not much later, when North American Aviation started producing rocket motors under a USAF contract, they were basing their work on the original V-2 motor which had, ironically, been based on the rocket motors of Robert H. Goddard when he worked out of Eden Valley, in Roswell, New Mexico, now the location of the above mentioned top-secret White Sands Proving Ground. Soon, NASA's improved rocket motors were using liquid hypergolic, self-igniting fuels, which the army then used in their Redstone/Jupiter developments, which led in turn to the first Titan ICBMs and, ultimately, the Apollo moon program.

All of this sprang indirectly from the US's neglected Robert H. Goddard; and, more directly, from the fruits of German World War II experimentation.

It was a matter of course, then, that when on 31 October 1947 the Russians launched their own V-2 rocket from Volgagrad, formerly Stalingrad, the United States had great cause for concern and, when it came to the first post-war UFO sightings, turned its suspicious gaze toward the Soviet Union.

The first post-war UFO flap came in 1946 when, throughout the summer and fall, thousands of 'ghost rockets' appeared in the skies over Scandinavia and western Europe. Mostly seen at night, they were reported as being 'cigar-shaped' and with flames issuing from the tail. Estimates of their speed ranged from that of a 'slow aeroplane' to 500 mph. In the month of July alone, the Swedish military received more than 600 reports, which encouraged the Swedish general staff to declare the situation 'extremely serious'. Then, when sightings of the unidentifieds spread out from Sweden to Finland and close to the Soviet border, the Americans also took the phenomenon seriously - certainly enough to express their fear that the rockets might be secret weapons developed by the Russians with the help of the captured German technical specialists and material.

Their fears were in no way eased by the knowledge that whereas the mysterious foo fighters had not shown up on radar, the ghost rockets certainly did, and therefore could not be classified as hoaxes, misidentifications or the products of mass hallucination.

The Soviets denied any knowledge of the rockets, but US suspicions remained unabated while the rockets continued to fly and were being reported from as far afield as Greece, Turkey, French Morocco and Spain, before gradually fading away the following year.

However, on 21 June 1947, when the 'ghost rocket' furore had barely died off, a harbour patrolman, Harold Dahl, accompanied by his fifteen-year old son and two crewmen, was on harbour patrol near Maury Island in Puget Sound, off Tacoma, Washington, when he observed six objects shaped like 'inflated inner tubes' hovering about 2,000 feet above his boat. Five of the objects were circling about the sixth as it descended to about 500 feet above the boat, where, appearing to hover magically, it was seen more clearly. The object appeared to be about 100 feet in diameter, metallic, with no jets, rockets, wings, or propellers, but with a 'hole' in the centre, or base, symmetrically placed portholes around the perimeter, and observatory windows on their underside. After discharging what appeared to be a cloud of aluminium-coloured debris, which littered the sea, where they gave off clouds of steam, suggesting that they were hot, the circular craft ascended to rejoin the others, then they all flew at high speed toward the open sea and soon disappeared.

Three days later, on 24 June, an American businessman, Kenneth Arnold, reported that when flying his private Piper Club aeroplane near Mount Rainier in the Cascades, Washington, searching for the debris of the Marine Corps C-46 transport that had crashed against the south shoulder of Mount Rainier the night before, he observed nine disk-shaped, apparently metallic, objects flying in ‘a diagonal chain-like line’ and making an undulating motion ‘like a saucer skipping over water’. According to Arnold’s report, the objects performed impossible manoeuvres in the sky, before flying off at supersonic speed to disappear in the direction of the Canadian border.

As Arnold had been a deputy sheriff and was a reputable businessman, as well as an experienced mountain air-rescue pilot, his story was taken seriously and the term ‘flying saucer’ came into being. It was therefore used widely over the next few weeks when the media spread Arnold’s story nationwide and encouraged a spate of similar sightings, many of which were hoaxes, some of which were by trained observers and seemed highly credible.

By this time the US military, while publicly ridiculing the reported sightings, were secretly in a state of panic over their own plague of UFO sightings: the first, on 28 June, over Maxwell Air Force Base in Montgomery, Alabama; the next, on 29 June, near Alamogordo, New Mexico, right over the top-secret White Sands Proving Ground; then, on 8 July, a whole spate of sightings of spherically shaped, white aluminium-coloured objects flying over Muroc Air Base (now Edwards AFB), the supersecret air force test centre in the Mojave Desert.

Because these particular sightings were made by

trained technicians and pilots, and because the reported objects were appearing increasingly over top-and-supersecret military research bases, there was a growing suspicion in intelligence circles that the men and material deported from Nazi Germany to Russia had led to a dangerous Soviet lead in space technology.

In a now declassified Memorandum for Record dated 25 April 1952, containing facts for discussion by the Special Study Group and marked for the attention of USAFE, West Germany, the Air Section, USFA, Austria, the Allied Air Forces, France, NATO, Italy, and the Joint Intelligence Bureau, London, the study of flying saucers, amongst 'other advanced aerial delivery systems' is recommended.

While on the one hand stating that 'current estimates do not reflect the possibility that the Russians may have overtaken the US in advanced guided missile research and development', the report goes on to say: 'The Air Force cannot assume that flying saucers are of non-terrestrial origin, and hence, they could be Soviet.'

This assessment is based on two factors. In the first instance, the memorandum cites the UFO report of an unnamed US Naval officer (probably Navy Commander R.B. McLaughlin) who tracked a 'saucer' with a theodolite and assessed it as flying at an altitude of 56 miles with a horizontal velocity of about 8,000 meters (5 miles) per second and a climbing speed of 4,400 meters (2.7 miles) per second. Stressing that the speed recorded by the theodolite was slightly higher than the speed required for the escape from the gravitational pull of the earth, the memorandum continues: 'It frequently has been stated that such velocities cannot be produced on Earth. Such a statement is correct insofar as our present engineering skills go, but it appears incorrect with respect to theoretical knowledge.' The memorandum then cites several propulsion methods by which, provided the engineering problems are solved, such speeds could be attained. These include ultra high speed engines using fuels composed of beryllium oxidized by ozone, liquid hydrogen enriched by stable hydrogen atoms, a gas consisting of pure hydrogen atoms, or a variety of ionized substances.

The Memorandum's second stand against the extraterrestrial hypothesis is based on the reports of astronomers, which at that time suggested strongly that even if traveling at the speed of light, any object coming from outside the planetary system would be 'ascertained by the astronomical patrol (daily photographs of the skies) at least four years in advance of its arrival'. The Memorandum concludes: 'These leads, coupled with the data of the Air Technical Intelligence Centre concerning Soviet progress in the design of missile engines, definitely underscore the immediate requirement for a thorough investigation of Russian capabilities in this field.'

The 'leads' mentioned include: firstly, Constantine E. Tsiolkovski's initial investigations in the field of high altitude and interplanetary flying, his anticipation of the need for rocket propulsion, and his known interest in 'circular, hyperbolic, and spherical airframes'; secondly, the formation, in April 1924, of a Soviet organization for the development of rockets and society for interplanetary travel, both of which were attached to the then Military Air Academy, which was interested in the military implications of these matters and scheduled the first experimental flights for 1928; thirdly, the fact that a patent for a 'flying saucer with a circular fixed wing' had been taken out in the United States on March 22, 1932; and, finally, the knowledge that 'the saucer sightings in the US tend to cluster around key development stations such as atomic plants, guided missile experimental areas, and Wright-Patterson Air Force Base'.

The Memorandum also points out that the Russian magazine, *Red Fleet*, in its 12 October 1952 edition, had announced that the Soviet Union was planning to build a 'moon rocket', that the world's only solar power institute was then at Tashkent, USSR, and that Russian efforts in the field of cosmic rays operated with a high degree of security.

The Memorandum concludes with the unequivocal statement: 'It must be remembered that the first sightings were made over Scandinavia, and in the US, over the Northwest. This would be in line with a hypothetical range extension from Soviet bases.'

In the words of Dr Eduard Ludwig:

> The surprise of scientists the world over at the astounding results of the German V-2 was no less than that which is produced today by the appearance of the mysterious 'flying disks'... The future will show whether the 'flying disks' are only the products of imagination or whether they are the results of a far-advanced German science which, possibly, as well as the nearly finished atomic bombs, may have fallen into the hands of the Russians.

Forthcoming events would prove that if not exactly right, certainly he was not far wrong.

In a series of interviews given to the West German press in 1952, a former Luftwaffe engineer, Flugkapitän Rudolph Schriever, then resident at Hökerstrasse 28 in Bremerhaven-Lehe, West Germany, claimed that in the spring of 1941, when an engineer and test pilot for the Heinkel factory in Eger, he started thinking of an aeroplane that could take off vertically like a helicopter. These thoughts led him to the concept of an 'arched, domed, and rounded cabin' in the centre of multiple, circular, adjustable wings that would be driven by a turbine engine, also located in the centre of gravity, under the capsule containing the pilot's cabin. A model of this vertical-rising 'flying top' was completed the following year and test-flown on 1 June 1942. This being successful, work began on a larger prototype, fifteen feet in diameter. Many engineers dealt with various aspects of the project in different areas of the occupied territories. By the summer of 1944, Schriever had been transferred to Prague, where with his colleagues, Walter Miethe (an engineer from the Peenemünde V-1 and V-2 program), another engineer, Klaus Habermohl, and the Italian physicist, Dr Guiseppe Belluzzo (from the Riva del Garda complex), he constructed an even larger, piloted model of his original prototype. Since by this time the first Messerschmitt jets were flying, Schriever and his team, now working in the East Hall of the BMW plant near Prague, redesigned Model 3, replacing its former gas-turbine engines with an advanced form of propulsion that utilized adjustable jets.

An article about 'Project Saucer' (*Projekt Untertasse*) was later published in *German Secret Weapons of the Second World War* (1959) by Major Rudolph Lusar, and included reproductions of the flying-saucer drawings of Schriever and Miethe.

According to Lusar, the flying saucer was constructed with 'special heat-resisting material' and consisted of 'a wide-surface ring which rotated around a fixed, cupola-shaped cockpit'. The ring consisted of 'adjustable wing-disks which could be brought into appropriate position for the take-off or horizontal flight, respectively'. Miethe then developed 'a discus-shaped plate of a diameter of 42 metres (138 feet), in which adjustable jets were inserted'. The completed machine had a height from base to canopy of 32 metres (105 feet).

Schriever claimed that his 'flying disk' had been ready for testing in early 1944, but with the advance of the Allies into Germany, the test had been cancelled, the machine destroyed, and his designs either mislaid or stolen. This ties in with the fact that the BWM plant stopped work on 9 May 9 1945, as the Russians advanced it was overrun by Czechoslovakian Patriots, and many of the Germans then fled for their lives. These included Schriever, who claims that the saucer prototype was blown up by his own men to prevent it from falling into the hands of the Russians. Schriever then fled to the west, reached the American lines, and eventually made it back home to Bremerhaven.

Schriever's recollection of the test flight date is contradicted in certain details by alleged eye-witness Georg Klein, a former engineer with Albert Speer's Ministry for

Armament and Ammunition, who told the press that he had actually seen the test flight of the Schriever disk, or one similar, near Prague on 14 February 1945.

A certain doubt may be cast on Klein's date, since according to the *War Diary* of the 8th Air Fleet, 14 February 1945 was a day of low clouds, rain, snow and generally poor visibility - hardly the conditions for the testing of a revolutionary new kind of aircraft. Nevertheless, according to author Renato Vesco, the test flight of a machine called the *Kugelblitz*, or Ball Lightning Fighter - which was rumoured to be a revolutionary kind of supersonic aircraft - was conducted successfully over the underground complex of Kahla (near the underground rocket complex of Nordhausen, where the Peenemünde rocket team were then located) in Thuringia, sometime during that February of 1945.

These various sightings could be explained by the fact that just as parts of Schriever's flying saucer project were being designed, tested and constructed in many different areas of the occupied territories, so other 'all wing' experimental prototypes were being developed by other designers.

One of those who may have been involved in Projekt Saucer is Heinrich Fleißner, of Dasing, Augsburg, in the Federal German Republic. Interviewed for the 2 May 1980 edition of *Neue Presse* magazine, the then 76-year old Fleißner claimed that he had been a technical consultant on a jet-propelled, disk-shaped aircraft that had been constructed by a team of technicians in Peenemünde, though the parts had been built in many other places. According to Fleißner, Hermann Göring had been the patron of the aircraft and had planned to use it as a courier plane. At the end of the war, the Wehrmacht destroyed most of the plans and a few of the 'unimportant' drawings fell into the hands of the Russians.

(The notes and drawings for Fleißner's flying saucer, first registered in West Germany on 27 March 1954, were assigned to Trans-Oceanic, Los Angeles, California on 28 March the following year and registered with the United States Patent Office on 7 June 1960.)

As early as 1939 Dr Alexander Lippisch, at Messerschmitt, Augsburg, was developing his Delta-Rocket Jet ME 163 and testing its 'circular wing' in the wind tunnel of the AVA company at Göttingen. Meanwhile, Arthur Sack, of Machern, near Leipzig, had for years been obsessed with the idea of disk-shaped aircraft (first conceived, in fact, by the 19th century German mathematician and aeronautical theorist Wilhelm Zachariae). He tested various models at the model-aeroplane competition at Leipzig-Mockau on 27 and 28 July 1939, with disastrous results. A larger, piloted model, the AS 6, was constructed at the Mitteldeutsche Motorenwerke factory in Leipzig and failed to fly during its test flight at the beginning of February 1944, on the airfield at Brandis, near Leipzig. He tried again at Brandis on 16 April 1944, but the aeroplane barely lifted off the ground. Shortly after, the Allied advance brought Sack's experimentation to a halt for all time.

Viktor Schauberger claimed to have designed and constructed a small, remote-controlled flying saucer in 1940 in the Kertl aircraft company in Vienna. Reportedly, during a test conducted in 1943, the saucer went through the ceiling, but by and large it was otherwise unworkable. Later, Schauberger was allocated some Czechoslovakian engineers to help him expand his project, but when the war came to an end, some of his plans went to the Russians and others were claimed by the Americans. According to Schauberger, when he went back to work on his flying saucer project in 1958, aided by his son, the American authorities invited both of them to the United States, where they remained for several months, working on various projects, none of which turned out well. Schauberger died later that year.

Hermann Klaas, from Mühlheim, West Germany, a biotechnician specializing in aerodynamic phenomena, is another who claims to have worked on various remote-controlled models for disk-shaped aircraft during World War II. The most common model was 2.4 metres in diameter and propelled by an electro-engine supplied by the Luftwaffe. According to Klaas, these models were similar to those then being developed by Schriever, Habermohl, Miethe, and Belluzzo in Böhmen (Czechoslovakia) and Breslau (now Wrocklaw, Poland).

The stories of Rudolph Schriever and Georg Klein therefore share common ground. In an interview given to the Zürich newspaper *Tages-Anzeiger* on 19 November 1954, Klein insisted that flying saucers were top-secret weapons of the US and Russia, based on the German prototypes. At Breslau, in May 1945, the Russians captured, along with many leading technicians, a 'scale model' of a 'pilotless, ray-guided disk' that had been built at Peenemünde. At the close of the war, Walter Miethe went to America with Werner von Braun, Dornberger, and hundreds of other members of the Peenemünde rocket program; and both the Russians and the Americans were therefore in possession of the technology. There were, Klein stated, two kinds of modern saucer: one with a diameter of about 52 ft and powered by five jets; the other with a diameter of about 138 ft and powered by twelve jets. Klein supported the view that the flying saucers could remain stationary in the air and make sharp, right-angled turns. Stability, he said, was attained with a device based on the principle of the gyroscope. Klein also insisted that flying saucers developed in Canada by John Frost, former colleague of Sir Frank Whittle, had reached speeds of up to 1,500 mph and were inspected by Britain's Field-Marshal Montgomery.

Lusar supports this story, as well as confirming that Schriever was involved in Projekt Saucer and Miethe, though initially working under Werner von Braun for the United States' first rocket centre in the White Sands Proving Ground, New Mexico, joined the A.V. Roe (AVRO-Canada) aircraft company in Malton, Ontario, reportedly to continue work on disk-shaped aircraft, or flying saucers - just as Habermohl was thought to be doing with the Russians.

US intelligence was seriously concerned by the possibility that the flying saucers being sighted by so many were not of extraterrestrial origin, but were based on the German designs and being constructed and flown by Russians - and, possibly, Canadians.

Their suspicions about Russian-made flying saucers would not have been eased by the fact that in August 1952 it was revealed on French radio and in the German magazine, *Der Flieger*, that according to Dr Waldermar Beck a flying saucer had crashed at Spitsbergen, Norway, and its remains had been studied by the Norwegian rocket expert, Dr Noreal, as well as some unnamed German experts. The flying saucer carried no crew and had been flown by a radio piloting system that malfunctioned. It was 47 metres in diameter and consisted of 'an exterior disk provided at its peripheral with 46 automatic jets'. The disk was designed to pivot around the central sphere, which contained the measurement and remote-control panel. According to Dr Noreal, the saucer had a radio piloting transmitter with a nucleus of plutonium transmitting on all wave lengths with 934 hertz, a measure that was then unknown. The steel used in its construction was of an unknown alloy. The measurement instructions on the control panel were in Russian.

Regarding US suspicions about Canadian flying saucers, a declassified CIA report based on 'unevaluated information' and dated 18 August 1953 reveals that they may have believed this was possible because: 'According to recent reports from Toronto, a number of Canadian Air Force engineers are engaged in the construction of a "flying saucer" to be used as a future weapon of war. The work of these engineers is being carried out in great secrecy at the A. V. Roe Company factories.' This is followed by the observation: '"Flying saucers' have been known to be an actuality since the possibility of their construction was proven in plans drawn up by German engineers toward the end of World War II.'

US concern was only increased when the former

Luftwaffe engineer, Rudolph Schriever, not long before he died, began talking to the media about Projekt Saucer. In another declassified CIA document dated 27 May 1954, it is suggested that Projekt Saucer resulted in three designs: 'One, designed by Miethe, was a disk-shaped aircraft, 135 feet in diameter, which did not rotate; another, designed by Habermohl and Schriever, consisted of a large rotating ring, in the centre of which was a round, stationary cabin for the crew.' The report does not describe the third design, but goes on to confirm that when the Soviets occupied Prague, 'the Germans destroyed every trace of the "flying saucer" project and nothing more was heard of Habermohl and his assistants'. The report also states that in Breslau, the Soviets managed to capture one of the saucers built by Miethe; and that Rudolph Schriever had died recently in Bremen-Lehe, where he had been living since the end of the war.

This unease at the possibility of highly advanced Soviet or Canadian flying saucers may have been heightened even more by the knowledge, related in the same report, that a recent issue of *Forces Aériennes Francaises* (a monthly periodical published by the Comité d'Études Aéronautiques Militaires - Study Committee on Military Aeronautics - which was headed by General P. Fay, Chief of Staff of the Air Force) contained an article suggesting that 'supersonic interstellar ships powered by cosmic energy are possible'. Since the article was written by Lieutenant Plantier of the Ecole de L'Air de Salon (a prestigious aeronautical school), its acceptance by the magazine was read as an indication that the French Air Force was admitting to the existence of flying saucers.

Certainly, by 28 August 1954, a formal US Headquarters Strategic Air Command 'Request for Intelligence Information' was asking for 'a summary of information of knowledge Russia has pertaining to flying saucers'.

To accept that the Soviets could have been flying disk-shaped craft based on the German designs, we have to accept also that the Schriever-Habermohl-Miethe-Belluzzo machine, even if completed, would have had the capabilities of the flying saucers sighted shortly after the war.

Not too much is known about the men who worked on Projekt Saucer. We know that Rudolph Schriever was a Luftwaffe engineer and test pilot who insisted, right up to the day he died, that he had worked on the project. Walter Miethe worked on the V-1 rocket program at Peenemünde (where the saucer was said to have been constructed) and was one of the engineers taken to America with Dornberger and von Braun; he was then hired by the A.V. Roe Company (AVRO-Canada), where he worked on the disk-shaped aircraft, the Avrocar.

Of particular interest regarding the Avrocar, or Omega, is that according to the West German magazine, *Hobby* (14 December 1977) another German engineer, Andreas Epp, who came from Schriever's home town of Bremerhaven, also worked on the Avrocar project.

Nothing is known about Habermohl, other than what can be gleaned from the many unsubstantiated reports claiming that he worked on the saucer project in Breslau, before being captured by the Russians. Nor is there any information on the background or fate of the Italian physicist, Guiseppe Belluzzo; though the fact that he was an Italian working for the Germans during the war suggests that he was involved either through the supersonic research centre at Guidonia, near Rome, where the Germans supervised extensive research in supersonic aerodynamics, or the underground laboratories at Riva del Garda where, as we have seen, many experiments regarding special heat-resistant metals and the boundary layer were undertaken.

As for Georg Klein, who says that he communicated frequently with Belluzzo, the nature of his involvement with Projekt Saucer is obscure, and we only know for certain that he was a former engineer with Albert Speer's Ministry for Armament and Ammunition, and that after the war he moved to Zürich, Switzerland, where he continued to work in engineering.

What *is* known, then, is that all four of them were in positions to at least have been involved in certain aspects of Projekt Saucer.

Germany had the advanced technology required to create the *Feuerball*, or foo fighter, but the capabilities shown by the flying saucers sighted after the war could only have come through a perfected means of controlling the boundary layer and creating frictionless air flow. Relative to this, it is known that throughout the war Nazi Germany's great wind tunnels were being used for extensive research into suction with regard to ultra-high speed flight - with impressive results.

Certainly, before the end of the war, the ME-109G modified fighter plane had flown a number of experimental flights using its compressor as a suction pump as a means of decreasing drag and increasing speed. It is also known that by 1944, professors Pradtl and Busemann had completed the plans for a high-speed fighter designed to dramatically reduce aerodynamic friction, if not obliterate it altogether. Thus by the closing months of the war there were many rumours in German aeronautical circles about the imminent appearance of radically different aeroplanes, without wings, tails, rudders or other surface protuberances and powered by special turbines or jet engines, that would move through the air 'like a sponge through water' or, as Sir Ben Lockspieser later put it: 'like a bar of wet soap slips through the fingers'. In other words: at ultra-fast speeds and with extraordinary manoeuvrability.

The Schriever-Habermohl-Miethe-Belluzzo flying saucer, or the *Kugelblitz* described by Renato Vesco in *Intercettateli Senza Sparare*, could have been just such an aircraft.

Indeed, while Vesco makes no mention of the Schriever-Habermohl disk, his *Kugelblitz*, or Ball Lightning Fighter, certainly appears to be the same machine. According to Vesco, the *Kugelblitz* was a larger, piloted version of the small, whirling, antiradar device, the *Feuerball*, which harassed Allied aircraft during the closing months of the war.

Projects that German scientists had been working on during the closing stages of the war indicate that this piloted 'flying saucer' could have had a form of radio that can cancel at the pilot's discretion the return signals, or blips, from the enemy's radarscope and thus render the saucer 'invisible' to the enemy. It could also have had electromagnetically or electroacoustically controlled firing weapons, cannons that spit ignition-damaging gas instead of shells, and possibly even the first, unsophisticated laser or pulse-beam weapons. Lastly, it could have been made from a combination of *Luftschwamm*, or aerosponge, and an alloy that could withstand enormous pressures and a temperature of 1000° Centigrade - as was being created in the immense underground Riva del Garda research complex. In short, a remarkably advanced, vertical-rising jet fighter, shaped like the contemporary flying saucer.

Did such a machine exist? It certainly seems so. We *do* know that a machine very much like it, supposedly designed and constructed by Schriever, Miethe, Habermohl and the mysterious Dr Belluzzo, was reportedly test-flown sometime in February 1945 in the area of the underground complex at Kahla, in the southern Harz mountain range of Thuringia. According to witness Georg Klein, the machine reached a height of about 40,000 feet at a speed of approximately 1,250 mph.

Flugkapitän Rudolph Schriever was adamant that while the flying saucer was destroyed to prevent it falling into the hands of advancing Soviet troops, the documentation survived and was widely distributed between the Allies and the Soviets, as were many scientists and much equipment. Georg Klein, who concurred with the basic details of this scenario, was equally adamant that 'the "saucers" are at present being constructed in accordance with German technical principles' and could 'constitute serious competition to jet-propelled aeroplanes'.

In short, the flying saucers were man-made.

Chapter 5

Spinning Disks and Flying Saucers

On 16 April 1897, at the height of the Great Airship Scare, the citizens of Linn Grove, Iowa, watched an airship pass slowly overhead, then land briefly a few miles outside town. When the airship took off again, it emitted 'two large boulders of unknown composition'. Similarly, one of the six objects seen by Harold Dahl on 21 June 1947 near Maury Island expelled a rain of 'small, whitish metallic fragments' that were obviously hot and gave off steam when they plunged into the waters of Puget Sound.

As we shall see, a 'whitish metallic' colouring is the one most attributed to flying saucers; but the importance of the Maurey Island case is that *some* form of debris was reported as having been spewed out of what seemed like an 'ailing' craft before it flew off and disappeared with the others.

Inexplicably, the US Fourth Air Force A-2 Intelligence Branch did not investigate the Maury Island sighting area until 31 July - ten days after the event - when their agents, Captain William Davidson and Lieutenant Frank M. Brown, failed to find the countless 'small, whitish metallic fragments', but were given what appeared to be 'pieces of porous lava' by the individual who had started the whole UFO scare with his more widely publicized sighting of 24 June - namely, Kenneth Arnold, who had been hired by *Fate* magazine to investigate the case.

Arnold sent his own UFO debris to be examined at the chemical laboratory of the University of Chicago, where the pieces were classified as 'slag of volcanic origin'. The rest of the debris, in the care of the A-2 intelligence agents, was lost when the B-25 taking them back to Hamilton Air Force Base in California crashed near Kelso, Washington. Later, authorities at McChord AFB confirmed that the aeroplane had been carrying classified material and that while the crew chief, Master Sergeant L. Taff, and a passenger, Technician Fourth Grade Woodrow D. Mathews, had managed to parachute to safety, the two intelligence agents had died in the crash.

This was singularly ironic in view of the fact that it was the aerial search for the debris of a crashed Marine Corps C-46 transport that had led Arnold to his momentous sighting of nine UFOs as they flew in formation over Mount Rainier, also in the Cascades, on the border between the United States and Canada.

Perhaps not surprisingly, shortly after the A-2 intelligence agents and their UFO debris were lost in that second air crash, Dahl and the man to whom he had submitted his written report, his direct superior in the Puget Sound harbour patrol, Fred L. Christman, admitted (reportedly under pressure from the Army's remaining A-2 intelligence agents) that the UFO fragments were only pieces of mineral formation picked up at random on Maury Island and shown to the press to heighten interest in the UFO story.

There the Maury Island Mystery ended.

These two incidents are among the very few in which UFOs have reportedly 'dropped' or 'expelled' debris, though others have left debatable physical traces of their presence. However, in general it has to be accepted that most UFO reports do not include debris, though the initial postwar sightings established the appearance, characteristics and capabilities of what we now view as being standard for UFOs, or flying saucers.

The Maury Island incident was exploited by various people to the degree where separating the truth from the fiction in the historical records is now virtually impossible. Nevertheless, while there are those who still think it was a hoax, it *was* the first major postwar UFO sighting; and Dahl's descriptions of the UFO, whether or not invented, set the pattern for most of the future descriptions of UFOs.

Dahl said that the Maury Island UFOs were shaped like 'inflated inner tubes' and had no structural protuberances, appeared to be about 100 feet across, had 'holes' in their centres and portholes around their perimeters, with an observation window in their undersides (possibly the 'hole' in the centre), and looked metallic. They could hover virtually motionless in the air and were seen to ascend rapidly and vertically.

When Kenneth Arnold saw UFOs four days later, neither he nor anyone else had heard of the Maury Island sighting. Nevertheless, Arnold, a trained mountain-rescue pilot, offered remarkably similar descriptions of the nine unknowns that he witnessed flying over Mount Rainier in the Cascades. At first assuming the distant objects were P-51s, Arnold then realised that they were devoid of tail assemblies or other protuberances - other than, in the words of Flammonde, 'an apparent cockpit with a full window canopy' - and that the whole fuselage of the craft resembled a single, particularly graceful, swept-back 'wing' or 'boomerang'. While the objects appeared to be capable of extraordinary aerial manoeuvres, they flew horizontally like 'speedboats on water' or like 'a saucer would if you skipped it across the water'.

Though Arnold had trained as a pilot, he was not a military man. For this reason, we turn to *The Report on Unidentified Flying Objects*, in which Captain Edward J. Ruppelt, the Air Force's most assiduous and honest UFO investigator, relates that four days after the Arnold sighting, on 28 June, at 3.15pm, an Air Force pilot, when flying his F-51 near Lake Meade, Nevada, saw a formation of five or six 'circular objects' off his right wing. That evening, four Air Force officers, two pilots, and two intelligence officers from Maxwell AFB in Montgomery, Alabama, saw a 'bright light' traveling across the sky, zigzagging with bursts of high speed, and making a sharp, 90-degree turn before shooting off.

On 4 July, at 11.00am, in Portland, Oregon, a carload of people driving near Redmond saw four 'disk-shaped objects' streaking past Mount Jefferson. At 1.05pm a policeman in the parking lot behind the Portland City Police Headquarters looked up to see 'five large, disk-shaped objects' flying at a high rate of speed and 'oscillating about their lateral axis'. Minutes later, two other policemen, both former pilots, saw three similar objects 'flying in trail' and four harbour patrol crewmen saw flying disks 'shaped like chrome hub caps' and 'oscillating' as they flew overhead. Numerous citizens of Portland saw similar objects at approximately the same time.

That night, a United Airlines crew flying near Emmett, Idaho, reported seeing five unidentified flying objects which were 'thin and smooth on the bottom and rough-appearing on top; two days later the crew of an Air Force B-25 saw 'a bright, disk-shaped object' flying lower than the aircraft; then a pilot flying across Fairfield-Suisun AFB, California, saw something that was 'oscillating on its lateral axis' as it traversed three-quarters of the sky in a few seconds.

However, the sighting that really made the Air Force sit up and take an interest in UFOs was the one that occurred four days later, on 8 July, at Muroc Air Base (now Edwards AFB), the supersecret Air Force test centre in the Mojave Desert, California.

At ten in the morning a test pilot observed what he thought was a weather balloon until he noticed that it was going *against* the wind. Studying it more carefully, he thought it was 'spherically shaped and yellowish white in colour'. It later transpired than ten minutes earlier several other officers and airmen had seen three similar objects, but of a 'silver' appearance, heading in the same direction. Two hours later, a crew of technicians on Rogers Dry Lake, adjacent to Muroc Air Base, observed a 'round object, white aluminium colour' in the vicinity of a formation of two P.82s and an A-26 aircraft which were carrying out a seat-ejection experiment. As the ejected experimental seat-and-dummy fell, the object followed it down, but drifting *against* the wind, until it was seen to have 'a distinct, oval-shaped outline, with two projections on the upper surface which might have been thick fins or nobs'. These projections crossed each other at intervals, suggesting 'either rotation or oscillation of slow type'. No means of propulsion were noticed and the object made no sound. It had the colour of an 'aluminium-painted fabric'. Four hours later, the pilot of an F-51 flying at 20,000 feet spotted a 'flat object of a light-reflecting nature' which had no vertical fin or wings. He tried to pursue it, but could not climb high enough.

Already, the basic characteristics of UFOs had a striking consistency. They were semi-circular or circular, usually domed or with viewing windows on the top or bottom, and could resemble either an inverted plate or two plates together, one placed upside down on the other. They were usually of a whitish-grey or metallic appearance. They flew horizontally with a slight bouncing motion, like 'speedboats on water' or 'a saucer would if you skipped it across the water'; but they could also change direction rapidly, ascend and descend vertically, and in general perform theoretically impossible aerial manoeuvres at remarkably low and high speeds. Most of them 'oscillated', but were silent and showed no means of propulsion.

If the Harold Dahl sighting at Maury Island was a hoax, it was a brilliantly conceived hoax indeed, because the UFOs described above were remarkably similar in configuration and envisaged potential to the 'flying wings' and 'humped airfoils' that were then being developed in the National Physical Laboratory and other aeronautical establishments through the US and Canada. In turn, these were based on the boundary-layer experiments that had already been conducted extensively in Nazi Germany.

By then, it had been widely accepted that control of the boundary layer was the key to hithertofore impossible high speeds and extraordinary manoeuvrability in flight; and that the 'suction' method - in which air is sucked through air vents, or slots, in the wing, to be expelled as added propulsion - was superior to the 'blowing' method of standard rotors, or propellers. Because of this, numerous experiments had been conducted on elliptical, boomerang-shaped, and 'humped' airfoils, or flying wings, lined with suction slots - resulting in such aircraft as the Armstrong Whitworth twin-engined, all-wing jet, the AW-52 Boomerang. When one of the AW-52 Boomerangs crashed, further development of the model ceased; but it was followed by aircraft with an even greater sweepback and a more strikingly 'triangular' form - such as the Hawker Siddeley Group's 'Aero Delta' aircraft, the Avro 698 and Avro 707B, as well as other 'flying wing' jet-propelled prototypes. Such aircraft, with their elliptical, semicircular, boomerang, or triangular shapes, undoubtedly were the forerunners of the completely circular, supersonic aircraft known as 'flying saucers' and seen mostly by trained observers over top-secret military establishments.

Nevertheless, while the abovementioned sightings offered purely visual support for the general appearance of the UFOs, the *physical* reality of the UFOs remained in doubt. Ironically, the removal of those doubts began with a 'classic' UFO encounter that may in fact have been a 'classic' case of misidentification.

It was also the first instance of a human death being caused by a UFO.

The 'Mantell Incident' began at 1.15pm on 7 January 1947 when the Kentucky State Highway Patrol phoned the control tower operators at Godman AFB, Louisville, Kentucky, to inform them that a lot of people from Maysville, a small town eighty miles east of Louisville, had reported seeing a strange craft. Though nothing was known to be flying in the area at that time, the state police called back about fifteen or twenty minutes later with more reports of a 'strange craft' seen over the towns of Owensboro and Irvington, west of Louisville. Most witnesses described the objects as being 'circular, about 250 to 300 feet in diameter' and moving westward at high speed.

While the control tower operators at Godman AFB still had no record of anything in the air, they deduced from the reports that as the UFO would have had to pass north of Godman to get from Maysville to Owensboro, it might return.

It did. At 1.45pm it passed over Godman and was witnessed by the control tower operators, the base operations officer, the base intelligence officer, and several other key personnel, all of whom, after studying the UFO through binoculars, decided that they could not identify it.

At 2.30pm four F-51s were despatched to take a look at the object and try to identify it. One of the aeroplanes was forced to return to base due to a lack of fuel, but the other three, led by the flight leader, Captain Thomas F. Mantell, climbed to 10,000 feet in pursuit of the object. At 2.45pm Mantell called the tower and said, 'I see something above and ahead of me and I'm still climbing.' This statement was confirmed by all of the people in the tower.

What is *not* confirmed by everyone is that Mantell then said, 'I've sighted the thing. It looks metallic and it's tremendous in size... Now it's starting to climb!' Everyone in the tower *did* agree that Mantell then said, 'I'm going to 20,000 feet.'

According to the statements they gave later, Mantell's two wing men were then at 15,000 feet and trying frantically to call their flight leader, who had climbed above them and was out of sight. By the time the wing men had returned to their base at Standiford Field, north of Godman, Mantell had crashed and died.

Though Mantell's disputed statement, 'It looks metallic and it's tremendous in size... Now it's starting to climb!' was spread far and wide, the official stance was that Mantell had mistaken the planet Venus for a UFO and blacked out due to lack of oxygen when climbing too high in pursuit of a UFO that wasn't actually there. However, ATIC's Project Sign team soon discovered that this could not have been possible. On the other hand, two people, including an astronomer, had reported seeing a balloon in the sky at the time and subsequent investigations by the Project Sign team revealed that a classified skyhook balloon project may have been operating out of Clinton County AFB in northern Ohio. As the winds were such that a skyhook balloon launched from Clinton County AFB could have been seen from Godman AFB even as high as 60,000 feet, it is possible that Mantell *could* have died chasing just such a balloon.

Two things cast doubt on this possibility. One is that few of those who knew Mantell, an experienced pilot, could imagine him spending so much time - nearly twenty minutes - in pursuit of a balloon without realising what it was. Indeed, according to Captain Ruppelt, one of Mantell's friends went on record as saying that Mantell was one of the most cautious pilots he had known and he could not conceive of him disregarding his shortage of oxygen.

'The only thing I can think,' Ruppelt reports this friend as saying, 'was that he was after something that he believed to be more important than his life or his family.'

According to Ruppelt, the second thing that casts doubt on the likelihood of Mantell chasing a skyhook balloon is that while the people who were working with the early skyhook projects claimed that they could remember operating out of Clinton County AFB in 1947, none of them were willing to be pinned down to that particular date.

Finally, in *The Report on Unidentified Flying Objects*, Ruppelt comments: 'Somewhere in the archives of the Air Force or the Navy there are records that will show whether or not a balloon was launched from Clinton County AFB, Ohio, on January 7, 1948. I never could find those records.'

Whether or not the unfortunate Captain Mantell died pursuing something 'metallic' and 'tremendous in size' will never be known, but certainly many of the UFOs being seen at that time fitted those two descriptions. Mantell's death at least rocked the Air Force and made them sit up and take notice of the UFO phenomenon - but what really got them moving was an extraordinary sighting that took place eighteen months later.

At 2.45am on 24 July 1948, in the middle of a

scheduled Eastern Airlines trip from Houston, Texas, to Atlanta, Georgia, the pilots, Clarence S. Chiles and John B. Whitted, saw an unidentified light straight ahead of them and closing fast. Chiles, the captain, quickly put his DC-3 into an evasive tight left turn. The UFO flashed by about 700 feet to the right and then pulled up in a steep climb.

Chiles and his co-pilot, Whitted, both got a good look at the UFO and later agreed that it had resembled a B-29 fuselage, with its underside emitting a 'deep blue glow' and a '50-foot trail of orange-red flame' shooting out the back. It also had 'two rows of windows from which bright lights glowed'. (Two years later, on 31 March 1950, the pilots of another DC-3, flying from Memphis, Tennessee, to Little Rock, Arkansas, almost collided with a UFO which they assumed was disk-shaped because of the 'circular arrangement of eight or ten "portholes", each one glowing from a strong bluish-white light' that seemed to come from the inside of the object.) Minutes after the sighting by Chiles and Whitted, a crew chief at Robins Air Force Base in Macon, Georgia, witnessed 'an extremely bright light' passing overhead and traveling at high speed. Another pilot, flying that night near the Virginia-North Carolina state line at approximately the same time as the DC-3 was 'buzzed' by the UFO, reported seeing 'a bright shooting star' in the direction of Montgomery, Alabama.

The sightings were correlated by ATIC and according to Captain Ruppelt their findings confirmed that the UFO which nearly collided with the airliner would have flown almost over Macon, Georgia, after passing that aircraft - and it had been turning in the direction of Macon when last seen.

Because the story of the crew chief at Robins AFB, 200 miles away, seemed to confirm the sighting, not to mention the report from near the Virginia-North Carolina state line, the Air Force was finally convinced that the UFO phenomenon was real, that it involved solid, moving objects, and that it warranted serious examination.

When ATIC's Project Sign submitted an official Estimate of the Situation, the UFOs stepped out of mythology and into reality.

The saucer-shaped configuration and manoeuvring capabilities of the UFOs had been verified, but confirmation of what appeared to be their unusually large size and remarkable top speeds was still missing. A Navy Commander, R.B. McLaughlin, had worked throughout 1948 and 1949 with a team of engineers, technicians and scientists on a classified skyhook balloon project, located in the Navy's top-secret guided-missile test and development area in the White Sands Proving Ground, New Mexico. On 24 April 1949, at 10.00am in an 'absolutely clear' Sunday morning, when McLaughlin and his team were preparing to launch one of their huge skyhook balloons (100 feet in diameter), the whole crew saw a UFO which, though high up, was clearly 'elliptical in shape' and had a 'whitish-silver' colour. With a theodolite, stop-watch, and 25-power telescope, they were able to track the UFO as it dropped from an angle of elevation of 45° to 25°, then abruptly shot upward and disappeared. Even after putting a reduction factor on the data recorded on the theodolite, McLaughin estimated that the UFO was approximately 40 feet wide and 100 feet long, had been at an altitude of fifty-six miles, and was traveling at seven miles per second, or approximately 25,000 mph.

According to Captain Ruppelt, there was some 'legitimate doubt' as to the accuracy of the speed and altitude figures that Commander McLaughlin's team arrived at from the data they measured with the theodolite. However, he points out that 'this doesn't mean much' and that even if they had been off by a factor of 100 per cent, the speeds and altitude of the UFO would be 'fantastic'. He also reminds us that various members of McLaughlin's team studied the object through a 25-power telescope and swore that it was a 'flat, oval-shaped object'.

Shortly after relating this information to the public in an article he wrote for the March 1950 issue of *True* magazine, Commander McLaughlin was transferred back to sea.

Nevertheless, his report had finally confirmed the extraordinary speeds and altitudes reached by UFOs.

Three years later, when the Robertson Panel submitted its infamous recommendations for a mass 'debunking' of the UFO phenomenon (see Chapter 12, pages 268-73), its conclusions flew directly in the face of the evidence presented by the Project Blue Book chief, Captain Ruppelt, who was convinced that the UFOs were actual aircraft of highly developed technology. While visual sightings of UFOs were by then in great abundance, what Ruppelt wanted were some sightings which would, in his view, produce enough data to confirm that they were intelligently controlled vehicles.

He found three such sightings.

The first occurred over Haneda AFB, now Tokyo International Airport, in Japan, in late August 1952. The UFO was first observed by two control tower operators who saw a large, brilliant light in the northwest over Tokyo Bay. The light, which was moving, was observed through 7 x 50 binoculars. It had a constant brilliance, was circular in shape, and appeared to be the upper portion of a large, round, dark shape which was about four times the diameter of the light itself. Then, when it moved, the tower operators saw a second, dimmer light on the lower edge of the dark, shadowy portion. This particular UFO was tracked simultaneously by radar and observed by intelligence officers as it flew back and forth across the central part of Tokyo Bay, sometimes almost hovering, then abruptly accelerating to 300 miles an hour. It was pursued by, and 'deliberately' eluded, an F-94 plane.

The sighting was thoroughly investigated by the FEAF intelligence officers in the area, then later investigated just as thoroughly by Captain Ruppelt. Both agreed that it was not a weather target, definitely not a star, and that visual and radar lock-ons had proved that it was solid *and* moving. They also proved that each turn the UFO made was constant, and that the straight 'legs' between the turns were about the same length. Indeed, Ruppelt later wrote that the sketch of the UFO's flight path reminded him very much of the crisscross patterns he used to fly during World War II - and that the only time the UFO had seriously deviated from this pattern was when the F-94 tried to pursue it.

The second sighting was one that occurred on the night of 29 July 1952, when an F-94 attempted to intercept a

UFO over eastern Michigan. This sighting was even more interesting in that there was a definite reason for every move the UFO made. First, it made a 180° turn because the F-94 was closing in on it. Next, it alternately increased and decreased its speed - but only increased its speed when the aeroplane was closing in on it and always slowed down when it was just out of range of the aeroplane's radar.

Adding weight to his argument that such movements could not have been random, Ruppelt submitted a third report - the one he called the 'best unknown ever' - a report of an F-84 pilot who chased an object right across Rapid City, south Dakota. According to the pilot *and* the radar operators who had located the object, the target accelerated and decelerated so that there was always *precisely* three miles between it and the F-84 - and it kept this up until the F-84 started running out of fuel and was forced to return to base. Later, both the pilot and the tower controller told Ruppelt that the UFO seemed to have some kind of automatic warning radar linked to its power supply.

This capability has been attributed to every modern UFO, from the German *Feuerballs* and *Kugelblitz* to the more advanced craft seen 'bobbing' over mountainous terrain or the buildings of military establishments.

By the mid-1950s ex-Air Chief Marshal of the RAF, Lord Dowding, was backing the UFOs, but reserved his judgement on what they were. Herman Oberth, the 'father' of German rocket development, publicly declared that they were interplanetary vehicles. In Belgium, a senator demanded an answer to the UFO mystery from the Secretary of Defence. In France, the French General Staff set up a committee, the *Groupment d'Études des Phénomènes Aériens*, to study UFO reports. In England, the aviation magazine, *Aeroplane*, examined the subject, but refused to come to any definite conclusion. In the Iron Curtain countries, UFOs were widely discussed - but purely as a form of capitalist propaganda. In the United States, two civilian UFO organizations were formed: The Aerial Phenomena Research Organization (APRO), located in Tucson, Arizona, and the National Investigating Committee for Aerial Phenomenon (NICAP), located in Washington, D.C. Both gained a wide membership, including noted scientists and former military and air force personnel, as well as a great deal of respect internationally for the sane and sober manner in which they investigated major UFO sightings.

The UFOs were widely reported as being flat disks, domed disks, double-domed disks, hemispherical disks, and spherical, elliptical, triangular, or cylindrical in general outline. They were capable of flying soundlessly at remarkable speeds and of making extraordinary manoeuvres. They could ascend and descend vertically, hover impossibly in mid-air, change direction abruptly, follow the terrain of Earth, seemingly automatically, and disappear in 'the blinking of an eye'. They were mostly silvery or a 'whitish-metallic' colour, had 'portholes' or other 'orifices' around their rims, and 'oscillated' around their lateral axes.

The most commonly reported shape certainly resembled the Germans' World War II 'wide-surface ring which rotated around a fixed, cupola-shaped cockpit' or 'large rotating ring, in the centre of which was a round, stationary cabin for the crew'. Last but not least, the UFOs fitting this description invariably showed up on radar screens, were confirmed by theodolites as physical objects, and appeared to fly away when pursued.

In short: the UFOs, or flying saucers, were not as 'alien' as they appeared to be... and possibly originated right here on Earth.

Chapter 6

The UFO Invasion

The guided missile test range at White Sands Proving Ground in New Mexico is spread over many square miles and, with its numerous cinetheodolite camera stations linked together by a telephone system, is fully equipped to track high, fast-moving objects. A cinetheodolite is similar to a 35mm movie camera, except that when a moving object is photographed with it, the developed photograph will also contain three readings that show the time the photo was taken, the azimuth angle, and the elevation angle of the camera. If two or more cinetheodolites photograph the same flying object, it is possible to obtain rough estimates of the object's size, speed and altitude – rough estimates because cinetheodolites do not give accurate readings and too many UFOlogists think they do.

Ruppelt, in *The Report on Unidentified Flying Objects*, relates two incidents which proved for him that the UFO phenomenon was based on sightings of real, solid objects.

On 27 April 27 1950, shortly after a guided missile had been fired from the White Sands Proving Ground and fallen back to earth, Air Force technicians spotted an object streaking across the sky. As most of the camera stations had already unloaded their film, only one camera was able to catch a shot of the UFO before it disappeared. That photo showed only a dark, smudgy object - but it also proved that the object had been moving. A month later, during another missile test, another UFO appeared, and this time two members of the camera teams saw it and shot several feet of film of the 'bright, shiny object' streaking across the sky. That film was subsequently processed and analyzed by the Data Reduction Group at White Sands. By putting a correction factor in the data gathered by the two cameras, they were able to calculate that the object was higher than 40,000 feet, was traveling over 2,000 mph, and was over 300 feet in diameter.

Ruppelt makes it clear that these figures were only estimates, based on the possibly erroneous correction factor. However, what they did prove is that *something* had been in the air and it had been *solid* and moving very fast. The photos were enough to convince Ruppelt of the reality of the phenomenon, but what shook the Air Force in general were two major flaps that came the following year: the Lubbock Lights and the Fort Monmouth sightings.

As related by Captain Ruppelt, the Lubbock affair began on the evening of 25 August 1951, when an employee of the Atomic Energy Commission's supersecret Sandia Corporation - one with a top 'Q' security clearance - looked up from his garden on the outskirts of Albuquerque, New Mexico, and saw a huge aircraft flying swiftly and silently over his home. He later described it as having the shape of a 'flying wing', about one-and-a-half times the size of a B-26, with six to eight softly glowing, bluish lights on the aft end of its wings.

That same evening, about twenty minutes after this sighting, four professors from the Texas Technological College at Lubbock - a geologist, a chemist, a physicist, and a petroleum engineer -observed a formation of lights streaking across the sky: about fifteen to thirty separate lights, all a bluish-green colour, moving from north to south in a semicircular formation.

Early in the morning of 26 August, only a few hours after the Lubbock sightings, two different radars at an Air Defence Command radar station located in Washington State showed an unknown target traveling at 900 mph at 1,300 feet and heading in a northwesterly direction.

On 31 August two women were driving near Matador, seventy miles north-east of Lubbock, when they saw a 'pear-shaped object' about 150 yards ahead of them, about 120 feet in the air, drifting to the east at less than the take-off speed of a Cub aeroplane. One of those witnesses was familiar with aircraft - she was married to an air force officer and had lived on or near air bases for years - and she swore that the object was about the size of a B-29 fuselage, had a porthole on one side, made absolutely no noise as it moved *into* the wind, and suddenly picked up speed and climbed out of sight in a 'tight, spiralling' motion.

That same evening, an amateur photographer, Carl Hart, Jr., took five photos of a V formation of the same bluish-green lights as they flew over his backyard. Finally, a rancher's wife told her husband (who related the story to Captain Ruppelt) that she had seen a large object gliding swiftly and silently over her house. That object was observed about ten minutes after the Sandia Corporation executive had viewed *his* object; it was described as 'an aeroplane without a body', and the woman said that on the aft edge of the wing were pairs of glowing lights -an exact description of the Albuquerque sightings made by the Sandia employee.

Subsequent investigation by the Air Force's Project Blue Book team confirmed that the Washington State radar lock-on had been a solid target - not a weather target. It was then calculated that an object flying between that radar station and Lubbock would have been on a north-westerly course at the time it was seen at the two places - and that it would have had a speed of approximately 900 mph, as calculated by the radar.

The five photographs taken by Carl Hart, Jr. were analysed by the specialist Photo Reconnaissance Laboratory at Wright Field. The results showed that the lights, in an inverted V formation, had crossed about 120° of open sky at a 30° per second angular velocity - which corresponded exactly to the angular velocity measured carefully by the four professors from the Technical College at Lubbock. Analysis of the photos also showed that the lights were a great deal brighter than the surrounding stars and that their unusual intensity could have been caused by an exceptionally bright light source which had a colour at the most distant red end of the spectrum, bordering on infrared.

As the human eye is not sensitive to such a light, the light could appear dim to the eye - as many of the Lubbock lights did - but be exceptionally bright on film, as they were on the photographs. While according to the Photo Reconnaissance Laboratory, at that time there was nothing flying that had those particular characteristics, Captain Ruppelt and his fellow investigators were startled by the discovery that the lights on the photos were strikingly similar to those described by the Atomic Energy Commission employee as being on the aft edge of the huge

UFO that passed silently over his house.

Did something solid pass over Albuquerque, New Mexico, and fly 250 miles to Lubbock, Texas, at an approximate speed of 900 mph? According to the witnesses, and to the radar and visual-tracking calculations, it did. The Lubbock files were also studied by a group of rocket experts, nuclear physicists and intelligence experts, and they were all convinced that the sightings had been of an enormous, solid object, most likely with a 'highly swept-back wing configuration' and with 'a series of small jet orifices all around its edge'.

According to Captain Ruppelt, the extraordinary findings of the Lubbock investigation, and the furore aroused by the sightings themselves, finally galvanized a harassed Air Force into action. However, official 'respectability' truly came to the UFO problem with the Fort Monmouth sightings that took place a month later at the Army Signal Corps radar centre at Fort Monmouth, New Jersey.

The flap began at 11.10am on 10 September 1951, when a student operator was giving a demonstration of automatic radar tracking to a group of visiting top brass. After spotting an object flying about 12,000 yards southeast of the station, the operator switched to automatic tracking, but failed to hold the object and, in his confusion, blurted out to the VIPs that the object was going too fast for the set - which meant that it was flying faster than any known jet. After three minutes, during which it continued to fly too fast for the automatic radar tracking, the UFO disappeared.

Checks with the weather department revealed that

there were no indications of the kind of temperature inversion that, by bending the light passing through it, can create unusual moving shapes or false radar images.

Twenty-five minutes later, the pilot of a T-33 jet trainer, carrying an Air Force major as passenger and flying 20,000 feet over Mount Pleasant, New Jersey, observed 'a dull, silver, disk-like object' below him. He described it as thirty to fifty feet in diameter. When the object descended toward Sandy Hook, the T-33 pilot went after it. As he approached, it stopped abruptly, hovered impossibly, then suddenly sped south, made a 120° turn, and vanished out to sea. The Air Force major confirmed this sighting.

At 3.15pm, back at the Fort Monmouth radar centre, a frantic call was received from headquarters, demanding that they pick up an unknown that was flying very high, to the north, roughly where the first UFO had vanished. A radar lock-on confirmed that the UFO was traveling slowly at 93,000 feet - or eighteen miles above the Earth - and it could also be made out visually as a silver speck.

No known aircraft of that period could fly eighteen miles above the Earth.

Next morning, two radar sets picked up another unknown that climbed, levelled out, dived and climbed again repeatedly, too fast for the automatic radar tracking. When the object climbed, it 'went almost straight up'. The flap ended that afternoon when the radar tracked another slowly moving UFO and tracked it for several minutes, before it disappeared.

Following the sightings, Major General C.P. Cabell, representing the Director of Intelligence of the Air Force, ordered an immediate investigation. In a matter of hours, two officers from the Air Technical Intelligence Centre (ATIC) at Wright-Patterson were on an aeroplane to Lubbock. Once there, they worked around the clock, interrogating everyone involved in the sighting - pilots, radar operators, technicians and instructors - and a couple of days later they were in the Pentagon, submitting their report to General Cabell and other high-ranking intelligence officers. Every word of that meeting was recorded, but the recording, as Ruppelt states, was 'so hot that it was later destroyed'.

Nevertheless, the Monmouth sightings, combined with the Lubbock sightings, compelled Major General Cabell to order ATIC to establish a new, more serious UFO investigations project. In April, 1952, Project Grudge was renamed Project Blue Book and Captain Edward J. Ruppelt was placed in charge. He was soon faced with the most frightening UFO flap of them all... and with the revelation that the US Government and the Pentagon were not as keen on official UFO investigations as they appeared to be.

In 1952, Washington DC was 'invaded' by UFOs to a degree that had not been duplicated before and has not been since.

By June of that year, the US Air Force's Project Blue Book was going strong under the leadership of Captain Edward J. Ruppelt and had received more official UFO reports than it had done in any previous month in its history. In fact, according to Ruppelt, the sheer number of reports was making Air Force officers in the Pentagon frantic.

By 15 June, the locations, timing, and sequence of the

reports indicated that the UFOs were gradually closing in on Washington D.C.

Throughout the afternoon of 15 June, reports of ‘round, shiny objects’ and ‘silvery spheres’ came in from all over Virginia, one after the other: 3.40pm at Unionville; 4.20pm at Gordonsville; 4.25pm at Richmond; then 4.43pm and 5.43pm at Gordonsville. At 7.35pm a lot of people in Blackstone, about eighty miles south of Gordonsville, observed a ‘round, shiny object with a golden glow’ moving from north to south. By 7.59pm the same object was observed by the people in the CAA radio facility at Blackstone. At 8.00pm a jet from Langley Air Force Base tried to intercept it, but five minutes later the object, moving too slowly to be an aeroplane, disappeared.

So inexplicable and disturbing were these reports that Captain Ruppelt was called to Washington to give a briefing in the restricted area of the fourth-floor ‘B’ ring of the Pentagon to General Samford, the Director of Intelligence, some of the members of his staff, two Navy captains from the Office of Naval Intelligence, and some others whom Ruppelt could not name for security reasons. That meeting resulted in ‘a directive to take further steps to obtain positive identification of the UFOs’.

Meanwhile, the sightings continued. By the end of June, it had become apparent that there was a considerable build-up of sightings in the eastern United States. In Massachusetts, New Jersey and Maryland jet fighters were scrambled almost nightly for a week, but always foiled when their radar-locks were broken by the abrupt, swift manoeuvres of the UFOs. On 1 July, many UFOs were sighted over Boston, then began working their way down the coast. The same day, according to Blue Book reports, two UFOs had 'come down across Boston on a southwesterly heading, crossed Long Island, hovered a few minutes over the Army's secret laboratories at Fort Monmouth, then proceeded toward Washington'. A few hours later, the first report from Washngton was submitted by a physics professor at George Washington University.

For the next couple of weeks, reports about Washington sightings poured in at the rate of twenty or thirty a day and, according to Ruppelt, 'unknowns were running about 40 per cent'. Finally, on the night of 19 July, the most highly publicized sightings in UFO history began.

At 11.40pm two radars at Washington National Airport picked up eight unidentified targets near Andrews AFB, Maryland. The objects were flying at approximately 100 mph to 130 mph, then they suddenly accelerated to 'fantastically high speeds' and left the area. They soon returned, en masse. During the night, tower operators and the aircrews of several airliners saw unidentified lights in the same locations indicated by the radar. Before the night was out, and while interceptor jets tried and failed to catch them, the unidentified targets had moved into every sector covered by the radarscopes, including the 'prohibited corridor' over the White House and the Capitol. A colourful climax was reached when, in the early hours of the morning, the operators in the control tower at Andrews AFB, in response to an ARTC traffic controller's query about a target directly over the Andrews Radio range station, located near their tower, reported that a 'large, fiery, orange-coloured sphere' was hovering in the sky directly above them.

Captain Ruppelt had not been informed of the sightings and only found out about them when he bought a newspaper at the Washington International Airport Terminal Building after a flight from Dayton, Ohio. He rushed immediately to the Pentagon where he had an urgent meeting with ATIC's Pentagon liaison man, Major Dewey Fournet, and Colonel Bower, an intelligence officer from nearby Bolling AFB. They confirmed that throughout the night the restricted corridor around the White House had been filled with interceptor jets trying to chase numerous UFOs, that the UFOs had been radar tracked all around Washington DC, that an analysis of the sightings had completely ruled out temperature inversions, and that the radar operators at Washington National Airport and Andrews AFB - plus at least two veteran airline pilots - had all sworn that their sightings were caused by the radar waves bouncing off solid objects.

On behalf of the Air Force, public relations officer Al Chops gave the press an official 'No comment' on the sightings. In the meantime, Captain Ruppelt tried to set up a thorough investigation, but was blocked whichever way he turned. He planned to go all over the area, to every sighting location, but he hardly got out of the Pentagon.

First, he called the transportation section for a car - and was refused. Next, he went down to the finance office to see if he could *rent* a car - and was refused that as well. Next, he was reminded that he was supposed to be on his way back to Dayton, and that if he didn't leave, he would be technically AWOL.Ruppelt gave up in disgust and returned to Dayton.

However, within a week to the hour of the first major

flap, another UFO 'invasion' took place over Washington DC - and this time it was even more impressive.

At approximately 10.30pm on 26 July, the same radar operators who had seen the previous UFOs picked up a lot of 'slowly moving' targets... but this time the UFOs were spread out in a huge arc around Washington - from Herndon, Virginia, to Andrews AFB.

In short, they had Washington boxed in.

By 11.30pm four or five of the targets were being tracked continually over the Capitol. F-94 interceptor jets tried and failed to catch them. Shortly after the UFOs left the sky over the Capitol, UFO reports came in from Langley AFB, near Newport News, Virginia, where the operators described them as unidentified lights that were 'rotating and giving off alternating colours'. Another F-94 was despatched from Langley AFB and visually vectored to the lights by the tower operators. The pilot reported that as he approached one of the lights, it went out 'like somebody turning off a light bulb'. No sooner had this happened, than the targets came back on the radarscopes at Washington National Airport. Again, F-94s were despatched to locate them - but each time they were vectored into the lights, the UFOs disappeared abruptly from the radarscopes and the pilots simultaneously reported that they had visually observed the lights blinking out.

This game of cat and mouse between the UFOs and the interceptor planes continued throughout the night until, just before dawn, the last of the UFOs disappeared from the radarscopes.

Throughout that same night, there was chaos in Washington.The press was furious because all reporters and photographers had been ordered out of the radar rooms at the time the Air Force interceptors were chasing the UFOs. However, once the press had gone, arguments blew up in those radar towers and in the Pentagon. According to Dewey Fournet, ATIC's Pentagon liaison man, everyone in the radar rooms had been convinced that the targets had been caused by solid, metallic objects and could not have been anything else - and whatever they were, they could literally hover in the air, then abruptly accelerate to thousands of miles per hour.

Soon, a story was circulating the President Truman had personally witnessed UFOs skimming right around the White House. There is no confirmation for such a story, but it is known that about 10.00am the next day, the President's air aide, Brigadier General Landry, called Intelligence at Truman's personal request to find out what was going on. Captain Ruppelt was the one who took that call, but he had to hedge his answers, because he could not explain the sightings away.

It was the Washington sightings more than anything else that made the Project Blue Book staff suspicious of the official Air Force stance on UFOs. In fact, Blue Book spent over a year investigating the sightings and some of the team were shaken by what they discovered.

For a start, when the tower operators at Andrews AFB were later interrogated about the 'large, fiery, orange-coloured sphere' they had reported seeing right over the Andrews Radio range station, located near their control tower, they completely changed their story and said that what they had really seen was a star.

Ruppelt found it had to credit that trained radar

operators would mistake 'a large, fiery, orange-coloured sphere' for a star; he was further disconcerted when he learned that according to astronomical charts there had been no exceptionally bright stars where the UFO was reported to have been seen. Ruppelt then found out, from what he claimed was a reliable source, that the tower operators had been 'persuaded' to change their stories.

Likewise, the pilot of an F-94C, who had told Ruppelt about vainly trying to intercept unidentified lights, later stated in his official report that all he had seen was a ground light reflecting off a layer of haze - a patently ridiculous statement, since both the pilot and the radar had confirmed that the lights had repeatedly disappeared and reappeared in the sky before eventually shooting away.

Regarding the Air Force's continuing insistence that the lights had been caused by temperature inversions, Blue Book checked out the strength of the inversions through the Air Defence Command Weather Forecast Centre - and at no time during that flap was there a temperature inversion strong enough to show up on the radar. Finally, no weather target makes a 180° turn and flies away every time an aeroplane reaches it.

The Washington sightings, according to Project Blue Book, are still unknowns.

While the UFO 'invasion' of Washington was unprecedented, it was followed by another series of sightings that would deepen Ruppelt's concern about what the UFOs were, where they came from, and who knew about them.

A couple of months after the Washington UFO

'invasion', at the beginning of September 1952, there was a build-up of UFO sightings from the southeastern United States, notably Georgia and Alabama. A disconcerting number of them were from the vicinity of the new, top-secret Atomic Energy Commission complex at Savannah River; many more were over Brookley Air Force Base near Mobile, Alabama. That same month, the NATO naval forces were holding manoeuvres - known as Operation Mainbrace - off the coast of Europe.

On 20 September, a US newspaper reporter and a group of pilots and flight deck crew on board an aircraft carrier in the North Sea watched a 'perfectly clear, silvery sphere' moving across the sky just behind the fleet of ships. The object was large and appeared to be moving rapidly, so the reporter shot several pictures of it. These were developed straight away and immediately studied by the intelligence officers on board the aircraft carrier. The pictures were excellent and the object shown looked like a large balloon - but no balloons were in the area and a later analysis of all the photographs proved conclusively that the object had been moving very fast.

The following day, six Royal Air Force pilots flying a formation of jet fighters over the North Sea saw a 'shiny, spherical object' coming from the direction of the NATO fleet. They took after it and lost it, but when they neared their base, one of the pilots noticed that the UFO was following them. He turned back towards it, but the UFO also turned away and outdistanced the RAF aeroplane in a matter of minutes.

Finally, on the third day of the NATO exercise, a UFO was observed near the fleet, this time over the Topcliffe

Aerodrome on the English mainland. A pilot in a British jet was sent in pursuit and managed to get close enough to describe the object as 'round, silvery and white' and to note that it 'seemed to rotate around its vertical axis and sort of wobble'. When he tried to get closer, the UFO shot off and soon disappeared.

According to what an RAF intelligence officer later told Captain Ruppelt at a Pentagon meeting, it was the Operation Mainbrace sightings that finally forced the RAF to officially recognise the UFO phenomenon. Though this was later denied by the RAF, Captain Ruppelt had other reasons to be particularly intrigued, and disturbed, by events that related the Washington UFO invasion to the Mainbrace sightings in his thoughts.

In *The Report on Unidentified Flying Objects*, Ruppelt reveals that prior to the famous UFO invasion of Washington on 20 and 27 July 1952, a scientist from an agency he could not name for security reasons told him with conviction: 'Within the next few days... you're going to have the granddaddy of all UFO sightings. The sightings will occur in Washington or New York - probably Washington.' Ruppelt also reports that in September of 1952, when the NATO naval forces were about to commence Operation Mainbrace, someone in the Pentagon mentioned that Naval Intelligence should keep an eye out for UFOs - which were subsequently observed by many involved in the operation. .

In other words, there were those in the White House and the Pentagon who seemed to have prior knowledge of when and where certain UFOs were going to appear. This led to the belief, widely suppressed at the time, that the US had its own flying saucers.

Chapter 7

The Man-Made Flying Saucers

US Intelligence concern that the flying saucers might be highly advanced, long-range, jet fighter or reconnaissance planes constructed in secret by the Soviets began with the Scandinavian 'ghost rockets' of 1947 and grew in the following years. This can be seen in a formerly classified Memorandum for Record dated 29 April 29 1952, requesting information on Soviet 'manned aircraft of unconventional design, orbital missile (including the Sanger global range bombing system) and orbital bombing platforms, and flying saucers'. This concern would only have been heightened by the reported crash of a flying saucer with Russian insignia at Spitzbergen, Norway, on 8 August the same year.

US Intelligence was aware of the fact that a patent for a 'flying saucer with a circular fixed wing' had been taken out by an American citizen (unnamed) as early as 22 March 1932.

The unnamed citizen was probably Jonathan E. Caldwell. This would explain why, on 19 August 1949, at the height of the immediate post-war UFO flap, the Air Force Command of Baltimore called a press conference to announce that two different types of prototypes which might solve the mystery of the flying saucers had been found in an abandoned farm near Glen Burnie, Maryland. According to the Air Force spokesman, both machines had been designed and constructed before the war by one Jonathan E. Caldwell, with the aid of a local mechanic, and one of the machines had actually been flown.

The machines had been abandoned for years and were falling apart, but as they were a combination of aeroplane and helicopter, with round wings and contrarotating propellers, it was the belief of Air Force intelligence that in flight they would have resembled flying saucers and therefore could have been the prototypes of the more advanced UFOs seen in the skies over the past few years.

This notion was quickly squashed when, less than twenty-four hours later, at another urgent press conference, a different Air Force spokesman announced that the Caldwell machines had ‘absolutely no connection with the reported phenomena of flying saucers’. What the Air Force spokesman did not mention is that Caldwell had constructed his ‘plane with circular wing of the “parasol” type’ (it was raised above the fuselage, like an umbrella) in 1932 and it was tested the following year by Professor J. Owen Evans in a wind tunnel in Los Angeles, then flown by the well known pilot, Jimmy Doolittle, displaying a top speed of 97 mph and a landing speed of 23 mph. In 1936, Caldwell produced a modified version of the prototype, but it crashed, killing the pilot, thus putting Caldwell out of business for good. When he left Glen Burnie, in 1940, he bitterly informed Professor Evans that only the lack of another $5000 had stood between him and ‘an astonishing result’.

Nevertheless, US military Intelligence continued to be anxious about the possibility of man-made flying saucers, and was further concerned because most of the saucer sightings in the US 'tend to cluster around key development stations such as atomic plants, guided missile areas, and Wright-Patterson Air Force Base'. It is clear, then, from these suspicions and other remarks sprinkled liberally throughout the now declassified intelligence documents of the period, that US intelligence findings 'seem to exclude extraterrestrial origin of the saucers'.

If on the one hand they were concerned with Soviet advancement in this field, they soon began suspecting that the saucers might be of US or Canadian origin. Regarding the former, as the US Navy, Army and Air Force were in constant competition with one-another, each would have been loath to inform the other of any secret projects in the pipeline. Thus, even at the top-secret White Sands Proving Ground, used extensively by the US Navy for their aeronautical and missile experiments, there were research projects that even the CIA could not learn about and, given Navy interest in vertical-ascending aircraft, they could have included saucer-shaped aircraft.

The first rumblings about Canadian flying saucer projects were made in a classified CIA memorandum dated 18 August 1953 - a year after the Spitzbergen flying saucer crash report. The CIA memorandum states: 'According to recent reports from Toronto, a number of Canadian Air Force engineers are engaged in the construction of a "flying saucer" to be used as a future weapon of war. The work of these engineers is being carried out in great secrecy at the A.V. Roe Company factories.'

This report was correct - as were the widespread suspicions that the US Navy was conducting experiments on saucer-shaped, vertical-rising aircraft in secret hangars in the vast White Sands Proving Ground.

One belief widespread in Intelligence circles was that the formation of the lights in the famous Lubbock sightings and others were not indicative of small glowing saucers, but of the many exhaust jets along the edge of a massive 'boomerang-shaped' aircraft, or advanced 'flying wing', which would, when viewed from certain angles, strongly resemble a flying saucer, or saucers. This belief went all the way back to the immediate post-war years, as can be gauged from a once secret, now declassified Department of the Army intelligence memorandum, dated 21 January 1948 and circulated to the intelligence chiefs of the US, Canada, and Europe.

In this document concern is expressed that 'the German High Command indicated a definite interest in the Horten type of flying wing and were about to embark on a rigorous campaign to develop such aircraft toward the end of the war'. After clarifying that these aircraft were the IX, or Go-8-229 and Go-P-60 night-fighter planes being produced at the Gotha (Erfurt) plant, the memorandum continues:

> This plant is now in the hands of the Russians. A recent report indicates that the Russians are now planning to build a fleet of 1800 Horten VIII (six engine pusher) type flying wing aircraft. The wing span is 131 feet. The swept back angle is 30°. The Russian version is reported to be jet-propelled.

Included in this secret memorandum was a request for

information on various technical matters relating to 'aircraft whose shape approximates that of an oval, disk, or saucer', including 'boundary layer control method by suction, blowing, or a combination of both' and 'special controls for effective manoeuvrability at very slow speeds or extremely high altitudes'.

The CIA were already holding copies of the lengthy paper presented by the Horten brothers at the Flying Wing Seminar in Bonn, Germany, on 14 April 1943, in which they confirmed that 'a sweptback wing without protrusions is suited to warding off cable barriers, balloon barrages etc... the sweptback wing has advantages at high Mach numbers' and 'sweepback becomes necessary for high-speed flight'. The writer of the Army intelligence memorandum, Colonel R.F. Ennis, GSC Chief, Intelligence Group, therefore also requested information on the 'present activities' of the Horten brothers, Walter and Rismer.

The fact that the Horten papers found in CIA files had not come from Germany, but from the Chance-Vought Aircraft Company, a division of United Aircraft Company, Stratford, Connecticut, is of particular interest as this company would soon be embroiled in the US man-made flying saucer controversy.

The correlation between flying 'wings' and flying 'saucers' is a logical outcome of the aeronautical development of that period. Renato Vesco quotes Charles Gardner, then considered Britain's best aviation editor, as saying:

> There is no doubt that the problem in passing through the 'sound barrier' will force us to make

> considerable modifications in the shapes of our flying machines... In order to overcome such difficulties many scientists have suggested a 'delta'-shaped wing or a right-angled triangle... without tail or fuselage... From the 'delta' to the semicircle and from this to the full circle are two clearly connected steps...

Various 'delta'-wing, semicircular, or 'boomerang' shapes were introduced shortly after World War II in the shape of such aircraft as the Armstrong Whitworth AW-52-G Bat - a 'twin-engined, all-wing jet' - and did indeed evolve into contemporary 'right-angled triangle' ultra-speed jet aircraft, such as the deadly Stealth night-fighter jets. What is not yet known is just how much has been done behind closed doors about the 'connected steps' from these semicircular, boomerang and triangular aircraft to the 'full circle' aircraft, or flying saucer.

We now know that such steps were certainly well under way in various top-secret establishments, first in World War II Germany, possibly then in the Soviet Union, and certainly in Canada and the US.

Evidence for US involvement with disk-shaped aircraft projects surfaced with information about the US Navy's Flying Flapjack, or Flying Pancake. Designed by Charles H. Zimmerman of the National Advisory Committee for Aeronautics and constructed in 1942 by the Chance-Vought Corporation, mentioned above, the Flying Flapjack, or V-173, was an experimental, vertical-rising, disk-shaped aircraft, a combination of helicopter and jet plane, powered by two 80hp engines and driven by twin propellers, with two fins (stabilizers) on either side of its semi-circular, or pan-cake-shaped, configuration. Reportedly it had a maximum speed of 400 mph to 500 mph, could rise almost vertically, and could practically hover at 35 mph.

A later, more advanced model, the XF-5-U-1, utilised two Pratt and Whitney R-2000-7 engines of 1,600hp each and was reported to be about 105 feet (30 metres) in diameter and have jet nozzles - resembling the 'glowing windows' seen on so many UFOs - arranged around its outer rim, just below the centre of gravity. It was built in three layers, the central layer being slightly larger than the other two. Since the saucer's velocity and manoeuvring abilities were controlled by the power and tilt of the variable-direction jet nozzles, there were no ailerons, rudders or other protruding surfaces. The material used was a metal alloy that had 'a dull, whitish' colour.

In short, a machine remarkably similar in appearance to those reported by so many UFO witnesses.

Information about the Flying Flapjack was released to the public in the April 1950 edition of the *US News and World Report* and it touched off some interesting speculations. The first of these arose from the retrospective knowledge that the US Navy had always expressed more interest in a vertical-rising aeroplane than the Air Force; they had, up to 1950, spent *twice* as much money as the Air Force on secret guided missile research; their top-secret missile-research bases were located in the White Sands Proving Ground - where the majority of military UFO sightings had occurred - and because they were not involved officially in UFO investigations, they could conduct their own research in a secrecy unruffled by the attentions of the media or the public.

According to the Project Grudge report for 1947, the UFO viewed over Muroc AFB on 7 and 8 July of that year was 'an oscillating object which flew *slowly* (author's emphasis) and had tactics unlike an ordinary aeroplane'. Some witnesses, all trained Air Force personnel, observed two disks at an altitude of about 8,000 feet, both manoeuvring in 'tight circles with varying speeds' and oscillating. Also, just like the XF-5-U-1, both disks had two fins on the upper surface.

Another interesting point is that the measurements taken by Navy commander R.B. McLaughlin and his team of Navy scientists of the UFO they had tracked over the White Sands Proving Ground in 1949 (two years after the Muroc sightings) corresponded closely, except for the speed, with the details of the original XF-5-U-1. It is also worth noting that initial reports of the extraordinarily high speeds recorded by McLaughlin turned out to be inaccurate and that later analysis of the data brought the speed much closer to that of an advanced jet plane or the original expectations for the Flapjack.

The *US News and World Report* also pointed out that the Air Force had called off official inquiry into the UFO phenomenon the previous December, even in 'the face of overwhelming evidence that the saucers are real'. This was seen by many as a clear indication that top Air Force officials now knew what the saucers are and where they came from. Therefore, while still denying that the Air Force was involved, they were no longer concerned about the saucers.

The article concludes: 'Surface indications, then, point to research centres of the US Navy's vast guided-missile project as the scene of present flying-saucer development.'

The production prototype of the Flapjack was due for a test-flight at Muroc AFB (now Edwards AFB) in 1947 - when the first 'flying saucer' sightings over that same base and at Rogers Dry Lake (then adjacent to Muroc, now part of Edwards AFB) were recorded. Whether such test flights were actually carried out has never been confirmed or denied by the US Navy. The only official statements given were to the effect that work on the Flying Flapjack had ceased the following year.

In an article published in the April 1950 issue of *Saucer News*, Dr Leon Davidson, then a chemical engineer at the Los Alamos Scientific Laboratory, claims that LCDR Picket Lumpkin, US Navy, told him that 'it became apparent that the desired speed characteristics could be attained with less difficulty in a jet-powered aircraft'. Whatever the reasons, LCDR F.M. Lloyd, also of the US Navy, informed Davidson that the project had been dropped officially on 12 March 1948.

The first version, the V-173, is stored with the Smithsonian Institution...But US involvement with saucer-shaped aircraft did not end with this prototype.

It is worth recalling that in the reports that started the modern UFO scare - the Harold Dahl and Kenneth Arnold sightings of June 1947 - both men observed the UFOs in the vicinity of Mount Rainier in the Cascades in the state of

Washington - which divides Oregon and Canada - and both stated independently that the UFOs flew away in the direction of the Canadian border. During the first week in July there were numerous reports of unidentified 'luminous bodies' in the skies over the Province of Quebec, Oregon and New England. The next major UFO flap was the 'invasion' of Washington DC in 1952; and while the official flap started on 19 July, there was a record, dated 17 June, of several hundred unidentified 'red spheres' that flew at supersonic speeds over the Canadian Air Base of North Bay in Ontario and then crossed over some of the south-eastern states. Finally, nearly all of the subsequent Washington DC UFOs were reported as flying away in a southerly direction; when they returned, en masse, on 26 July, their disappearance in a general southerly direction - toward the Canadian border - also applied.

It is, therefore, a matter of considerable interest that on 11 February 1953, the Toronto *Star* reported that a new flying saucer was being developed at the AVRO-Canada plant in Malton, Ontario.

The US and Canadian governments both denied involvement in any such project, but on 16 February, after freelance photographer Jack Judges had taken an aerial photograph of a flying-saucer resting outdoors in the Avro-Canada plant in Malton, the Minister for Defence Production, C.D. Howe, admitted to the Canadian House of Commons that AVRO-Canada was working on a 'mock-up model' of a flying saucer, capable of ascending vertically and flying at 1500 mph (2400 km/h). By February 27, Crawford Gordon Jr., the president of AVRO-Canada, was writing in the company's house journal, *AVRO News*, that the prototype being built was so revolutionary it would 'make all other forms of supersonic aircraft obsolete'. The aircraft was called the 'Avrocar'.

Soon, the Toronto *Star* was claiming that Britain's Field Marshal Montgomery had become one of the few people to view Avro's mock-up of the flying saucer (Georg Klein started telling the same story in 1954 in Zürich, Switzerland, though who picked it up from whom it a moot question) and a few days later Air Vice Marshal D. M. Smith was reported to have said that what Field Marshal Montgomery had seen was the preliminary construction plans for a 'gyroscopic fighter whose gas turbine would revolve around the pilot, who would be positioned at the centre of the disk'.

Confirmation that the craft actually existed came via the April 1953 issue of the *Royal Air Force Flying Review* which contained a two-page report on the Avrocar (also dubbed the 'Omega'), including some speculative sectional diagrams. According to this report, the building of a prototype had not yet commenced, but a wooden mock-up had been constructed behind a closely guarded experimental hangar in the company's Malton plant, near Ontario. The aircraft described had a near-circular shape, measuring approximately forty feet across, and was being designed to attain speeds of the order of 1,500 mph - more than twice that of the latest swept-wing fighters. It would be capable of effecting 180° turns in flight without changing attitude.

In early November 1953, Canadian newspapers were reporting that a mock-up of the Avrocar, or Omega, had been shown on 31 October to a group of twenty-five

American military officers and scientists. By March the following year, the American press was claiming that the US Air Force, concerned at Soviet progress in aeronautics, had allocated an unspecified sum of money to the Canadian government for the building of a prototype of their flying saucer, that the machine had been designed by the English aeronautical engineer, John Frost - who had worked for AVRO-Canada in Malton, Ontario - and that it would be capable of either hovering virtually motionless in mid-air or flying at a speed of nearly 2,000 mph.

This story was followed by Canadian press assertions that their government was planning to form entire squadrons of AVRO-Canada's flying saucers for the defence of Alaska and the far regions of the North because they required no runways, were capable of rising vertically, and were ideal for 'subarctic and polar regions'.

Unexpected disappointment came when, on 3 December 1954, it was announced that the 'saucer project' had been dropped. Confirming this decision, the Canadian Minister of Defence pointed out that the project would have cost far too much for something that was, in the end, 'highly speculative'.

However, this announcement was contradicted less than a year later, when, on 22 October 1955, US Air Force Secretary Donald Quarles released an extraordinary statement though the press office of the Department of Defence. Among other things, he said that an 'aircraft of unusual characteristics' would soon be appearing; that the US government had 'initiated negotiations' with the Canadian government and AVRO-Canada for the preparation of 'an experimental model of the Frost flying disk', and that the aircraft would be mass-produced and used for 'the common defence of the sub-arctic area of the continent'.

In February 1959, after a long silence, the press was receiving ambiguous US Air Force statements about a revolutionary new aircraft that had been undertaken jointly by the US Air Force, the US Army, and the Canadian government. Then, on 14 April, during a press conference in Washington DC, General Frank Britten implied that the first test flight of the aircraft was imminent and that it was destined to 'revolutionize traditional aeronautical concepts'.

In August 1960 the Air Force, giving in to public pressure, allowed reporters to view the prototype of the machine that had so fascinated them and their readers. What the news hounds were shown was a crude experimental aircraft that combined the characteristics of air-cushion machines - a crude flying saucer based on the principles of the jet ring and barely able to rise above the runway. Small wonder, seeing this, that they did not appear unduly surprised when, in December the following year, the Department of Defence announced that they were withdrawing from participation in the project.

So what, exactly, was the Avrocar, which may, or may not, have been what the reporters saw in August 1960? In the words of the *Royal Air Force Flying Review*:

> Apart from the platform of this aircraft, the most revolutionary feature of the project is the use made of the gyroscopic effect of a revolving power plant to acquire stability. The power plant housing

> rotates inside a stationary wing of near-circular platform whereas hitherto it had been assumed that such an aircraft would employ a swiftly rotating wing. The pilot of the saucer is seated in a central plastic capsule, which presumably can be ejected should the aircraft find itself in difficulties, and a gas turbine power plant of unconventional design revolves around this capsule at several hundred revolutions per minute. Surrounding the rotating power plant housing and forming the 'rim' of the saucer is the stationary wing, a series of slots in the leading edge which feed air to the turbine. Part of the intake of air is compressed and fed to combustion chambers in the wing and ejected through a series of exhaust orifices lining the outer rim of the disk. The remainder of the airflow appears to be fed over a series of vertical deflector vanes in the 'flattened' trailing edge of the aircraft for control purposes. A tripod-type launching gear is planned to enable the saucer to take off vertically.

The writer was careful to point out that:

> Although quite a number of aircraft featuring circular, disk-shaped or annular wing forms have been built and flown, the aerodynamics of such shapes cannot yet be considered as fully established, and the design problems facing the young Avro Canada design team in bringing this revolutionary project to fruition are of

considerable magnitude.

This may have been true. Details released later by the A.V. Roe Company (AVRO-Canada) stated that the Avrocar, powered by three 1,000-hp Continental J69-T-9 turbojets, was planned to have a maximum forward speed of 300 mph and a range of 1,000 miles; but when test flown in 1960, it never did more than 'hover within ground effect' and was subsequently abandoned as a failure.

The prototype was placed on display for all to see at the Army Transportation Museum at Fort Eustis, Virginia.

In 1954 the Canadian Government announced that the 'flying wing' or 'highly swept-back wing configuration' controlled by a series of small jet orifices located all around its edge, as suggested by the Lubbock sightings of 1951, was exactly the kind of thing they had tried unsuccessfully to build. According to the statement, the project for the development of that 'saucer-like craft' had been taken over by the US Air Force.

Under pressure from the media to reply to this allegation, the US Air Force finally admitted that they had taken over the project, but insisted that it had been dropped at an early stage and that the crude prototype on display at Fort Eustis, Virginia, is the only one they managed to complete.

However, while the Canadian and US governments have insisted that they are no longer involved with flying saucer construction projects, there are many who believe that they are lying, and that the Canadian, British, US and even Soviet governments are continuing to work on highly advanced, saucer-shaped, supersonic aircraft based on the work done in Nazi Germany. What happened to the original Projekt Saucer team supports this: Habermohl was captured by the Russians and taken back to the Soviet Union, along with over 6000 German technical specialists of all kinds, to work on similar projects; Miethe went to the United States with Werner von Braun and other German rocket scientists and ended up working for Avro-Canada, in Malton, Ontario; and Rudolph Schriever insisted right up to his death that the Soviet Union and United States were both working on flying saucer construction projects based on material captured by them during the war.

In fact, the April 1953 edition of the *Royal Air Force Flying Review* stated that it was 'common knowledge' that aircraft designers throughout the world were then devoting increasing attention to 'flying saucers' when considering flying speeds of more than twice that of sound. It also contained a short report about man-made flying saucers that had recently skimmed over the rooftops of Belgrade, Yugoslavia. Reportedly, these were experimental models made by the Yugoslavian Air Force; they were less than twelve inches in diameter, weighed just over 4lb, had a top speed of 31 mph, and were controlled by radio - crude versions of the German *Feuerball*.

It seems clear, therefore, that work on 'circular flying wings' of various shapes and sizes was going on in America and Canada - and may have been going on elsewhere, notably in Soviet Russia. Also, there is a growing body of evidence that the Pentagon knew what the flying saucers were and where they came from, despite the lack of communication between the US Air Force and US

Navy. Dr Leon Davidson points out that interservice rivalry between the two was intense and that the former would not have informed the latter about their secret aviation developments, such as the Flying Flapjack, even after the experimental models had been sighted over The White Sands Proving Ground.

Captain Ruppelt, when head of Project Blue Book, was adamant that, at least with regard to the United States, UFOs were spotted most frequently, by trained observers, over areas vital to the defence of the country. In his own words: 'The Los Alamos-Albuquerque area, Oak Ridge, and White Sands Proving Ground rated high. Port areas, Strategic Air Command bases, and industrial areas ranked next.'

This concentration of UFOs over top-secret military establishments in particular leads to one of two conclusions. The first is that the Russians or Canadians were using flying saucers to spy on US military establishments. The second is that US flying saucers were being constructed in, and tested over, top-secret areas such as the White Sands Proving Ground.

Chapter 8

UFO Landings and UFOnauts

Perhaps the world's best known and most respected UFOlogist is the astronomer, Dr J. Allen Hynek, whose involvement began in 1948 when he became the astronomical consultant to the United States Air Force (USAF) on their UFO research project. After the termination of Project Blue Book, Hynek became critical of the Air Force's methods and conclusions. In 1973 he became the Founder and Director of the Center for UFO Studies (CUFOS) and since then he has been a fulltime UFOlogist.

While Hynek adheres to no particular theory regarding the nature of UFOs, he believes firmly in the reality of the phenomenon and that the solution to the mystery could lead to a 'quantum jump' in human understanding. He is the author of two of the most reliable books on the subject: *The UFO Experience: A Scientific Inquiry* (1972) and *The Hynek UFO Report* (1978). However, he first became publicly well known in 1977 through the release of Steven Spielberg's blockbusting UFO movie, *Close Encounters of the Third Kind*, for which he was the technical advisor.

The title of the movie was taken from one of the four terms coined by Hynek to describe the major forms of UFO contact: Close Encounters of the First Kind (CE-I), which are UFO sightings at close range without tangible physical evidence; Close Encounters of the Second Kind (CE-II), which are UFO sightings at close range accompanied by tangible physical evidence; Close Encounters of the Third Kind (CE-III), which are close range sightings of UFOs and one or more UFOnauts (UFO crew members); and Close Encounters of the Fourth Kind (CE-IV), which are the abductions of human beings by UFOnauts.

The question of contact with UFOs or their occupants is a vexing one, particularly since the earliest reported close encounters were undoubtedly hoaxes and even the more persuasive cases can seem fantastic. The incident that set the pattern for most contemporary hoaxes, as well as the basic appearance of the 'alien' UFOnauts, was the notorious 'Aztec' case of 1948. In *Behind the Flying Saucers* (1950), the author, Frank Scully, formerly Hollywood's *Weekly Variety* columnist, alleged that 'the first saucer to land on this earth' crashed east of Aztec, New Mexico, in 1948, and was found virtually intact, with sixteen dead aliens, or UFOnauts, inside. The UFOnauts were only three-and-a-half feet tall and had 'flawless teeth' and unusually pointed features, but otherwise resembled human beings. According to Scully, the flying saucer, which was 99 feet in diameter (with all of its measurements reportedly based on a system of nines, rather than tens), was dismantled and the pieces, along with the remains of the sixteen aliens, were transported in secret to Muroc Dry Lake (now Edwards AFB), then on to the legendary top-secret 'Hangar 18' in Wright-Patterson AFB in Dayton, Ohio. Scully also alleged that there had been three other flying saucer landings during the same period and that a total of thirty-four dead aliens had been found and were also being preserved at Wright-Patterson.

Scully's book became a bestseller, but little substantiation could be found for his claims. Two years later, the investigative reporter, J.P. Cahn, revealed that Scully had received most of his dubious information from Silas Newton and Dr Gee, later identified as Leo A. Gebauer. In fact, both men were experienced confidence tricksters who had been arrested that very year for trying to sell worthless war surplus equipment as oil detection devices; and it is highly probable that they based their whole story on the better documented 'Roswell Incident', discussed below.

Nevertheless, Cahn's exposé of the Aztec case as a hoax did not stop the continuing flow of UFO 'crash' stories and rumours that alien corpses - at least those captured in the United States - were being preserved in Hangar 18 in Wright-Patterson AFB, Dayton, Ohio. As late as 1978, the UFOlogist and author, Leonard Springfield, was claiming that he had reports from 'twenty-five unimpeachable sources' that 'spaceships and frozen alien corpses' were being held at Wright-Patterson. A year later, William Spaulding, aerospace engineer and Western Division Director of the widely respected and scientifically-based organization, Ground Saucer Watch (GSW), was claiming that he was in possession of signed affidavits from 'retired colonels in military intelligence' attesting to the fact that a crashed disk and alien entity had been retrieved and transported to CIA headquarters at Langley, Virginia, from which it would, according to legend, have been shipped on to Wright-Patterson for examination and preservation in Hangar 18.

All requests to Wright-Patterson AFB for information

regarding Hangar 18 are routinely given the reply that it doesn't exist. However, according to news commentator and reporter, Robert D. Barry, quoted in Timothy Green Beckley's *The Riddle of Hangar 18* (1981), one of his interviewees, a Civil Air Patrol Cadet on special training at Wight-Patterson in 1965, saw 'the famous hangar with the tall wire fence around it... completely around it... and all windows knocked out and replaced with concrete'. Also, on 24 October 1974, the syndicated news broadcast 'Earth News' revealed that a 'press spokesperson' for Senator Barry M. Goldwater had confirmed that 'the senator was once denied permission to the Wright-Patterson Air Force Base's Hangar 18. (Goldwater, a former Republican presidential candidate who took the UFO phenomenon seriously, eventually became a member of the Board of Governors of the National Investigations Committee on Aerial Phenomena [NICAP]).

While no more evidence for the existence of Hangar 18 and its extraordinary contents has been forthcoming (interested readers could try asking Wright-Patterson AFB for information on Building 18-A, Area B), further 'respectability' for the UFO-landing theory came with Gordon Cooper, the astronaut who claimed that he had seen a UFO while orbiting Earth in the Mercury 9 spacecraft on 16 May 1963. Later, as a guest on the *Merv Griffith Show*, Cooper boldly announced that in the early 1950s, while in a jet fighter group in West Germany, he had been one of many witnesses to a series of unidentified objects that 'would stop in their forward velocity and change 90°, sometimes in the middle of their flight path'. Later, Cooper told journalist Lee Spiegel that while at the Edwards Air

Force Base Flight Test Center in California, either in 1957 or 1958, a team of photographers assigned by him to photograph the vast dry lakes near Edwards 'spotted a strange-looking craft above the lake bed'. The object was 'hovering above the ground. Then it slowly came down and sat on the lake bed for a few minutes'. It was 'at least the size of a vehicle that would carry normal-sized people in it' and was also 'a typical circular-shaped UFO' which 'took off at quite a sharp angle and just climbed straight out of sight'. In Cooper's words: 'There were always strange things flying around in the air over Edwards.' According to Cooper, the film of the UFO taken by his photographers was forwarded to Washington D.C. for evaluation -but no report came back and the movie has certainly not resurfaced.

Other 'landing' and 'crash' stories abound, but are similarly lacking in substantiating details or verifiable names. For instance, in *The Riddle of Hangar 18*, author Timothy Green Beckley relates a story about Charles Wilhelm, executive director of the Ohio UFO Investigators League who, according to Beckley, claimed to have 'recently conversed with a radio electronics expert who was in the army in the mid-1950s and said that he was flown to Fort Monmouth, New Jersey' where, in the company of 'nine others, plus a major who was setting up the projector', the 'electronics expert' watched 'a special film' in order to 'analyze from the film anything that he could define from his experience in radar technology'. The film showed 'a strange, disk-shaped object with two guards, one on each side of the craft. The ship was sitting on two large blocks, and the technician estimated the craft to be fifteen to eighteen feet in diameter. Its surface was smooth, except for some tool marks around the door entrance. A ramp extended to the ground. The UFO was either silver or light grey in colour.' After showing the interior of the craft, which was relatively bare, except for some control levers, the camera was moved back outside where it focused on 'a table with three small bodies laid out'. All were approximately five feet tall, with abnormally large heads and human features. When the movie was over, 'the major' in charge would only say that the craft and its occupants had been found in 'New Mexico'.

This is an intriguing tale, but like so many other 'landing' or 'crash' stories it raises more questions than it answers. When was 'recently'? Who, exactly, was the 'electronics expert'? Who was 'the major'? Who were the 'nine others'? Precisely where and when in New Mexico was the object found? And last but not least, how could the unnamed 'electronics expert' possibly apply his 'experience in radar technology' to his viewing of a movie film of the supposed exterior and interior of a flying disk?

The mixture of unsubstantiated facts and disguised speculation is one of the major obstacles in any examination of the 'landing' or 'crash' UFO stories. Nevertheless, there is a growing body of evidence that some close encounters are genuine, as are certain rare cases of UFO landings or crashes, or even the capture of UFO and their occupants.

Dr J. Allen Hynek claims that genuine UFO landings took place at Cannon Air Force Base, New Mexico (18 May 1954), at Deerwood Nike Base (29 September 1957), and at Blaine Air Force Base (12 June 1965). However, even Hynek can only offer unnamed 'independent sources' for such reports and makes it clear that none of them were transmitted to Project Blue Book.

According to articles written by journalists David Branch and Robert E. Klinn and published in the *Santa Ana Register* (California), on 15 and 23 November 1972, reports of the landing and take-off of two UFOs from Holloman AFB, located in the White Sands Proving Ground, New Mexico, were suppressed by the authorities. The first of these incidents reportedly took place shortly before 8.00am. on an unspecified day in September, 1956, when a 'domed, disk-shaped' aircraft landed about fifty yards from US 70, about twelve miles west of Holloman AFB. The ignition systems and radios of passing cars went dead and the peak-hour commuter traffic backed up as amazed witnesses - including two air force colonels, two sergeants, and dozens of Holloman employees - watched the UFO for over ten minutes, before it took off with a 'low whirring sound'.

Shortly after the disappearance of the UFO, word of the sighting flew from Holloman to Washington DC and the area was soon inundated with air force intelligence officers and CIA agents. Base employees who had witnessed the sighting were sworn to secrecy and the Pentagon's evaluation team wired a report stating that the UFO was 'not any type of aircraft under development by the US or any foreign terrestrial power'.

Two years later, in the summer of 1958, a mechanic at Holloman AFB was working on a grounded Lockheed F-104 jet interceptor when he saw a disk-shaped object hovering silently over the tarmac. After watching the object retracting its 'ball-like landing gear', he called another mechanic and both of them watched the UFO take off vertically at great speed. During a subsequent interrogation, both men identified the craft type they had seen from a book of over 300 UFO photographs. They were then informed that the personnel in the base control tower had observed the same object for two or three minutes. They were also warned not to discuss the incident and then made to sign a statement swearing them to secrecy.

The most striking feature of the landed and crashed UFO stories is that the most substantiated ones invariably have taken place, at least with regard to the US, on or near military and Air Force establishments in the top-secret White Sands Proving Ground. The UFO 'crash' at Roswell, New Mexico, was just such a case; the famous UFO 'landing' at Socorro, New Mexico, was another, even more disturbing, example.

The so-called 'Roswell Incident' was the first in which an official statement about a flying saucer landing was released to the public. According to Charles Berlitz and William Moore, who researched the case for their book, *The Roswell Incident* (1980), there was a considerable build-up of UFO sightings in the south-western area before the actual Roswell incident. 25 June 1947: a saucer-shaped object 'about one half the size of the full moon' was observed by a local dentist as it moved south over Silver City, New Mexico. 27 June: a disk-shaped object was witnessed in the vicinity of Bisbee, in south-eastern Arizona, near the New Mexican border; and a series of eight or nine 'perfectly spaced disks' traveling at high speed with 'a wobbling motion' were observed passing over Warren, Arizona. By 9.50 that morning, a 'white disk glowing like an electric light bulb' was observed as it passed over Pope, New Mexico. Minutes later, the same, or a similar, object was spotted over the White Sands Proving Ground by Captain E.B. Detchmendy, who reported it to his commanding officer. At 10.00am. a female witness reported a similar object passing over San Miguel, New Mexico. The following day, Captain F. Dvyn, when flying in the vicinity of Alamogordo, New Mexico, in the White Sands Proving Ground, reported 'a ball of fire with a fiery blue trail behind' as it passed *beneath* his aircraft. The next day, Army Air Force pilots were sent on an unsuccessful search for a UFO reported to have fallen near Cliff, New Mexico. That same day, a team of naval rocket-test experts working at the White Sands Proving Ground reported seeing a 'silvery-coloured disk' perform a series of manoeuvres at high altitude over the secret test range. Thirteen silver, disk-shaped objects were then witnessed by a whole neighbourhood as they flew over Albuquerque, New Mexico, on 30 June; a 'bluish disk' was seen 'zigzagging' across the sky over Albuquerque on 1 July; and on 2 July, at approximately 9.50pm, a married couple, Mr and Mrs Dan Wilmot, witnessed 'a large, glowing object' as it passed over their house in South Penn Street, Roswell, New Mexico.

This latter sighting marked the true beginning of the Roswell Incident.

Dan Wilmot and his wife later described the UFO as 'a big glowing object' that was shaped 'like two inverted saucers faced mouth to mouth' and glowing 'as if lit from the inside'. Though Wilmot described the object as being perfectly silent, his wife thought she had heard a 'slight swishing sound' for a brief moment, as the object passed overhead. It was heading northwest, towards Corona, New Mexico, and passed over their house and out of sight in forty to fifty seconds.

Nearly a week later, on 7 July, at 4.00pm, Lydia Sleepy, the teletype operator for Radio KOAT, Albuquerque, New Mexico, received a call from Johnny McBoyle, reporter and part owner of sister station, KSWS, in Roswell. Clearly excited, he told her that a flying saucer had recently crashed near Roswell, that he had been out there and seen it, and that it looked like 'a big, crumpled dishpan'. According to McBoyle, 'some rancher' (W.W. Brazel) had 'hauled it under a cattle shelter with his tractor' and the army had since gone out there to pick up the object and seal off the whole area.

McBoyle asked Sleepy to get his message out on the teletype right away, but when she tried to do so, she was blocked by the incoming message of an unidentified sender: 'ATTENTION ALBUQUERQUE: DO NOT TRANSMIT. REPEAT DO NOT TRANSMIT THIS MESSAGE. STOP COMMUNICATION IMMEDIATELY. When Sleepy relayed this message to McBoyle, he changed his mind about transmitting the news of the UFO crash, said that obviously they were not supposed to know about it, and told her to forget what she had heard.

This attempt to comply with the authorities was rendered redundant when, the following day, without the authorization of his commanding officer, Lieutenant Walter

G. Haut, public information officer of the Roswell Army Air Base (now Walker Air Force Base) released the following press statement:

> The many rumours regarding the flying disk became a reality yesterday when the intelligence office of the 509th Bomb Group of the Eighth Air Force, Roswell Army Air Field, was fortunate enough to gain possession of a disk through the co-operation of one of the local ranchers and the Sheriff's office of Chaves County.
>
> The flying object landed on a ranch near Roswell sometime last week. Not having phone facilities, the rancher stored the disk until such time as he was able to contact the Sheriff's office, who [*sic*] in turn notified Major Jesse A. Marcel, of the 509th Bomb Group Intelligence office.
>
> Action was immediately taken and the disk was picked up at the rancher's home. It was inspected at the Roswell Army Air Field and subsequently loaned by Major Marcel to higher headquarters.

Lieutenant Haut would soon have cause to regret his hasty public announcement. While his press release was being enthusiastically picked up by the world's news agencies, the Roswell *Daily Record* of 8 July was confirming that the Intelligence Office of the 509th Bombardment group at Roswell Army Air Field had come into possession of the crashed saucer; that according to information released by the department, the disk had been recovered on a ranch in the 'Roswell vicinity' after an 'unidentified rancher' had notified Sheriff George Wilcox that he had found the crashed object on his land; that intelligence officer Major Jesse. A. Marcel had led the official recovery team and, after inspecting it, had arranged for it to be flown by aircraft to 'higher headquarters'; and that no details of the saucer's construction had been revealed.

By this time, Johnny McBoyle of Radio KSWS in Roswell had informed Lydia Sleepy of Radio KOAT in Albuquerque that he had seen an aeroplane, which he knew was destined for Wright Field (now Wright-Patterson AFB) in Dayton, Ohio, take off with the object, or parts of it, on board. However, he had not been able to get near the aeroplane because it was surrounded by heavily armed guards.

Another article in that day's edition of the Roswell *Daily Record* revealed that Mark Sloan, operator of the private airfield at Carrizozo, thirty-five miles south-west of the reported crash site, in the presence of flying instructor Grady Warren and pilots Nolan Lovelace and Ray Shafer, had witnessed a flying saucer speeding over the airfield at 10.00am at an altitude of about 4,000 to 6,000 feet. Sloan estimated that it was moving at between 200 mph and 600 mph and 'oscillating' as it travelled on a south-west to north-west course.

While no missile tests were being conducted at that time, there were violent thunder and lightning storms north-west of Roswell. Those could have accounted either for some of the reported UFO sightings or for the crash of *some* kind of aircraft.

Rumours began circulating to the effect that Brigadier

General M. Ramsey, commander of the Eight Air Force District at Fort Worth, Texas, and Lieutenant General Hoyt Vandenberg, Deputy Chief of the Air Force, had expressed their displeasure to Colonel Blanchard, commander of the Roswell Air Base, over his public information officer's unauthorized press release. Because of this, they had demanded that the man who located the crash debris, Major Jesse A. Marcel, personally fly it to Carswell Air Force Base, Forth Worth, Texas, for General Ramsey's personal inspection, before flying it on to Wright Field (Wright-Patterson AFB) in Dayton, Ohio, where it would undergo 'further analysis' under the personal supervision of General Vandenberg.

So widespread and persistent were these rumours that General Ramsey was driven to assuring the public, via a hook-up with Fort Worth's Radio WBAP, that the crashed flying saucer was in reality no more than a crashed Rawin weather balloon, that the remaining pieces of it were in his office, where they would probably remain, and that the 'special flight' to Wright Field had been cancelled.

This statement was supported with an invitation to the press to come and photograph General Ramsey and his assistant, Colonel (now retired Brigadier General) Thomas Jefferson Dubose, posing in the former's office with the debris of a real Rawin balloon. Colonel Blanchard, commander of the Roswell Air Base, went unexpectedly, or conveniently, on leave at the same time as Major Marcel was flying the crash debris to Carswell AFB, Forth Worth. He was replaced in his absence by the base deputy commander, Colonel Payne Jennings, who spent most of his time repeatedly telling the press that Blanchard was 'unavailable for comment'.

No sooner had the crash remains been delivered to Carswell, Forth Worth, than the base A-2 Division (Intelligence) chief, Colonel Alfred E. Kalberer, started making public appearances at various Fort Worth civic organisations, assuring them that there was no need for hysteria over crashed flying saucers. According to the records of the Forth Worth Army Air Base, while Kalberer was thus engaged, Colonel Irving, Assistant to the Chief of Staff, HQ Strategic Air Command (SAC), paid a visit to General Ramsey at Fort Worth for a discussion on an undisclosed subject, widely believed to have been the debris, and/or remains from the crash near Roswell.

In the days that followed, contrary to what the Army Air Force was trying to say about Rawin weather balloons, the word of numerous witnesses indicated that there may in fact have been *two* crash sites, both of which were connected with the same incident. There were also rumours about 'a large flying saucer' and the remains of a number of small, humanoid creatures dressed in one-piece uniforms.

So what actually happened?

The first available information on the Roswell crash came from Major (now retired Lieutenant Colonel) Jesse A. Marcel, who at the time of the incident was the ranking staff officer in charge of intelligence at the Roswell Army Air Base. In interviews conducted between Marcel and UFO investigators William Moore and Stanton Friedman throughout 1979, Marcel confirms that he first learnt about the crash when, on 7 July 1947, he received a call from the

Chaves County sheriff's office, in Roswell, informing him that a local rancher, W.W. Brazel, had come in to report that something had exploded 'over' his ranch, located on the south-east side of Corona, near Roswell, during a violent electrical storm several days before. According to Brazel, there was 'a lot of debris scattered everywhere'.

Brazel had not informed anyone before because he lived alone on his sheep ranch, thirty miles from the nearest town, and had no telephone.

On the instructions of his base commander, Colonel Blanchard, Marcel and a Counter-Intelligence Corps (CIC) agent named Cavitt followed Brazel out to the crash site, the former in a '42 Buick staff car, the latter in a Jeep Carry-all. In response to later enquiries about flying saucers and their occupants, Marcel stuck to his story that they found 'a lot of wreckage, but no machine'. Marcel was also adamant that whatever it was, the object had exploded above ground level and disintegrated before it hit the ground (thus confirming Brazel's description of an explosion 'over' his ranch), with the wreckage scattered over an area of about three-quarters of a mile long and several hundred feet wide. It was, he insisted, 'definitely not a weather or tracking device, nor was it any sort of plane or missile'.

The debris picked up was enough to fill the Carry-all and the trunk and back seat of the Buick. It included small beams, or rods, of an unknown material, which had indecipherable hieroglyphics embedded in them. They 'looked something like balsa wood, though they were not wood at all. They were very hard, although flexible, and would not burn'. Marcel's hieroglyphics were 'little numbers with symbols that we had to call hieroglyphics because [we] could not understand them... They were pink and purple. They looked like they had been painted on'. But: 'Those little numbers could not be broken, could not be burned'. There was also a lot of 'unusual parchment-like substance which was brown in colour and extremely strong' and 'small pieces of a metal like tinfoil, except that it wasn't tinfoil... it was so light it weighed practically nothing'. Yet, as they were to find out later, the foil could neither be bent nor even dented with a 16lb sledgehammer. Also found was 'a black, metallic-looking box several inches square' and with no apparent opening. From this material, Marcel was only able to ascertain that the object had been big and constructed possibly from unknown materials. He could not judge its shape or general appearance.

The material was driven back to the Roswell Army Air Base, where reportedly it was stored in Hangar 84, which to this day remains sealed, unused, and off-limits.

The following afternoon, on orders from Colonel Blanchard, it was loaded onto a B-29 and flown to Carswell AFB, Forth Worth, Texas. There, after informing the press that the debris was from a crashed Rawin weather balloon, General Ramsey and his assistant, Colonel Dubose, staged their photo session. However, according to Marcel, after taking one photograph of him with a very small portion of the less interesting, albeit genuine wreckage, 'they cleared out our wreckage and substituted some of their own. Then they allowed more photos. Those photos were taken while the actual wreckage was already on its way to Wright Field.'

Marcel was adamant that 'it was General Ramsey who put up the cover story about the balloon just to get the press off our backs.'

Meanwhile, the unfortunate farmer, W.W. Brazel, was regretting having reported the incident. Shortly after leading Marcel and Cavitt out to where the wreckage was found, he was taken into custody and held incommunicado for almost a week. When he came out, on 15 July, he refused thereafter to talk to anyone about the crash.

Brazel died in 1963, but in an interview given to William Moore in 1979, Brazel's son, Bill, confirmed that for most of his remaining life his father had been 'very reluctant to talk about it at all... He took the most part of what he knew to the grave with him'. According to what Brazel *did* tell his son, the military, after locking him in a room and refusing to let him out, interrogated him for a week and then swore him to secrecy. 'He said they had told him to shut up because it was important to our country and was the patriotic thing to do, and so that's what he intended to do. He was very discouraged and upset by the way they had treated him.'

Nevertheless, from what he could piece together from the various things his father told him over the years, Bill Brazel was able to confirm in just about every detail what Marcel had revealed about the crash, including the fact that in the middle of a lightning storm on the evening of 2 July 1947, his father had heard 'an odd sort of explosion, not like ordinary thunder' and that the following morning he had found 'this collection of wreckage scattered over a patch of land about a quarter mile long or so, and several hundred feet wide'. Bill Brazel's vivid recollections of the debris shown to him by his father match in almost every detail those given by Marcel. He also recalls his father saying that 'from the way this wreckage was scattered, you could tell it was traveling an airline route to Socorro, which is off to the south-west of the ranch.'

While there is no evidence whatsoever that dead aliens or UFOnauts were found at the Brazel site, Brazel's remark about 'an airline route to Socorro' is of interest in view of the fact that rumours have persisted to this day about another possible crash near Socorro, New Mexico, shortly after the crash near Roswell. It was widely believed that this was either a different disk entirely or the same disk which, after being damaged by an aerial explosion while flying over the Brazel ranch, had managed to fly for another 150 miles westward, before crashing.

The only evidence for this second crash is the word of Socorro civil engineer G.L. 'Barney' Barnett, who was working for the federal government in the area when he saw a disk-shaped object at rest on the Plain of San Augustin, west of Magdalena, New Mexico, on the morning of 3 July 1947.

Barnett died in April 1969, but was described by his boss, J.F. Danley, as 'a good man... one of the most honest men I ever knew'. Yet according to Danley, Barnett excitedly told him in the 'early summer' of 1947 that the flying saucers were real and he had just seen one. Danley instantly dismissed this as a joke, but a little later, when he asked Barnett if he had meant what he said, Barnett, now cooled down, would only add that he had seen a crashed object out on 'the Flats' (the Plain of San Augustin), that it had looked like a saucer, and that he didn't want to talk about it anymore.

However, Barnett later talked to other friends. While living in Socorro, he and his wife, Ruth, had become close friends with L.W. 'Vern' Maltais and his wife, Jean Swedmark Maltais. Interviewed by William Moore in 1979, the Maltaises confirmed that Barnett, a veteran of World War I, former commander of the American Legion Post at Mozquero, New Mexico, and engineer for the US Soil Conservation Service for twenty years, was the conservative, quietly self-assured type, not given to the spreading of wild rumours. Nevertheless, in February 1950, when the Mailtaises were visiting him and his wife in Socorro, Barnett told them that when working near Magdalena one morning, he saw 'a large metallic object' about a mile or so away on the flat desert land of 'the Flats'. Thinking it was a crashed aeroplane, he approached it and found himself looking at 'some sort of metallic, disk-shaped object about twenty-five or thirty feet across'. Even as he was studying it, some members of an archaeological team from the University of Pennsylvania arrived to study what they, too, had assumed was a crashed aeroplane.

Barnett was adamant that there were dead bodies both inside and outside the crashed flying saucer, which was made of 'a metal that looked like dirty stainless steel'. The bodies were 'like humans, but... the heads were round, the eyes were small, and they had no hair. The eyes were oddly spaced. They were quite small by our standards and their heads were larger in proportion to their bodies than ours. Their clothing seemed to be one-piece and grey in colour.'

While Barnett and the others were studying the crashed saucer and its strange occupants, all dead, 'a military officer drove up in a truck with a driver' and was followed by other military personnel. Barnett and the group from the University of Pennsylvania were told that it was their patriotic duty not to tell anyone what they had seen; then they were made to leave. The area was then sealed off and, presumably, the bodies and wreckage were removed by the military.

The basic scenario, therefore, is that somewhere between 9.45 and 9.50 on the evening of 2 July 1947, a UFO passed over Roswell, as witnessed by the Wilmots, then ran into storm lightning north of the town. As witnessed and heard by Brazel, it suffered some kind of explosion - either caused by a lightning bolt or by an internal malfunction - which sent debris raining down on the flatlands of Brazel's ranch, near Corona. The damaged UFO then managed to fly as far as the Plain of San Augustin, near Magdalena, west of Socorro, where it finally crashed, resulting in the deaths of all crew members, whether alien or human.

As the intact, albeit damaged, saucer-shaped craft had crashed in Magdalena, it was easily traced and a military group from Alamogordo, in the White Sands Proving Ground, was able to get there quickly and remove the remains. However, since only debris had fallen near Brazel's ranch, and as Brazel had not notified the authorities until several days later, when the latter would have assumed that the event had been well suppressed, it was news of the Roswell crash, and not the Socorro crash, that inadvertently leaked and led to the now famous Roswell Incident. Although there appears to be no evidence for the second crash, other than the word of Barnett, there is plenty of evidence pointing to the fact that *something* crashed, if not in Socorro, then in Roswell, New Mexico, on 2 July 1947. Neither a weather balloon nor missile, it became the subject of a widespread cover-up.

Interestingly, the most persuasive case to date of a CE-III, or close encounter of the third kind, also took place in Socorro, New Mexico, nearly two decades later, on 24 April 1964.

The Socorro sighting is described by Dr J. Allen Hynek as 'one of the soundest, best-substantiated reports' and the only 'landing, trace and occupant' case listed as 'unidentified' in the Project Blue Book files.

In a sworn affidavit dated 8 January 1967, Opal Grinder, manager of the White Brothers' service station in Socorro, claimed that on Friday, 24 April 1964, at approximately 5.50pm to 6.00pm , the driver of a 1955 model Cadillac, which had a Colorado licence plate and also contained the driver's wife and three boys, stopped at Grinder's service station for gas. The agitated driver told Grinder that 'something traveling across the highway from east to west' almost 'took the roof off' his car as he was driving just south of town, north of the airport. He suspected the object had either landed or crashed, as he had also seen 'a police car head off the road and up a hill in that direction'. Continuing into town, he had met another police car heading in the same direction. To Grinder's suggestion that he might have seen a helicopter, the unnamed man said, 'That sure would be some funny helicopter!'

Given that Grinder's affidavit was made out three years after the incident, the sketchiness of the scenario is understandable. However, when speaking to Ray Stanford and other investigators a few days after the incident, Grinder's descriptions were more precise. According to these, the object observed flying only a few hundred feet to the north-east of the north-bound Cadillac at 5.45pm on 24 April was 'egg-shaped, had a smooth aluminium or magnesium-like surface, and seemed to be a little longer than the four-door Green 1955 Cadillac in which the family was riding'. The craft dropped to barely ten feet above the ground, flew directly at the Cadillac, and passed silently within ten feet of its top, almost touching the tip of the radio antenna. It streaked onward a few hundred yards to the south-west, where it stopped abruptly, hung in midair for about thirty seconds, then descended vertically, silhouetted by the low afternoon sun, to land just beyond a small hill which hid it from the view of those in the Cadillac.

The driver of the Cadillac and his wife then observed a white Pontiac police car as it turned off a north-south road that ran west of US Highway 85, cut across rough terrain, and headed for the rise beyond which the strange flying object had landed. Thinking that perhaps they had seen some 'new type aircraft' that was being developed in the area, the driver of the Cadillac kept driving toward Socorro, eventually passing another police car. This one, which was from the New Mexico State Police, was moving urgently in the opposite direction, also heading for where the strange aircraft had descended.

Once in Socorro, the driver of the Cadillac stopped at the Whiting Brothers' service station on the north side of town, where he told the manager, Opal Grinder, what he had seen and complained that someone was flying 'a funny looking craft' dangerously low over the highway on Socorro's south side, had landed, and was probably being checked out by the officer of the pursuing police car. Then the driver of the Cadillac continued his journey with his family.

The man in the white Pontiac police car was Lonnie Zamora, a 31-year old Socorro policeman described in a subsequent report by investigating FBI agent J. Arthur Byrnes Jr as 'a sober, industrious and conscientious officer, and not given to fantasy'.

Zamora's extraordinary experience had begun at approximately 5.45pm when he set off in pursuit of a speeding black 1964 Chevrolet, following it south, after pulling away from the west side of the courthouse. About a minute later, at approximately the same time as the unknown man from Colorado had sighted his UFO, when Zamora was a half mile south of Spring Street, he heard a roar and noticed a brilliant blue 'cone of flame' low to the south-southwest, at a distance of approximately 2,400 feet. As Zamora was wearing prescription glasses with green sunshades, he was at this stage unable to distinguish the difference between the flying object's body and the 'blue cone of flame' shooting out of it. However, as the flame was over the location of a dynamite shack owned by the town mayor, Zamora assumed that the dynamite was blowing up, so instead of continuing his pursuit of the Chevrolet, he turned off the paved road and headed across the rough terrain, toward what now looked like a descending flame and sounded like a 'continuous roaring'.

Because of the position of the speeding Chevrolet, it is

unlikely that its driver would have either seen or heard the descending object.

Zamora drove across the rough terrain, toward the roaring 'flame', for about twenty seconds. By this time he was able to note that the flame was definitely 'bluish, very brilliant, a little orange around the edges, more so near the bottom' and that it was 'sort of motionless, but appeared to *descend slowly*'. He could not see the bottom of the flame, which had just descended behind a hill; nor did he notice smoke; but some dust seemed to be moving over the area where it had landed.

The 'flame' disappeared completely behind the hill, but the roaring continued as Zamora tried more than once to make his Pontiac climb the steep, gravel-covered slope. Then, as he finally began to ascend successfully, the roaring of the hidden 'flame' died away.

Turning over the hilltop, Zamora saw a 'shiny type object' down in the ravine, or arroyo, to the south-west, at a distance of about 150 yards. He stopped his car for a few seconds, in order to study the object. At first he thought it was 'an overturned white car' with the far end raised higher than the nearest one. Then he saw two people in white coveralls very close to the object.

As if having heard Zamora's arrival, one of the persons turned and looked straight at his car, then jumped slightly, as if startled by seeing it there.

Zamora had only stopped for a few seconds. Now, as he started forward again in his car, he noted that the object was 'like aluminium - it was whitish against the mesa background, but not chrome' and it seemed oval or 'egg-shaped' with support legs extending obliquely from it.

The people in white coveralls looked like normal human beings, but 'possibly they were small adults or large kids'.

As he drove on again, Zamora descended into a dip and temporarily lost sight of the object and the two people beside it. Worried that he might have come across a top-secret experimental vehicle from the White Sands Proving Ground, and wanting one reliable witness other than himself in case of trouble with the authorities, he radioed to the sheriff's office that he was checking a possible 10-40, or accident, down in the arroyo, and wanted New Mexico State Police Sergeant Samuel Chavez to come alone to the location.

As his message was being relayed to Chavez by Ned Lopez, the Socorro chief dispatcher, Zamora stopped his car again and started to get out, still talking on the radio. He dropped the microphone accidentally and leaned down to retrieve it. Even as he was straightening up, he heard 'a heavy slam, metal-like, heavier than a tank hatch... then another slam, real loud'. He was now completely out of his car and could see the object in clear view, about fifty feet away in the arroyo, with two of its four extension legs extending obliquely down to the ground. He could also see, for the first time, a large, red insignia on one side of the object's otherwise smooth, featureless, egg-shaped body.

The two people in white coveralls had disappeared - a fact which, combined with the metallic 'slamming' noises heard by Zamora, made him assume that they had entered the strange craft by some unseen door.

He had only taken two or three steps toward the object when he heard 'a roar... not exactly a blast, very loud roar...

not like a jet... started low frequency quickly, then rose in frequency (higher tone) and in loudness, from loud to very loud'. At the same time he saw 'bright blue flame' shooting out from the underside of the object and it started to rise vertically from the ground.

Thinking that the object was about to explode, Zamora threw himself to the ground. He felt a wave of heat, but when no explosion came, though the roaring continued, he got up again and ran back to his car. Bumping into it while glancing fearfully back over his shoulder, he lost his glasses and sunshades. Picking them up, and determined to keep the car between himself and the ascending object, which he still felt might explode, he ran north across the mesa, glancing back two or three times to observe that in about five or six seconds the object had risen level with his car, about twenty feet above the bottom of the arroyo, and was still roaring and shooting flame from its underside.

About fifty feet from his car, when just over the rim of the hill, Zamora turned back toward the object, but shielded his eyes with his arm in case it exploded.

At that moment, the roaring stopped and was replaced with a 'sharp tone, a whining sound' that went 'from high tone to low tone in maybe a second, then *stopped*'. Then there was silence.

Zamora saw that the object was no longer rising, though it was still moving: heading away quickly, in perfect silence, west-southwest, passing over, or rather south of, the dynamite shack as it flew away.

Realizing that the object was in flight and not exploding as he had feared, Zamora raced back to his car, picked up his glasses from where they had fallen, and once more radioed the Socorro sheriff dispatcher, Ned Lopez.

Lopez later confirmed that he had received the call from Zamora, breathlessly telling him to look out the window of the sheriff's office to see if the object was in sight. As Lopez was at the north window, not the south, and therefore could not see the object, he asked Zamora what kind of object it was. Zamora said, 'It looks like a balloon.'

Yet even as he was talking to Lopez, Zamora was watching the UFO disappearing in the distance. According to what he later told investigator Ray Stanford, it stayed about ten to fifteen feet above the ground, following the terrain, until it was near the perlite mill on the west side of US 60, about a mile away. There, it suddenly 'angled up at a steep climb and got small in the distance, over the canyon or mountain that way, *very fast*'. He remembered it as 'a bright, whitish oval getting smaller and smaller as it sped away, upward and over the mountains'.

Approximately one minute and fifty seconds after Zamora had first heard the roar and seen the 'flame' in the sky, the UFO was gone.

Sent urgently to the landing site by the message relayed through dispatcher Ned Lopez, New Mexico State Police Sergeant Sam Chavez reached Zamora just after the UFO had disappeared. Even as Chavez was approaching Zamora, the latter was making a sketch of the red insignia he had seen on the object before it took off. Though he had remained calm enough to do this, he was, according to Chavez, as 'white as a sheet' and in a cold sweat.

Examining the landing site with Zamora, Chavez also saw that the brush was smouldering in several places, after being ignited by the flame, and that there was what appeared to be a 'quadrangle' formed by four heavy, wedge-shaped imprints in the soil.

Zamora's radio transmissions had been heard by others, including State Police Senior Patrolman Ted V. Jordan, who arrived at the landing site shortly after Chavez, in the company of Socorro Under-sheriff James Luckie. A cattle inspector named White, who had also heard Zamora's radio calls, turned up at the landing site; and just after 6.00pm FBI agent J. Arthur Byrnes arrived to investigate.

All of these witnesses were able to confirm that the brush had been scorched by flames and that the pad prints, or landing imprints, had been made, in the words of Ray Stanford, 'by wedge-shaped units being forced by great weight, down into the rather well-packed soil of the ravine'. The wedges had a horizontal length of 12 to 16 inches, a horizontal width of 6 to 8 inches, and a vertical wedge-depth of 4 to 6 inches, though this latter measurement was impossible to define accurately because of the inward falling of the soil. According to the detailed account in the 28 April 1964 edition of the local biweekly newspaper, *El Defensor Cheftain*, the landing gear imprints 'did not appear to have been made by an object striking the earth with great force, but by an object of considerable weight settling to earth at slow speed and not moving after touching the ground'.

Though some of the bushes were still smouldering when Chavez, Jordan, Luckie and White were present, they all agreed that there was 'no odour whatever that would indicate that combustion of any conventional fuel had caused the burn damage'.

Jordan was particularly impressed by the fact that the flame described by Zamora had obviously 'sliced' a large greasewood bush, located almost centrally in the landing gear quadrilateral, without leaving any signs of turbulence, such as that which would have been caused by normal rotors or jet exhausts.

Jordan also took Polaroid pictures of the landing site and the four imprints within minutes of arriving on the scene.

The details of the Socorro sighting and the landing site itself were investigated thoroughly not only by FBI agent J. Arthur Byrnes, but by Ray Stanford (later to become director of Project Starlight International and editor-in-chief of its *Journal of Instrumented UFO Research*, then in Socorro on behalf of the National Investigations Committee on Aerial Phenomenon [NICAP), and Dr J. Allen Hynek, in his official capacity as consultant to the US Air Force (USAF).

Examination of the landing site revealed that the diagonals of the quadrilateral formed by the four landing marks intersected almost exactly at right angles. This led Hynek to speculate:

> One theorem in geometry states that if the diagonals of a quadrilateral intersect at right angles, the midpoints of the side of the quadrilateral lie on the circumference of a circle, and it is thus of considerable interest that the centre of the circle so formed [on the Socorro landing site] virtually coincided with the principal

> burn mark on the ground. Under certain circumstances the centre of gravity of the craft would have been directly over the centre of the circle, hence making the presence of the burn mark more significant.

At Hynek's request, USAF'S Project Blue Book chief, Major Hector Quintanilla, contacted the National Aeronautics and Space Administration (NASA), the Jet Propulsion Laboratory (JPL), and fifteen industrial firms in the vicinity to find out if they had been conducting any experiments with lunar landing models. They all said, 'No.'

In *Socorro Saucer* Ray Stanford claims that by 7.20pm. on the evening of the sighting, FBI agent J. Arthur Byrnes and US Army Captain Ord/C, Richard T. Holder, up-range commander of the White Sands Stallion Site, had met in the Socorro County Building where they proceeded to interrogate Zamora. In the course of this interrogation, Byrnes told Zamora that it would be better if he did not 'publicly mention seeing the two small figures in white' and Captain Holder 'recommended' that in future Zamora refuse to describe the insignia he had seen on the side of the vehicle to anyone other than official investigators.

What was the insignia?

Red in colour and approximately one-and-a-half feet tall, the insignia described and sketched by Zamora was an 'inverted V', or a vertical arrow, with a line under it, vertical lines on each side, and a parabolic arc over the point of the arrow. While author and computer scientist Jacques Vallee states that it is similar to a medieval Arabic sign for Venus, author and engineer Leon Davidson insists that it is confirmation that the UFO was a man-made craft. To support his claim, he points out that by moving and rotating the lines of the drawing, the initials 'CIA' and 'AD' can be formed, the latter representing the initials of Allen Dulles, then head of the CIA. To this intriguing theory, Ray Stanford adds the notion that the parabolic arc above the arrow, or inverted V, could have represented a 'stylized cross-section of the body of the craft (or a pressure wave)' while the arrow, or inverted V, with a line under it, could indicate that 'a *vertical thruster* was centrally located in it'. Stanford also believes that the placing of the symbol on the side of the craft, just above the thruster orifice on its underside, could have been a warning that the thruster was located there; while the use of red for the symbol could have been a danger sign, just as it is with current aircraft (and other) symbols.

The implication, therefore, is that the Socorro sighting was of a highly sophisticated, piloted, man-made craft that had flown from, and returned to, somewhere in the White Sands Proving Ground.

Chapter 9

UFOnauts and Close Encounters

There are a couple of sound reasons for concentrating on UFO sightings and encounters only in the US. The first is that while UFO landings and crashes have been reported from other countries, the US remains the most free with its information and, with the introduction of the Freedom of Information Act, has become even more so for the researcher. The second is that while we accept that highly advanced, disk-shaped aircraft may have been, or are being, created in countries other than the US, notably the Soviet Union, the available evidence makes us concentrate on the thread that leads logically from Germany's World War II technology to the US Navy's Flying Flapjack and the Canadian Avrocar, then on to the reports of UFO sightings, landings or crashes in the vicinity of the many top-secret military establishments scattered around New Mexico.

Most US atomic and space research, aircraft and missile development, and radar electronics and advanced weaponry experimentation takes place in New Mexico. It was from Eden Valley, near Roswell, south-east of Albuquerque, New Mecico, that Robert H. Goddard shot his first rockets skyward in the early 1930s. Shortly after World War II, the Roswell Army Air Field (now the Walker Air Force Base) became home to what was then the only combat-trained atom-bomb group in the world: the 509th Bomb Group of the US Army Air Force. Albuquerque itself is the home of the top-secret Kirtland AFB/Sandia National (Atomic Energy) Laboratories complex, located just south of the city, and the Manzano Nuclear Weapons Storage Facility, located to the east of Kirtland. New Mexico also contains the 'scientific community' of Los Alamos, created by the Manhattan (Atom Bomb) Project in 1943; once a 'secret city', it is still a highly restricted area, noted for its many atomic-energy laboratories. Two hundred and fifty miles south of Los Alamos is the White Sands Proving Ground, the US government's first rocket centre. The town of Alamogordo, lying between the Proving Ground and the site of the first atomic explosion, still proudly advertises itself as: *Home of the Atomic Bomb, Centre of Rocket Development*. The Proving Ground, which measures 4,000 square miles, has on its western border the Organ Mountain (so named because its closely bunched peaks are said to resemble organ pipes) and is otherwise a wasteland of sand and sagebrush out of which have sprung the numerous restricted US Army and Air Force bases, including Holloman AFB, the location for several UFO sightings, as well as many of the US Naval Research Laboratory's top-secret experimental establishments.

Because of the proliferation and secret nature of these research centres, certain UFOlogists assume that the great number of UFOs observed over them – sightings reported mostly by base personnel – is an indication that the saucers are spy craft crewed by extraterrestrials. However, continuing space exploration has revealed that no planet known to us holds any form of life (many extraterrestrial theories and 'close encounter' stories have been discredited in the past decade by our growing knowledge of the Moon,

Mars, and Venus) and that the problems of traveling to other galaxies are at this point seemingly insurmountable. Therefore we would appear to have increasingly valid reasons for believing that the 'circular, hyperbolic and spherical' craft of highly advanced capability are most frequently observed over top-secret military establishments because they are designed, constructed, tested and perhaps even used there, safe behind guarded fences, their reality confused by a constant smokescreen of disinformation.

If many of the sightings and encounters have taken place in such establishments, there have been even more extraordinary incidences elsewhere – Close Encounters of the Fourth Kind (CE-IV), or personal contact with, or abduction by, UFOnauts (UFO occupants, or crew members) – and since some of them, on first reading, appear to make mockery of the very idea of 'man-made' saucers, it is to them that we must now address ourselves.

One of the first and most famous contactee cases was that of George Adamski, a self-styled 'professor' in oriental mystical philosophy who founded his own cult (The Royal Order of Tibet), set it up as a religious community in California, then moved to Mount Polomar where, while working at a hamburger stand, he managed to convince many visitors, including journalists, that he was actually an astronomer at the famous observatory on the peak of the mountain.

In 1946 Adamski had written an unpublished novel, *Pioneers of Space*, which was about an imaginary journey to the Moon, Mars and Venus. It is very likely that this work of fiction was the basis of Adamski's later, hugely successful 'non-fiction' book, *Flying Saucers Have Landed* (1953), purporting to be a true account of how Adamski, in the company of friends (not including co-author Desmond Leslie), spied 'a gigantic spacecraft' near Desert Centre, California. Fearlessly approaching the saucer, Adamski met with a male Venusian with whom he communicated telepathically and with sign language. After explaining that the radiation from the fallout of Earth's atom-bomb tests was damaging the other planets in the solar system and that he had come to Earth to stop such tests, the Venusian gave Adamski a tour of the inside of his spacecraft. Before the spacecraft took off, Adamski was able to take a lot of photographs, but as one camera was out of focus and the other not working properly, he only managed to obtain a single, blurred photograph of the flying saucer, which was later widely derided as a fake. Adamski was also able to take a plaster-of-paris cast of the alien's footprint, though it was never satisfactorily explained why he had taken plaster-of-paris into the desert in the first place.

Adamski followed *Flying Saucers Have Landed* with two more books: *Inside the Spaceships* (1955), and *Flying Saucers Farewell* (1961). In these, he described his deepening friendship with the Venusians and numerous journeys made with them in their 'gigantic spacecraft' to the Moon, Mars and Venus, all of which contained wondrous cities and civilizations, none of which were remotely like the planets we now know so well. Other authors, including Truman Bethurum, Daniel Fry, Orfeo Angelucci, and Howard Menger, followed with similar tomes, most of them capitalizing on Adamski's contention that Jesus had been an alien spaceman and that the aliens were trying to save mankind from self-destruction through atomic warfare or fallout; but the (all male) authors also added the novelty of beautiful female extraterrestrials with whom they invariably had intimate relationships. In the age of the Cold War, with the atomic threat hanging over mankind, such books made for popular escapist reading.

As such early 'contactee' cases were fanciful nonsense, we can safely ignore them and instead turn to three of the most baffling 'abductee' cases on record: the New Hampshire case of 19 September 1961; the Pascagoula case of 11 October 1973; and the Alamogordo case of 13 August 1975.

Barney Hill was a black, 39-year old who worked for the United States Post Office. His wife, Betty, Caucasian, was a 41-year old State of New Hampshire social worker. On the night of 19 September 1961, when driving from Canada to New Hampshire along US Highway 3, through the White Mountains, they were tracked by a 'spinning' white light. When the light eventually approached their car, the Hills saw that it was 'a large, disk-shaped craft with windows around its rim'. Six beings, wearing dark uniforms, were watching them from the windows. According to the Hills' initial recollection, the craft was now hovering in the air fifty feet away, so they stopped to let Barney get out and look at it through his binoculars. As he did so, the object descended vertically and landed. 'Two fins, each bearing a red light, were slowly extending from the right and left of the craft. Another extension was lowered from its base.'

Terrified, Barney jumped back into his car and drove off quickly. He and Betty heard 'an irregular beeping sound' coming from what seemed to be the trunk of their car, and both experienced a 'tingling sensation and drowsiness'. Aroused by another series of beeps, they discovered that they had travelled thirty-five miles and could not recall what had happened in between. Also, their wristwatches had stopped running.

Ten days later, Betty began to suffer from vivid dreams in which she and Barney were taken aboard a flying saucer and medically examined. About a month after the incident, she and Barney realised that the trip from Canada to Portsmouth had taken at least two hours longer than it should have.

Beginning in December 1963, almost two troubled years after the UFO sighting, Betty and Barney were hypnotised repeatedly, in independent sessions, by Boston psychiatrist, Dr Benjamin Simon. Over the course of many sessions, Barney and Betty revealed separately that during the missing two hours of the night of 19 September 1961 they had been taken aboard a 'spacecraft' by 'humanoid' creatures with 'large eyes that reached around to the side of the head, no nose, and a mouth that was a slit without lip muscles'. The humanoids communicated telepathically. Betty and Barney were medically examined by the humanoids, shown a map consisting of dots, which they were told were galactical travel routes, then returned to their car. From inside the car, in the company of their visibly frightened dog, they were able to watch the 'spacecraft' ascending again, increasing in brilliance and resembling 'a glowing orange ball' as it left.

At the end of the many hypnotic sessions, Dr Simon's conclusion was that the Hills had 'undergone an imaginary experience caused by fear after an actual UFO approach'.

However, under posthypnotic suggestion, Betty Hill drew the star map she had been shown aboard the spacecraft and the results appeared to suggest something she could not possibly have known about: the stars Zeta 1 and Zeta 2, located in the Reticulum constellation and long held to be prime candidates as a possible source of extraterrestrial life.

While there are arguments against this interpretation of the map drawn by Betty Hill, and while the New Hampshire case in general has its detractors, it has become one of the most famous and controversial UFO 'abductee' cases on record. Almost as well known is the Pascagoula case. This began on the evening of 11 October 1973, when two shipyard workers, Charles Hickson and Calvin Parker, were fishing off a pier on the Pascagoula (Singing) River, just outside the city of Pascagoula, Mississippi – an area with a heavy concentration of government space research and military installations. Hearing a sudden buzzing noise, Hickson and Parker looked behind them to see a large eggshaped, or oblong, craft that was glowing a bluish-white as it hovered about three feet above the ground near where they were sitting. Paralysed with fear, both men watched as a door in the craft opened and three beings emerged and *floated* up to them. These creatures then took hold of Hickson and Parker (the latter had fainted), and 'floated' them into the UFO where, in a brightly lit room that had 'no corners or edges' (ie., circular), the still conscious Hickson was 'levitated' into a horizontal position and given what appeared to be a medical examination by a free-floating device. About twenty minutes later, both men were deposited back on the river bank, the UFO left the area ('straight up'), and Parker then regained consciousness.

Hickson and Parker were interrogated separately by intelligence officers at Keesler Air Force Base and the case was later investigated by J. Allen Hynek, representing the National Investigations Committee on Aerial Phenomena (NICAP), and University of California civil engineering professor James Harder, a consultant to the Aerial Phenomena Research Organization (APRO). While certain discrepancies in the reports indicate that Hickson and Parker may have been party to a hoax designed to lure tourists to the town, Hynek remained open-minded about it and Dr Harder, after hypnotizing both men, said, 'They are not unbalanced people, not crackpots... Hickson and Parker have been through a terrifying experience.'

Whether hoax or reality, the descriptions given of the UFOnauts are of particular interest. The creatures were less than five feet tall, with grey, wrinkled skin. Their heads were round-shaped, with no necks. They had 'pointed protrusions' jutting out where their ears should have been. They had no eyes. There was only 'a small opening' under the nose where the mouth should have been, though this could have been a covering made either from thin metal or 'wrinkled' material 'like an elephant's skin'. The 'shapeless' legs of the creatures ended in round feet with no toes. Most remarkably, they had unusually long arms with what resembled 'claws' instead of human hands.

Based on the descriptions obtained by Hickson and Parker during the hypnotic sessions, Dr Harder preferred to describe the UFOnauts as 'automata' with 'pincers at the end of armlike appendages'. It was his belief that they were 'advanced robots' and that it was perfectly natural for the terrified Hickson and Parker to have projected human characteristics onto them.

This leads us naturally to the Alamogordo case, which has striking similarities to those mentioned above. On 13 August 1975, at about 1.15am, US Air Force Sergeant Charles L. Moody was watching a meteor shower over the desert near Alamogordo, New Mexico, when he saw 'a glowing, metallic, disk-shaped object' descend about 300 feet away, to an altitude of fifteen to twenty feet. Judged by Moody to be about fifty feet long and eighteen to twenty feet wide, it 'wobbled on its own axis' before moving steadily toward him. Unnerved, Moody attempted to drive away, but was unable to start his car. The UFO stopped its advance about seventy feet away, thus enabling Moody to see 'a rectangular window' and, framed by it, shadows resembling human forms.

By this time, a high-pitched whining sound could be heard. When it stopped abruptly, Moody felt a numbness creeping over his body. The next thing he remembered was the object rising into the sky and disappearing into the distance. When Moody turned the ignition key in his car, it worked normally, letting him drive back to his house, though still feeling terrified. Checking his wristwatch as soon as he arrived home, he saw that he had somehow lost about ninety minutes.

In the days immediately following the event, Moody suffered various psychosomatic illnesses. On the recommendation of his physician, he practised self-hypnosis and eventually pieced together just what had happened to him on the night of August 13. According to these recollections, shortly after the whining of the UFO had stopped and Moody felt the numbness creeping over him, two creatures, both about six feet tall and wearing skintight black clothing, approached his car. After a brief struggle, Moody was somehow rendered unconscious and awoke on a slab inside the craft, feeling paralysed. Looking down at him were the two creatures who had captured him, plus another one, only five feet tall and wearing a silvery white suit. Like the other two creatures, he had a large hairless head, a protruding brow, roundish eyes, small ears and nose, and very thin lips. His skin was whitish-grey'. The creature seemed to speak telepathically.

When the terrified Moody agreed not to resist, the shorter UFOnaut, whom Moody assumed was the leader, relieved his state of paralysis by applying a 'rodlike device' to his back. Moody was then shown around the ship and noticed a 'sweet, stifling odour'. He was informed that the UFO's 'mother ship' was located 400 miles above the Earth (Moody later changed this figure to 6,000), promised a future meeting with the occupants, and told that 'future contact with Earthmen' would not be attempted for another twenty years. Finally, after telling Moody that he would have no recollection of this experience until about two weeks later, the short UFOnaut placed his hands on the sides of Moody's head and rendered him unconscious. Moody awoke in his car just as the UFO was leaving.

The delayed recollections, psychosomatic illnesses and need for hypnotic retrieval of the experience make this similar to the New Hampshire case in particular. However, in all three cases communication was made by telepathic means and those abducted underwent some kind of physical examination. The creatures in the New Hampshire case had 'large eyes that reached around to the side of the head, no nose, and a mouth that was a slit without lip muscles'. The creatures in the Pascagoula case had 'no eyes. There was only a small opening under the nose where the mouth should have been', though this could have been a covering made either from thin metal or wrinkled material, 'like an elephant's skin'. In the Alamogordo case, the creatures had 'roundish eyes, small ears and nose, and very thin lips' with 'whitish-grey' skin.

Such descriptions, albeit distorted by terror and confused recollection, are surprisingly similar to one-another, as they are to the other famous abductee cases. For instance, in the Kelly-Hopkinsville, Kentucky, incident of 21 August 1955, the UFOnaut observed by teenager Billy Ray Sutton was about four feet tall and had 'a round head' with pointed ears, and 'long arms' with 'clawlike' hands. Bullets seemed to ricochet off it and similar UFOnauts, as if they were 'covered in nickel-plated armour', and they appeared to be able to 'float' like the creatures in the Pascagoula case. In the Cisco Grove, Placer County, California, case of 4 September 1964, the UFOnauts observed by three hunters were over five feet tall and dressed in silvery-white uniforms with hoods or helmets that went straight up from their shoulders; but they were accompanied by short, stocky, 'robotlike' creatures that were 'dark grey or black' in colour, had no discernable neck, but possessed 'enormous, glowing eyes' above 'a square, hinged jaw which dropped open to form a triangular hole in the face'. What appeared to be a cloud of steam emitted from the hole. In the Betty Andreasson case of 25 January 1967, the UFOnauts were approximately four feet tall and had ‘pear-shaped’ heads with narrow chins, ‘holes’ for noses, ‘scarlike slits’ for mouths, and ‘large, almond-shaped eyes slanted around to the sides of their heads’ (exactly like those in the New Hampshire case of 1961). In the Falkville, Alabama, case of 17 October 1973, the UFOnaut observed up close and photographed by Police Chief Jeff Greenshaw was like ‘a man wrapped in aluminium foil’. It had ‘an antenna’ on its head but was otherwise featureless, and walked with ‘a stiff and mechanical gait’.

It is clear, then, from these descriptions and others, that the UFOnauts observed by the majority of contactees and abductees are either normal, albeit tallish, creatures very much like human beings or short creatures with certain human characteristics but also possessing bizarre, even nightmarish physical attributes. Though Dr Harder describes the latter as ‘automata’ and believes them to be ‘advanced robots’, contactee descriptions of ‘wrinkled’ and ‘whitish-grey’ skin, ‘like an elephant’s skin’, suggest that they may be cyborgs – half man, half machine.

If this were the case, neither the tall, human-like creatures nor the short, robotlike creatures would necessarily have to be extraterrestrials; they could in fact come from right here on Earth. However, the theory of Earthly origin would still be confronted with the other seemingly ‘magical’ or ‘impossible’ aspects of so many contactee and abductee reports, including paralysing or mesmerizing ‘devices’ and ‘beams of light’; levitation; telepathic communication; and information about the supposed extraterrestrial origin of the UFOs and their occupants.

Yet all of these aspects of the reports may be explainable within the present technology.

The brain controls most of our bodily functions, including what we see, hear, smell and feel. Yet since the brain is rarely used at even a *tenth* of its full potential, by awakening certain dormant areas of it, or by deadening others, either electrically, by the use of drugs, or through hypnotic suggestion, the scope of both our senses and our capabilities can be dramatically expanded or reduced, and our whole mode of behaviour changed. Such methods of affecting the brain can also induce pleasure, fear, many other emotions, and even physical pain; they can therefore be used to 'reward' or 'punish' the subject in a Pavlovian manner and by so doing completely control him.

Regarding the most common form of mind-control, namely hypnotism, the same principles apply, the only difference being that the sensations are induced, or recalled, by a process of suggestion, rather than by physical means. However, through routine hypnotism the subject can be directed to go to sleep or waken up, feel non-existent pain or ignore applied pain, turn as rigid as a plank, relive long forgotten experiences or forget past experiences, and frequently do what he would not normally contemplate. So real can the hypnotic experience be that a hypnotised subject, if told that he has just been scalded, will actually come out in blisters. Alternately, the same subject can be burned or pierced with needles and experience no pain at all; nor will he be marked with the burning or piercing when snapped out of the trance state.

It is a common misconception that only certain kinds of individual can be hypnotised. In fact, any intelligent adult and most children over the age of seven can be hypnotised. Only the mentally retarded and the psychotic can *resist* being hypnotised. Hypnotisability is in no way a sign of weak will. Indeed, the more intelligent and imaginative the individual, the better a subject he will be – but certainly most individuals can be hypnotised, whether or not they want to be.

There are three prime states of hypnotism: light, medium and heavy, the latter being a state of somnambulism.

Contactees frequently tell of how, though frightened, they felt drawn toward the UFOnauts or, at least, felt compelled to obey them – even when it seemed that the UFOnauts had not actually *spoken*. Another common denominator in the contactee experience is the feeling of remoteness, of divorce from the self, with the contactees invariably behaving as if they are zombies.

This is often the case with the (often rapidly flickering) 'beams of light' that emanate from the UFO – often accompanied by 'eerie' sounds – or from the hands of, or apparatus used by, the UFOnauts. When the contactees are struck by the flickering beam of light, they are either rendered unconscious (to reawaken elsewhere, usually in a daze) or placed into a state of what can only be described as fully conscious suspended animation: they are aware of what is happening to them, but unable to resist it in any way. In this condition, they are often convinced that they are 'floating' or 'gliding' between their captors and into the UFO; and that their captors are not actually speaking to them, even though they, the abductees, can somehow 'hear' what their captors are saying.

Such sensations are fully consistent with the hypnotic state. Once a person has been conditioned to accept the hypnotic state, a simple phrase or gesture (the waving of a hand; a light touch on some part of the face or head) can be used to put them into a hypnotic trance – but still awake, with eyes open.

As the often reported 'beams of light' emanate from the UFO and not the UFOnauts, we will return to them in a subsequent chapter. For the moment, let us concentrate on the other widely reported UFOnaut method of mesmerizing, which is the pressing of the contactee's neck, either by hand or with some kind of metallic device. This either renders the contactee unconscious or without will while still fully conscious.

Although this seems singularly mysterious, it is in fact another standard form of hypnotism: the 'instantaneous technique' or the 'carotid procedure', both of which are based on simple biology: the hypnotist merely applies pressure to a blood vessel near the ear, thus inhibiting the heart rate, interfering with the circulation of blood to the brain, and rendering the subject dazed and confused, and susceptible to suggestion.

'Wide awake' hypnosis is a commonplace hypnotic state in which the subject knows exactly who he is, where he is, and what he is doing – even though only capable of doing what he is instructed to do by the hypnotist. This particular form of hypnotism can even be applied to a sleeping subject. The hypnotist simply attracts the attention of the sleeper with some sort of physical contact, hypnotises him by repeatedly telling him that he can hear the hypnotist's voice, has him perform what is required of him, then very gently puts him back to sleep. He will later waken up in a normal fashion, but with absolutely no recollection of being hypnotised or what he did while in the hypnotic state.

The 'amnesia' or bewildering, though uncomfortably familiar 'nightmares' suffered by so many contactees (as with Betty and Barney Hill) could be either a form of remote-controlled brain implantation, as discussed below, or a form of post-hypnotic suggestion. In this condition, the victim can be conditioned to remember nothing about what has happened to him – or, for the hypnotist's purposes of disinformation, to remember *some* of it, but only enough to confuse or frighten him or those who listen to him, because what he recollects will seem so senseless, bewildering, and therefore frightening.

Normal hypnosis could certainly account for this. However, electric brain implantation would be an infinitely more powerful and lasting way of doing the same thing.

As early as 1932 Dr Walter Hess had devised the modern technique of electrode implantation, thereby demonstrating that most of man's functions and emotions can be influenced by stimulation of specific areas of the brain. A simple method of doing this is to inject radiopaque materials into the intercerebral spaces inside the skull to facilitate, by X-ray, the visualization of various parts of the brain. This is done with a stereotaxic skullcap (similar devices are often described in UFO abductee reports) which, utilizing minute spikes that pierce the scalp, takes

X-rays from many different angles and makes geometrical calculations to give three-dimensional coordinates for the positioning of the electrodes. The steel electrodes, which are as thin as hairs (small enough to be placed inside an individual nerve cell) are guided into the skull by micromanipulators, after which they can release the light electric current required for stimulation of the chosen area.

A state of constant drowsiness can be brought about by the electric stimulation of the caudate nucleus, the nucleus reticularis, or the inferior thalamus. Conversely, a similar stimulation of the mesencephalic reticular formation will induce instant arousal. Another example is the hypothalamus: the area of the brain which controls our most basic, primitive needs. By stimulating the appropriate areas of the hypothalamus with submicroelectric electrodes, the controller can regulate the subject's blood pressure, heart rate and respiration; control his sleep or appetite, even the diameter of his pupils; can place him into a state of suspended animation or make him work till he drops. In short, he can totally control the subject's bodily and mental functions and even, with the aid of the appropriate computer-controlled interfacing equipment, do so from a distance, with the subject (or victim) not knowing that he is under control.

The possibility of physical and mental control of human beings was already well developed by the mid-1960s, with many bio-engineers claiming that computer and human brain would soon be directly linked. Said R.M. Page of the US Naval Research Laboratory: 'The information which a machine can obtain and store from a person in a few minutes will exceed the fruits of a lifetime of man-to-man communication.' As to method: 'The coupling mechanisms to carry out the functions will be myriad, including in some cases electrical connections to the body and brain. Some connections may be wireless, with imperceptible transmitting elements implanted in the body.'

While such research work was clearly under way in the top-secret experimental establishments of the White Sands Proving Ground (where the US Naval Research Laboratory, among others, has its own research centres), ESB, or electrical stimulation of the brain, was becoming dangerously innovative elsewhere. The suggestion that computer-controlled electrodes be implanted in the brains of babies a few months after birth, thus robotizing them for life, was made by the American electronics engineer Curtiss R. Schafer in a paper he presented before the National Electronics Conference in Chicago. In a similar mood, Dorman S. Isreal, a fellow of the Institute of Radio Engineers, proposed that 'newborn infants can be operated on and the latest submicroelectrical equipment installed in the brain and at certain critical points in the spinal column' in order to give them the benefits of 'non-radio communicative powers' and also enhance their creativity ability.

While such suggestions may have been made half in jest, it was already clear by the early 1970s that such proposals were being taken seriously by many scientists and that much of the experimentation was moving beyond the already controversial area of vivisection and into the human arena, with subjects wired for electrosleep, electroprostheses, electrovision, electroanalgesia, electroanaesthesia and, increasingly, electrosociology.

In the field of electrosociology, Dr Jose M.R. Delgado, professor of physiology at the Yale University School of Medicine, and Dr James Olds of McGill University in Canada, both experimented extensively with the so-called 'pleasure centres' of the human brain, as did Dr Robert G. Heath of Tulane University. Meanwhile, Dr C. Norman Shealy, chief of neurosurgery at the Gunderon Clinic in La Crosse, Wisconsin, had perfected electro-analgesic techniques to the point where they were being applied to humans, mainly through the implanting of a .8 to 1.2 stimulating electrode in the spine rather than the brain. Regarding electrosociology, a team of doctors at Massachusetts General Hospital and Boston General Hospital were 'pacifying' violent human subjects with the implantation of electrodes into the rostral part of the caudate nucleus of the brain.

Such experiments had been going on for years – overtly in animals, covertly in human beings, with the latter experiments usually cloaked in secrecy. What *is* known is that electrodes implanted in the human brain have been used successfully to activate paralysed and artificial limbs; to control otherwise uncontrollable muscular spasms, as in Parkinson's Disease; to pacify violent mental patients and prisoners; and even to initiate 'thought control' between a human controller and a computer.

Given that any form of human brain manipulation can have frightening social and political ramifications, many of the experiments on humans have been conducted behind closed doors, most notoriously in mental institutions and state prisons, where prisoners receive certain benefits for becoming so-called 'voluntary' guinea pigs. The results of such experiments are rarely discussed openly, but given what has already been accomplished in these fields, it is safe to assume that remote-controlled 'programming' of individuals is well within reach and may, indeed, now be widespread.

Certainly it is no secret that the reflexes and appetites of animals have been controlled at a reasonable distance by a controller seated behind a computer-linked console. Such an animal can be made to sit, stand, play, fight, collapse in terror, eat, or starve itself to death. Regarding human beings, by the end of the 1960s it was still only possible (in unclassified experiments) to stimulate specific areas of the brain and do so under immediate visual control. However, the possibility of long-distance control of implanted human beings was being explored in many areas; and though it was generally believed that the particular response required would be programd at the time of the implantation – fed into the brain via the computer – and would be limited to one or two responses only, those were early days and the reports were only of known experiments.

On the assumption that great advances have been made since then, it should now be possible to implant an electrode, or electrodes, in the brain of a human subject and then program him to feel pain or terror each time he attempts to recollect what his controller wants him to forget. This could certainly account for the many reports of amnesia, followed by headaches, nausea, terror or acute bewilderment, when the contactees have tried to recall exactly what had happened to them.

In *Phoenix* and *Genesis* (Books Two and Three in the *Projekt Saucer* series), I offer the present state of progress on prosthetics and other surgical nightmares as a possible explanation for the physical appearance and peculiar abilities of the UFOnauts. Since the reality of such creatures borders on science fiction, rather than fact, it will be instructive to look back at the work that was being done in those relatively early days in the various areas relating to UFOnaut appearance and capability.

By 1980 in the field of prosthetics work had been progressing with remarkable speed and success on the artificial heart (South Africa's Dr Christiaan Barnard completed the first human heart transplant in 1967), lung, gut and gill, as well as artificial cells, blood vessels, intestines and even skin. Artificial bones, joints and sockets were being used with increasing success, the main alloys being of the cobalt and chromium variety: tantalum, titanium, niobium and molybdenum. Blood vessels, heart valves, bone, skin, blood and even the cornea of the eye were all being preserved artificially. Skin, stored in DSMO for periods of years, had already been grafted successfully to the human body by researchers at the University of Pennsylvania School of Medicine. Bone frozen for years and revived with cobalt radiation had also taken when grafted to the body. Likewise, red blood cells had already been freeze-dried for years and as early as 1980 tissue banks were becoming commonplace. Indeed, as long ago as 1980, even before my novel *Genesis* was published, the US Navy tissue bank was able to supply some 3,000 square inches of human skin to Brazilian fire victims.

In external prosthetics, the myoelectric control of

limbs was racing ahead. The Soviets were making the greatest advances in this particular field and had already perfected a hand-arm prosthesis in which all five fingers were capable of closing around objects of variable shape with the precision of a human hand. British scientists had developed, among other advanced prosthetics, myoelectric arms with interchangeable hands; while in the United States, a team of scientists and engineers from Harvard, MIT, and Massachusetts General Hospital, had developed a sophisticated myoelectric arm that could move at any angle, speed or force simply by being *thought* into action. The arm picked up muscle signals generated to the natural stump, transmitted them to a small amplifier, and used it to drive a compact electric motor. The machinery for all of this was housed inside a flesh-coloured, fibre-glass casing that resembled a real arm.

However, researchers at the Powered Limbs Unit of West Hendon Hospital, near London, England, were soon advancing on the above by developing an implantable electrode, or transmitter, called an Emgor. This used a resonator circuit that did not require batteries to detect myoelectric signals, thus obviating the need for frequent surgical intervention to replenish the power source.

Regarding the extent to which some surgeons would go openly in this kind of development, and to which some patients would willingly let themselves be used in the desperate hope of prolonging their lives under any circumstances, it should be noted that according to *World Medicine*, 1 March 1966, 'lower body prosthetics' had already been developed to the point where some surgeons were willing to perform hemicorporectomies: amputation of the entire lower half of the body, including legs, rectum and genitalia. This procedure had already been offered to patients in a prominent New York hospital as an alternative to death by abdominal cancer. Among those who accepted the offer was forty-nine year old James Cavorti who, 'after months of the most mutilating and demoralizing operation known to surgical science, returned home with a complete lower-body prosthesis to support his sixty-pound torso'.

David Fishlock, who recounts the above story in his book, *Man Modified: An Exploration of the Man-Machine Relationship* (1971), gives other chilling examples of just how much certain individuals may be willing to let themselves be butchered or mutilated if they have strong enough reason (one of his examples being that certain, perfectly sane, professional deep-sea divers would be willing to 'face the hazards of using their lungs as gills, in order to breathe underwater'); but both Fishlock and Vance Packard, author of *The People Shapers* (1978), show a healthy concern for the dubious attitudes and ethics of the 'bio-medical engineering' profession.

Living in a democratic society, it is hard to imagine that the involuntary use of human experimental 'animals' could take place anywhere other than in a Nazi concentration camp. However, as Fishlock makes clear: 'Even today there are people who believe that convicts, especially the criminal lunatic, and even conscientious objectors, should be compelled to lend themselves to science.' As an example of a much milder and widely accepted form of this, Fishlock points out that destitute citizens in the US can acquire a measure of care and attention in exchange for 'freedom of access to their bodies'. (Such 'access' would include the selling of blood, as well as laboratory sex with other humans or with the aid of prosthetics, frequently while being photographed and filmed.) In order to emphasise that many other scientists would be willing to go, and have gone, much farther than this, Fishlock tells us that in *Human Guinea Pigs* (1967) by Dr M.H. Pappworth: 'His search through a portion of the medical literature of recent years has yielded a wealth of evidence that experiments are made freely by a small number of medical research teams in the USA and Britain, on the sick and dying, on geriatric patients, on criminals, even on infants and pregnant women.'

The extent to which highly educated and supposedly civilized men will go to create a Brave New World is detailed in even more nightmarish detail by Vance Packard in *The People Shapers*. As this book was published sixteen years ago, it is chilling to read what had already been seriously considered up to that time. One of Packard's more illuminating examples is the 'amiable and highly respected' New York psychiatrist, Willard Gaylin, who 'explored at length' the possibilities of 'harvesting' the living dead and preserving them in special 'bioemporiums' that would house 'living cadavers' attached to respirators. In the words of Packard: 'Since their brains had stopped functioning they would be legally dead. But they "would be warm, respiring, pulsating, evacuating, and excreting bodies"' and could therefore be maintained for many years as 'a source of spare parts' and for medical experimentation of all kinds.

We are reminded by Packard that in the Cleveland

Clinic's Department of Artificial Organs, not only medical specialists, but 'mechanical, electrical, chemical, and biomedical engineers, as well as biochemists and polymer chemists', were, in their busy operating theatres, enthusiastically engaged in 'surgery connected to the development of artificial substitutes for other vital organs such as the liver, lungs, pancreas, and kidneys'. Conveniently within walking distance of the Cleveland Clinic's Department of Artificial Organs are the Neurosurgical Research Laboratories of the Cleveland Metropolitan General Hospital, where great interest was being expressed, as far back as 1967, in the possibility of transferring the entire head of one human being to another. Switching human *brains* from one head to another would be complicated and costly; but as Packard explains: 'By simply switching heads, on the other hand, only a few connections need to be severed and then reestablished in the neck of the recipient body.'

Robert J. White, then professor of neurosurgery at Case Western Reserve Medical School and head of the Cleveland Metropolitan General Hospital's live brain transplant research team, informed Packard that he preferred to call the procedure 'a cephalic transplant' because 'the phrase "head transplant" seemed to give some people the shivers'. The good doctor might have felt this way because in the same hospital some 'isolated' animal brains were being kept in cold storage while others, less lucky, were 'functioning, warm brains' that were being 'kept alive by hookups to blood machines or to live individuals of the same species. What is going on mentally inside those disembodied brains is a matter of speculation'.

In 1908 the American vascular surgeon, Charles Guthrie, grafted an extra head onto a dog, thus creating a two-headed animal; and in 1968 a team of Russian surgeons, led by Professor Anatoli Kanevsky, repeated the experiment more than once, then proudly reported that their twin-headed dogs ate, slept and performed their physiological functions normally, as if nothing had happened.

Nevertheless, while in those early experiments the head transplants did not survive long, brain-wave and chemical tests showed them to be functioning normally while alive and, according to Packard, 'somewhat better than before they were "isolated"', though possibly feeling 'bored and lonely, living on old memories.'

Certainly, with regard to the Cleveland Clinic's monkeys with transplanted heads, Professor White was adamant that the brains remained operational as far as the eyes, ears, nose, face and tongue were concerned. If a monkey was aggressive before the head transplant, it would remain that way after the transplant; if gentle before the transplant, it would remain so afterwards. Also, most of the heads that had been transplanted showed 'every indication of being alert to what was going on'. In other words, the transplanted heads would make sounds, accept and chew food, and track a human being with their eyes as he or she walked past them. So, though the monkeys with transplanted heads lived only a week, they were functioning properly while still alive.

At the time of these experiments, in the early to mid-1970s, it was known that the recipient body would remain out of contact with the brain 'until scientists master the problem of regenerating severed spinal cords'. However, it was White's belief that if we could grow spinal cords, we could 'transplant heads of humans with hope of achieving reasonably normal people'.

Indeed, in June 1976, even as Professor White was conducting his head transplant experiments with monkeys, a Soviet scientist, Levon A. Matinian, reported at the fourth biennial conference on Regeneration of the Central Nervous System that he had succeeded in regrowing the spinal cords of rats. Given that *Science News* described this achievement as one of 'monumental importance', it has to be accepted that more work in this area has continued behind closed doors and may now be remarkably well advanced.

Were this not enough, Packard informs us of the following: In one medical experiment, 'the heads of eight live young fetuses were cut off and then injected with radioactive compounds to study brain metabolism'. At a hospital for elderly chronic patients in Brooklyn, 'live cancer cells were injected into debilitated patients who did not suffer from cancer' in order to determine if cancer could be so induced. And at an institute for mentally retarded children on Staten Island, some of the children were injected with live hepatitis virus.

Last but not least, Packard points out that: 'A recent issue of *Modern Medicine* reported that most doctors favour experimentation on humans, even on prisoners, children, the mentally retarded, and other captive subjects, as long as there is peer review.' As in practice, peer review committees consist 'overwhelmingly of fellow staff members', Packard was of the opinion that little legal, ethical, religious, or scientific restraint would be placed on such gruesome activities.

If such experiments were taking place in public hospitals and institutions so long ago, who is to say that even more ambitious experiments were not taking place behind the guarded fences and locked doors of the world's most secret military and scientific establishments? As David Fishlock reminds us: 'Men accustomed to solving the most intricate problems that aerospace and weapon technology could conceive turned with confidence to those of medical engineering.'

They certainly did. Remote-controlled robots are called 'phantoms' and at least two decades have passed since NASA's Manned Spaceflight Centre, in cooperation with the Illinois Institute of Technology Research in Chicago, produced 'a very sophisticated phantom' that resembled 'a human being in shape and size and in the way it moves its thirty-five joints, thirty-three of them fitted with strain-gauge torque sensors. In fact, it does almost anything but walk…' By the mid-1960s those primitive robots, or phantoms, had evolved into 'master-slave manipulators' called CAMS, or Cybernetic Anthropomorphous Machine Systems, which were designed to 'unite man's complex of sensory mechanisms with the power and versatility of a machine'. Used mostly for work in environments hostile to man (the sea bed, outer space, the handling of radioactive and other dangerous substances), the CAMS, or 'slave' machine, is operated by remote-control and 'mimics its master's arm, finger and thumb movements with such finesse that it can twirl a hula-hoop with its one digit'. This man-machine coupling was so efficient that 'the man need not think about the machine at all; he simply concentrates on the task'.

The early CAMS were operated through hydraulic servo-mechanisms that had their limitations, but progress was soon made on the 'sensitive coupling of the operator's nervous system' to powered manipulators that were even more versatile than human limbs. Interested in remote-controlled machines that could assist in the 'hostile' environment of a nuclear accident or attack, the US Air Force Weapons Laboratory soon produced 'an eleven-ton monster with two manipulators, each having six degrees of freedom and a nineteen-foot reach'. Not to be outdone, the UK Atomic Energy Research Establishment, at Harwell, England, created a 'remote inspection vehicle' which 'moves with the profile of a crawling man to gain access, but once in position can stand erect in order to deploy its "eyes" and "arms"'.

In an aerospace conference given in Boston in 1966, engineer William E. Bradley, who developed the idea of cable-less man-machine manipulator systems for the US Defence Department's Institute for Defence Analysis, stated his belief that man and machine would eventually be linked in such a way that by performing the manoeuvres himself, the man would cause them to take place, through the machine, at a distance of thousands of miles. This concept soon led to the weapon-aiming system devised by the Philco Corporation for the US Air Force, in which the pilot's helmet is coupled by a servo-system that enables him to aim and fire his weapons automatically by merely swivelling his head until a camera located in his helmet shows the target.

Meanwhile, back on Earth, the sponsorship of the US Army and Navy had led to General Electric's development of the exo-skeleton, or external skeleton, a 'walking manipulator' that gave its human wearer a 'lifting capacity of three-quarters of a ton' and could be used for heavy labour and underwater work. Once the operator stepped inside his hydraulically powered skeleton, a weight of 1,500 pounds would feel no heavier than 60 pounds and he could raise it six feet in as many seconds. When the man moved inside the skeleton, he looked like some kind of space-age monster.

By 1967, according to the 3 June issue of *Nature* magazine, an American Air Force scientist had taught people, himself included, to 'think' simple messages into a computer, using short and long bursts of alpha activity in a form of Morse code. When the computer reprinted what had been 'thought' into it, the first step had been taken in the 'thought control' of man-machine manipulators and advanced prosthetics. At approximately the same time, the scientists of many countries were experimenting with the control of myoelectric prosthetics with tiny sensors buried under the skin and capable of relaying EMG. (Electro-Miography) signals to an electronic circuit outside the body.

In the Neurological Prostheses Unit of Britain's Medical Research Council, Professor G.S. Brindley was attempting to 'implant electrode arrays in the brain which, when stimulated, might enable the patient to perceive sensations similar to those caused when lightwaves fall on the eye' – in other words, to cure blindness. Also, by the mid-1960s corneal transplants were commonplace, as was the deep-freezing of blood to preserve it for years, and the preservation and grafting of human skin. At approximately the same time work was racing ahead on the artificial larynx, lung, kidney, and heart, alongside the rapid development of miniaturized pacemakers and other sensors that could be implanted in the stomach, chest, or other areas under the skin. The discovery, in 1960, of 'acquired immunological tolerance' had already opened up the prospects for organ transplantation and now, thirty years on, the advances in this field are startling, if not always publicized.

Unconsciously indicating that the market for spare parts was about to expand, surgeons began to talk openly about the need to view persons suffering irreversible brain damage as an invaluable source of human organs. As Fishlock points out in *Man Modified*: 'Once the technical problems of transplantation are resolved, as is already the case with the kidney, the case purely on grounds of logic for regarding the unconscious cerebral cripple as a source of spare parts to be "cannibalized" may become overwhelming.' Fishlock also reminds us that many transplant surgeons had already expressed their belief that the most 'suitable and prolific' source of spare parts could come, ironically, from the most common 'mismatch' between man and machine – the young victims of automobile accidents, particularly those who die from brain damage. To this end, one London surgeon had even suggested having 'collection points' along motorways to 'harvest this valuable crop of bio-mechanisms'.

In a CIBA. Symposium on 'Ethics in Medical

Progress' held in London in 1966, Dr Joseph Murray pointed out that the physiological requirements of space travel may have to be met with 'the grafting of accessory organs' such as extra adrenal glands and lungs. His view was supported by Dr Nathan S. Kline and Dr Manfred Clynes, both of the Rockland State Hospital in Orangeburg, New York, who insisted that the true conquest of space will only come when we 'equip man with exogenous components that would extend the self-regulating functions of the body far enough to adapt to a fresh environment'. In other words, a 'Cyborg'.

The astonishing surgical and bio-engineering advances mentioned above were all made before 1967. Since then, the transplanting of hearts, kidneys and other organs has become commonplace, the artificial womb has been created, natural skin can be grown in laboratories, plastic surgery has become an art form, sperm banks are big business, genetic engineering and cloning have created a vast new industry, and computer intelligence has reached the point where there is genuine fear that it will soon start 'reproducing' itself and eventually break away from human control. Indeed, according to Ray Hammond in *The Modern Frankenstein: Fiction Becomes Fact* (1986) the interaction of man and machine is now so advanced that 'for practical purposes the "cyborg" is already here'.

If we assume that what we already know is only the tip of the iceberg, and that the bulk of the iceberg is hidden from view, we must accept that what is hidden from us by government and military scientists may be even more bizarre, and possibly more terrifying, than what has already been described. We should also bear in mind that the US Navy, Air Force, Army and government agencies such as NASA – all with top-secret research establishments in the White Sands Proving Ground and similar areas – have a particular need for advanced man-machine manipulators or cyborgs. Finally, we should note that if the necessary experiments are remotely like those performed openly, and described above, the moral, ethical, legal and theological ramifications would be enough to ensure that most of the work was performed in strict secrecy and, as with the UFOs, protected behind a smokescreen of official disinformation and ridicule.

Given these considerations, it is within the bounds of possibility that the small 'claw men' and creatures seemingly without eyes or mouths, as described by so many UFO contactees, could be cyborgs: half man, half machine – the result of decades of secret prosthetic experiments even more advanced that those mentioned above.

Theoretically, the lungs of such creatures would be partially collapsed and the blood in them artificially cooled. The cyborgs' respiration and other bodily functions would then be controlled cybernetically with artificial lungs and sensors which maintain constant temperature, metabolism and pressure, irrespective of external environmental fluctuations – thus, even if not protected by an antigravity (or gravitic) propulsion system, they would not be affected by the extraordinary accelerations and direction changes of their craft. The cyborgs would have no independent will, but could be remote-controlled, both physically and mentally, even across great distances, by computer-linked brain implants. Since this operation would render the mouth and nose superfluous, these would be sealed (possibly with the 'metallic' or 'wrinkled grey skin' coverings described by so many contactees) and completely non-functioning.

To the mesmerized or terrified abductee, such unfortunate creatures would certainly look like 'aliens' or extraterrestrials.

On the understanding that research into the physical and mental mutation of human beings commenced as far back as the early 1960s and continues to this day behind closed doors, we can assume that the 'secret' work is even more advanced than the 'known' technology, which already includes genetic engineering and the cloning of life. If this is the case, it is possible that the UFOs and their 'alien' occupants – a mixture of normal humans and cyborgs – are members of a secret, Earth-bound society determined to pursue its research regardless of moral, ethical and religious considerations.

It is therefore possible that those abducted by UFOs are taken away for a variety of reasons: to undergo brain implantation and be returned to the real world as remote-controlled slaves who appear perfectly normal to those who know them; to be used as living subjects for even more advanced surgical, psychological and genetic experiments of the kind that would be morally unacceptable in normal society; or to be killed and used as a source of spare bodily parts for the cyborgs required by that society to work on the sea bed or in outer space.

This is not as far fetched as it may seem. Indeed, as shown in *The Human Body Shop: The Engineering and*

Marketing of Life (1993) by Andrew Kimbrell, a host of startling new discoveries, including the cloning of life forms and fetal tissue transplants, has led to what amounts to 'a new industrial age – a marketing revolution based on the manipulation and marketing of life'. This includes 'the sale and manipulation of blood, organs, and fetal parts'; the marketing of 'human reproductive materials – semen, eggs, embryos, and children'; and, finally, the 'new biotechnology business of selling and engineering human biochemicals, genes and cells'.

As the human body is rapidly becoming no more than a 'commodity' in a 'free market', it is not beyond the bounds of possibility that a secret, totalitarian society, based on a highly advanced technology and the control of mind and body, could be abducting people to be used as more fodder for their on-going experimentation and ever broadening mind control.

In short, the 'aliens' who abduct humans in their UFOs may not be alien or extraterrestrial. Like the UFOs themselves, they could come from right here on Earth.

Chapter 10

UFO Technology

Discussing the cinetheodolite photos taken at the White Sands Proving Ground in April and May of 1950, Captain Ruppelt notes: 'By putting a correction factor in the data gathered by the two cameras, they were able to calculate that the object was higher than 40,000 feet, traveling over 2,000 mph, and it was over 300 feet in diameter.' Ruppelt makes it clear that these figures were only estimates, based on the possibly erroneous correction factor. However, what they *did* prove is that the object had been solid and moving very fast through the air.

Those and other sighting estimates serve to remind us that many of the supposedly 'remarkable' speeds assessed from cinetheodolite data (and all too often taken as gospel by proponents of the extraterrestrial hypothesis) are inaccurate. In fact, many trained observers believe that the UFOs have lower, therefore more technologically feasible, speeds than they are widely credited with, though they are still craft of extraordinary capability.

In order to assess whether or not such craft could have been built right here on Earth, we first have to assess exactly what they are in relationship to the present technology. We know that by and large they are disk-shaped, but depending on the angle of view they can appear to be round, oval-shaped, spherical, or like a cylinder viewed from one end. Kenneth Arnold's momentous description of the horizontal flight of the UFOs being like 'a saucer would if you skipped it across the water' remains the most apt, since the UFO, with its central, non-revolving dome, certainly resembles either one plate placed upside down (dome on top) or two plates placed one upon the other, the top plate resting upside-down on the lower one (dome top and bottom). Analysis of the many sightings suggests that the standard UFO (there are exceptions) has a diameter about ten times its thickness. While attempts to judge the size of any object in high-speed flight are bound to be problematical, it is now widely accepted that the bonafide 'unidentifieds' range from diameters of two feet (which would be something like the German remote-controlled *Feuerball*) to 300 feet (for which the only remote comparison with present aircraft is the Lockheed C-5A Galaxy heavy-logistics transport aircraft: wingspan nearly 223 feet; length nearly 248 feet.)

It is assumed that UFOs between one and three feet in diameter are remote-controlled sensing devices. They could in fact be highly complex Cybernetic Anthropomorphous Machine Systems (CAMS), either flying with their long axis vertical or flying in the direction of their axis. Controlled by Remote Manipulator Systems (RMS), not much different from the ones widely known, they would most likely be used for reconnaissance and basic manual tasks, such as the gathering of soil or plant samples. The larger (but still relatively small) UFOs of between six to fifteen feet in diameter are, depending on size, either remote-controlled or single-pilot craft, used for more complex reconnaissance and collection purposes. The 'standard' model, about twenty-five to thirty-five feet in diameter, would be more like a jet fighter, with defensive or attack capabilities. This model revolves around its axis, and is piloted either by human pilots, by the kind of cyborgs described in the previous chapter, or by a combination of both.

The large UFO, from about 100 feet to 300 feet in diameter and two or three stories tall inside, would be the equivalent of the above mentioned Lockheed C-5A Galaxy heavy-logistics transport aircraft, though even more spacious, with many crew members, and probably used as a transport and refuelling craft.

Whether or not such a craft as a 'command' or 'mother' ship actually exists is a matter of pure speculation; but those reported have been as much as a mile in diameter and were seen to discharge and receive the smaller UFOs, often in large numbers. If they exist, they could be self-generating airborne colonies, capable of drifting in outer space or of hibernating on the sea bed, manned by a large crew of humans and cyborgs, the heavy labour performed by 'programd' slaves or CAMS. If this were the case, they would contain accommodations, workshops, laboratories, medical quarters, cryonics preservation units, various hangars, and a selection of the other, smaller disks.

The exterior surface of the UFOs is invariably described as smooth and seamless. When doors open, they usually do so in the side, sometimes falling down like ramps, or in the base, like trapdoors; but in the former instance, once the door closes again, no joins or dividing lines can be seen. It is not known what the composition of the UFO's structure is, but it is usually described as metallic, aluminium, chrome, silvery, shiny, whitish-grey, or white. The surface, no matter the colour, sometimes has a soft glowing or luminous aura around it, while in other cases the 'aura' is blinding white, dazzling, intensely luminous, or like burning magnesium. Multicolored lights are often described, sometimes flashing simultaneously, sometimes sequentially, but these appear to be separate lights, emitting from specific parts of the craft. They are not produced by the composition of its surface material.

The colours suggest an exterior surface made from some kind of metal. For instance, the bright aluminum surfaces of an airliner, when viewed under an overcast sky or through atmospheric haze, will take on a dull grey, or even dark grey, appearance.

Nuclear physicist James M. McCampbell, whose speciality is planning and managing large-scale projects involving advanced technologies, is the author of *Ufology* (1976), the only book devoted solely to the physical nature of UFOs. In it he says: 'Some hints as to the actual metal of UFOs might be inferred from the properties required by their flight characteristics and mode of propulsion. These include lightness, strength and resistance to heat. McCampbell believes that the metal would have to be composed of elements that are already known, even if 'technological superiority may be evidenced by unusual purity or new mixtures and crystal structures'. He proposes magnesium and titanium.

This is interesting in that one of the most extraordinary metals now in existence is Nitinol, described by *Science Now* as 'the magic metal' because, though a simple, light alloy of nickel and titanium, it possesses properties that have perplexed the most knowledgeable minds in metallurgy for nearly thirty years. Nitinol is 'a metal with a memory' that can be made to remember any shape it is bent into and will always return to it after being heated. Nitinol also has the ability to 'learn' and if heated and crumpled enough times will not only remember its original shape but gradually 'learn' to remember its crumpled form as well. The aerospace industry has been using this 'magic metal' for years. In the words of *Science Now* (No.2): 'The speed and reliability of Nitinol's shape-changing response, the metal's lightness and its total resistance to metal fatigue make it an invaluable material for use in spacecraft.'

Dr James Harder, in his article 'Looking at the Evidence', published in *Worlds Beyond* (1978), claims that a piece of metal shot off a UFO over Washington in 1962 was found to be 'magnesium orthosilicate, with some tiny round occlusions'; another fragment recovered in Sweden was 'a chunk of tungsten carbide, one of the hardest metals known, next to the diamond'; and some fragments found in Brazil were of 'ultrapure' magnesium. Harder also points out that abductees taken aboard UFOs invariably describe the floor as being 'very hard and cold' and the materials they encounter 'metallic or hard plastic'. Other than that, it is certainly worth recalling that the 'tiny round occlusions' found in the magnesium orthosicilate suggest some form of porous metal, or *Luftschwamm*, which was, as we now know, a mixture of magnesium and aluminium.

The use of a porous metal with high heat resistance and a composition that charges the air around it could account for UFO speed and lack of noise. James M.

McCampbell believes that the presence of a UFO in flight must be 'telegraphed' ahead to the gas molecules in the air; a force exerted by it then moves the molecules out of the way, and, after passage of the UFO, the air closes in behind it. By such means 'the UFO could slip through the atmosphere with little expenditure of energy and no shock wave would be created on its leading edge'. It is McCampbell's belief that the plasma on the surface of the UFO, or the radiant energy that stimulates it, is responsible for this. He points out that as early as 1968, the Northrop Corporation was reportedly experimenting with electromagnetic fields to 'modify the air stream around supersonic aircraft to prevent shock waves'. It is also reported that by 1976 the North American Rockwell Company, under US Air Force sponsorship, had developed a radar-absorbing material composed of 'advanced structural plastics' and possessing 'special electrical properties'. The material had been created not only to make aircraft lighter, but to make them 'invisible' to enemy radar.

A contemporary example of this attribute can be found in the F-117a Nighthawk, or Stealth night-fighter, which has often been mistaken for a UFO because of its appearance and capabilities. First test-flown on 18 June 1981, but kept secret from the public until 1989, the Stealth is a Delta-wing aircraft with a pyramidal structure that gives it a flying saucer appearance when viewed from most angles. With a wingspan of 43 feet 4 inches and a length of 65 feet 11 inches, the F-117a Nighthawk is powered by two General Electric turbofans, armed with two laser-guided smart-bombs, has a low radar profile in flight and, because of its exceptional streamlining, makes little noise. Painted stark black with a special anti-radar paint, the F-117a Stealth is as near to an 'invisible' supersonic aircraft as it is possible to imagine within the known technology. However, as the authorities have finally let it be shown to the public, after years of denials regarding its very existence, it has almost certainly been superseded.

Its successor is possibly the Aurora - an officially non-existent supersonic aircraft often seen flying over Scotland and its off-shore waters. Invariably described as big, black and triangular, with no wing surfaces or tail surfaces, two thirds the size of the Stealth night-fighter (which would make it about ninety feet long), the Aurora is possibly radar invisible (at least its presence in the skies has been denied by all radar operatives under its flight path) and witnesses have reported that it makes no noise when in flight.

This mysterious, supersonic, silent aircraft, recorded as flying as fast as 6 Mach, is most frequently sighted in the vicinity of RAF Machrihanish, located on the tip of the Mull of Kintyre. Jointly owned by the United States, RAF Machrihanish is one of the most secret NATO air bases in Europe.

The Pentagon, which for years denied the existence of the F-117a Nighthawk, is now insisting that the Aurora does not exist.

The UFO's ability to 'just disappear' or 'blink out like a light bulb' is often attributed to its extraordinary speed (which is certainly one cause, as we shall see), but it may also be related to its oddly 'glowing' colours. Another form of apparent 'invisibility' is that many UFOs, while not seen by those who have accidentally photographed them, have shown up mysteriously on developed film.

With regard to this apparent 'invisibility', official analysis of the photographs taken of the Lubbock lights during the famous sighting of August 1951 revealed that what the photographer had picked up was an exceptionally bright light source which had a colour at the most distant red end of the spectrum. This suggests that it was infrared - or something similar to infrared - which in turn means that the object would be dim to the human eye but bright on the photograph.

Let us take this hypothesis further by going beyond the known spectrum. If the UFO could produce such light, and do so at will, it would in effect be capable of materializing and disappearing in the wink of an eye, even when *not* moving fast. As previously noted, the UFOs are usually described as being surrounded by glowing colours: blue, green, yellow, orange, red. Assuming that they are constructed with a metal composed of already known elements - possibly of unusual purity and radical mixtures - we can also assume that what we are *not* dealing with is a magical metal that can actually transmit light.

As electrical discharges of unusual strength will sometimes lead to a soft, white glow, a corona, near high-voltage transmission lines, it can be assumed that they have either some sort of negative potential that causes electrons to leak into the atmosphere surrounding it, an alternating potential that agitates gas atoms in the surrounding atmosphere to their ionization potential, or even an alternating current within the UFO's own shell which draws radiant energy from the surrounding atmosphere.

This would account for a white glow.

However, let us assume that the UFO's luminosity is not caused by an unknown composition, but by the natural air closely surrounding it. If atoms are sufficiently agitated by the absorption of electromagnetic radiation, a few of their electrons will be elevated out of their normal orbits, or possibly removed from the atom completely; then, as more electrons fall back in these empty spaces, a certain amount of energy will be released and radiated away as photons. Within the visible region, a stream of such photons having the same wavelength and frequency will be seen by the human eye as an unusual, glowing colour, ranging all the way from violet to red. This is a form of electromagnetic radiation - and unusual traces of electromagnetic radiation have often been found upon examination of reported landing sites.

As the magnetic field in interstellar space is extraordinarily weak, we can assume that the UFO, which certainly leave Earth's atmosphere on occasion, would not be using electromagnetic propulsion and that the traces of electromagnetism found after so many sightings are related solely to the craft's composition. Assuming, therefore, that the UFO is made of some exceptionally pure composition of metals - say, aluminium, magnesium, titanium or strontium - and that the material is electronically charged, the UFO would often appear to be white or silvery up close, a dull or dark grey when viewed through atmospheric haze, and just as often be surrounded by a glowing halo of various colours. If such a craft also had the capability of creating a colour source beyond the known spectrum and turning it on and off at will - it could be dim, or even invisible, to the human eye, show up on normal film, and yet materialize in our visible spectrum as required.

This may have been the case with the UFO sighted over Lubbock in August 1951 - as well as in many similar sightings. It may also explain the relative 'invisibility' and 'silence' of the Aurora, presently being sighted by so many, even as the Pentagon insists that it does not exist.

Though the 'glowing' colours indicate an unusual composition of otherwise known materials, they could also be indicative of the UFO's mysterious propulsion system. UFOs have unusual and remarkable flight characteristics, including the ability to hang nearly motionless in the sky, settle gently on the ground, rise vertically, and make sharp, right-angled turns. Such manoeuvring capabilities, combined with the absence of air blasts, smoke and sonic booms, indicates that they are certainly not propelled by orthodox engines or rockets.

In a declassified, formerly secret Department of the Army Intelligence Memorandum, dated 21 January 1948, information was requested on various possible propulsion systems for 'oval, disk, or saucer-shaped aircraft'. Among the systems to be investigated were 'jet propulsion engines including turbo jets, rockets, ram-jets, pulse jets, or a combination of all four'. Nuclear propulsion (atomic energy) was also to be investigated on the grounds that 'atomic energy engines would probably be unlike any familiar type of engine, although atomic energy might be employed in combination with any of the above types'. How the UFOs are propelled remains a mystery, but it is known that since that Memorandum was written and distributed, many experiments have taken place in advanced ion propulsion, electromagnetic and microwave propulsion, in certain cases nuclear fusion pulse rockets, and even antigravity, or gravitic, propulsion.

Ionization and electromagnetic discharges could be another cause of the plasma-like glowing that so fascinates UFO witnesses; the use of an anti-gravity shield, or gravitic propulsion, could account for the UFO's lack of turbulence and sonic booms.

McCampbell reminds us that according to technical analysis, the lift-off of the average UFO would require as much energy as the detonation of an atomic bomb, would cause the body of the UFO to heat up to about 85,000°C, and would naturally lead to intense deposits of radioactivity (often found on or near UFO landing sites). However, with an antigravity shield reducing the mass of the UFO to almost zero, it would require only a modest force to reach exceptionally high accelerations.

The UFO does not defeat gravity entirely. If it did so, it would continue to float upward into the atmosphere, instead of hanging motionless in the sky. Nevertheless, it must *almost* defeat gravity and could therefore be using some form of gravitic protection, or propulsion.

How would this work?

Gravity is the force that draws all bodies in Earth's sphere toward the centre of the planet. Where gravity exists, so does the inertial force, which is 'proportional and directionally opposite to the accelerating force'. According to Einstein's principal of equivalence, it is not possible to distinguish between the two: gravitational mass and inertial mass are, to all intents and purposes, identical. This being the case, if we manage to nullify the effect of gravity on a certain mass, we will also nullify the inertial mass that would normally act against it. So if we activate a so-called gravity 'shield' around our UFO, thus reducing its mass respecting gravity and the inertial force to almost zero, we will produce what McCampbell has termed 'neutral buoyancy' in the atmosphere.

Very modest forces exerted upon this virtually massless UFO would produce extremely high accelerations. In fact, a vehicle so shielded could accelerate out of sight faster than the human eye can see' Also, by applying 'a small force in the direction of flight', the gravity-shielded vehicle could be brought to an abrupt halt; while 'applying the force traversely would produce astonishing, sharp, nearly right-angle turns'.

As the inertial mass of such a craft would decrease the higher it goes, we can assume that such a mass would be reduced to nearly zero by the time it reached the limits of Earth's atmosphere. This could be the explanation for the UFO's widely reported 'two-stage' take-off: a slow rise to a hundred feet or so, then a sudden acceleration and disappearance. Finally, since the UFO's performance is related directly to Earth's gravity, and as the pull of gravity varies slightly from place to place, the UFO in horizontal flight would often appear to rise and fall slightly: the increase and decrease of gravitational pull would effect its inertial mass and makes it 'wobble' or bob up and down. This would also explain why the UFO appears to be able to follow the profile of the terrain below it automatically.

An antigravity shield would certainly account for the

UFO crews' apparent ability to withstand the extraordinary speed and direction changes of the machines. As the inertial mass is also nullified, the gravity-force would apply simultaneously to the crew *and* the UFO; as it provides a cushion of air around the saucer, it also prevents the UFO from heating up.

Antigravity, or gravitic propulsion, is not as revolutionary as it sounds. As far back as 1965, when UFO sightings over secret military bases were at their peak, there were at least forty-six unclassified G-projects being undertaken in the US alone - by the Air Force, the Navy, the Army, NASA, the Atomic Energy Commission, and the National Science Foundation. Given that these were only the unclassified projects, considerably more advanced projects could have been completed in any one of the top security research establishments, including those scattered throughout the White Sands Proving Ground.

Nuclear physicist Stanton T. Friedman has made the point that since you do not need right-angle turns and hovering capabilities when you are in interstellar space, there may be different kinds of, or a combination of, UFO propulsion systems. A gravitic propulsion system would undoubtedly make sense for flight within the pull of Earth's gravity; but for interstellar flight (assuming the UFOs make such flights), staged fission or fusion-propulsion systems would do the job. As someone who worked on both systems for General Electric and others, Friedman is able to point out that by 1978 the most powerful nuclear reactor to be tested in the Free World was the Phoebus 2-B nuclear-reactor rocket-propulsion system built by the Los Alamos

Scientific Laboratory. That system, which operated at a power level of forty-four hundred million watts - twice the output of the Grand Coulee Dam - was under six feet in diameter.

According to Friedman, fusion is even more exciting. 'If you use the fusion process properly, you can kick particles out of the back end of a rocket that have *ten million* times as much energy per particle as they can get in a chemical rocket.' With relevance to the enormous power of fusion being packed into the relatively small confines of a UFO, Friedman reminds us that a quasar represents the energy of a galaxy in something the size of a single star; and that when we moved from the atomic to the nuclear world, we 'went down in size and way up in energy per particle'. Thus, when we go down from the nuclear world to the subnuclear world (which we are now doing), we will 'go down in size again and up in energy again'. In other words, fusion will present us with a form of enormous power that can be contained in minute housing.

'Fusion is something we know about,' Friedman says. 'H-bombs are fusion devices; the Sun is a fusion factory... We know how to do it.'

Friedman also suggests in his article 'Flying Saucers Are Real' (1978) that a propulsion system based on the ionization of the air could solve all the problems of high-speed flight. 'About ten years ago, an electromagnetic submarine was built in California. I believe you could build an analogous airborne system where you create an electrical conducting fluid, similar to the seawater around the submarine, by ionizing the air.' With ionized air, as opposed to 'neutral' air, it would be possible to interact with the electrically conducting fluid, or the electric and magnetic fields, thereby reducing heating and drag, increasing lift, and eliminating sonic boom.

According to Friedman, the UFO's frequent changes in colour, extraordinary flight characteristics, and absence of noise indicate the presence of ionized air and high magnetic fields. While he leans toward the extraterrestrial hypothesis, he does believe that 'there are a number of professional people working at a secret project, using the data input from the Aerospace Defence Command and others, trying their darnest to build a flying saucer'.

The 'spinning' of the UFO could be an integral part of its propulsion system. The only time a UFO does *not* spin is when it is resting on the ground. In most reports the UFO starts spinning as it lifts off the ground, with the rotations becoming faster as it ascends. In some cases, the whole UFO spins; in others, the outer rings spin around a fixed cockpit or central dome. According to McCampbell: 'It is easy to imagine that rotation of the entire vehicle, or a major component, would be used to achieve stability in the air; that is, to maintain the axis of rotation in a constant direction due to the angular momentum.' Clearly, since the passengers, or crew, could not be subjected to the rotation of the outer surface of the vehicle, the interior portions of the UFO would be uncoupled from the exterior and we can thus think of the craft as operating like a gigantic gyroscope.

Regarding this, Renato Vesco tells us that in 1945, along with reports of 'constant-velocity airfoils, one with an elegant two-pointed meniscus shape and the other with a curious if not monstrous-looking mushroom shape', there were leaks about the construction of an experimental 'independent, gyroscopically stabilized cabin' that was 'ringed with a rotating organ of large dimensions, as in the Italian-German projectiles and the Fireballs, involving the need for autonomous and automatic stabilization'. At that time, the US National Physical Laboratory's division of applied physics was investigating the 'direct gyroscopic stabilization' research material of the captured Kreiselgeräte GmbH, located in Berlin Britz. That company (now liquidated) was so-called because it had designed and constructed the Kreiselgeräte: a mechanism that could reduce the oscillations of a violently shaking body to under one-tenth of a degree. Such a device, if applied to a fixed central cupola, or dome, placed within a rotating circular wing, or disk, would, at least in theory, have supported the often reported view that 'seen from below, the UFO seemed to spin rapidly on its own axis, except for the central part, which appeared to be stationary'.

Reports indicate the presence of strong gusts of hot or cold air as the UFO descends, ascends, sweeps past, or passes overhead. The currents are often strong enough to bowl people over, bend trees, make grass and plants flutter wildly, and suck snow, water, sand, and loose materials up into the air. On odd occasions, trucks and cars have almost been lifted off the road by a UFO passing over overhead. According to McCampbell, the UFO can not only lift vehicles off the road, but 'seems to impart a torque, or turning force to them, as confirmed by the spinning and swirling of other objects'. This phenomenon shows that the unknown force 'prevails within a cylindrical zone having the same diameter as the UFO and extending from it to the ground'. What is most puzzling about this force is that instead of acting downward, as would be the case with jet exhausts, it acts upward, thus causing rotation to the objects affected. The force is also selective in what it affects, favouring electrical conductivity as a 'responsive item'. Thus, stone or dry sticks are not so affected (unless wet); the human or animal body, metals, and water are. This suggests that the UFO may indeed be defeating gravity in some manner and, if so, is sharing this achievement with the 'responsive items' directly below it, which in turns suggests 'gravity damping by electromagnetic radiation'.

More support for the presence of electromagnetic radiation comes from the charred grass and plants often found where UFOs have landed. As the roots of grass so affected are charred, but the blades are not damaged, it is possible that we are dealing with induction heating from a 'powerful, alternating magnetic field'. This offers the possibility of microwave propulsion. McCampbell points out that electromagnetic energy in the range of about 300 to 3000 MHz or higher seems to be responsible for stimulating coloured halos around the UFOs; producing a dazzling, white plasma on the vehicle's surface; turning off automobile headlights and stopping internal combustion engines; precipitating wild gyrations of compasses and magnetic speedometers; interfering with radio and television reception; disrupting transmission of electrical power; charring or calcining grass roots, insects and wooden objects; heating bituminous highways to the point of flame-up; heating the human body internally and causing people to feel electrical shocks; and inducing temporary paralysis in witnesses. Medical experiments have also shown that when pulsed at a low audio frequency, electromagnetic energy is capable of stimulating a humming or buzzing sound in the human ear - one of the few sounds attributable to UFOs.

In summary, the microwave energy radiating from UFOs may be an integral part of a propulsion system that is capable of greatly diminishing gravitational and inertial forces, furnishes the required thrust for acceleration, and moves air out of the flight path to minimize drag, shock waves and sonic boom. While such a system may be well in advance of the *known* technology, McCampbell is of the opinion: 'It does not appear to be so far distant that a well-organized and adequately funded research program could not make it available to humanity.'

Stories of contactees being mesmerized or temporarily paralysed by 'beams of light' or unfamiliar sounds (including the 'humming' or 'buzzing') emanating from UFOs are common. While such stories seem uncomfortably close to science fiction, they could be perfectly true. Lasers can concentrate high energies in narrow beams, have extremely pure colours, and produce well-ordered, regular light-waves - just like the beams of light emanating from UFOs. Also, it is now well established that under certain conditions light and sound can have extraordinary mental *and* physical effects on normal, healthy people.

For instance, a light flickering somewhere in the alpha-rhythm range, between eight and twelve cycles per second, can cause extremely violent reactions in the person exposed to it, including jerking limbs, faintness, lightness in the head, or unconsciousness. It is therefore possible that the mysterious beams of light described by so many contactees are strobe lights or laser beams which flicker on and off at the particular rate which affects the brain's basic rhythmic patterns and place the subject into a hypnotic trance. As for the strange humming, buzzing or 'vibrating' sounds which also appear to affect the contactees, laboratory tests have revealed that infrasounds, which are just below the limit of human hearing (thus making the listener imagine that he is *feeling* the sound, like a 'vibration') can affect humans in the same way as flickering lights: either hypnotizing them, stunning them, rendering them unconscious, or paralysing them while leaving them fully conscious.

Certain low frequency sounds can lead not only to a change in the brain's rhythmic patterns, but to actual physical changes, such as the breaking of glass, the deadening of ignition systems (also caused by electromagnetic energy, as explained above), and even the killing of human beings or animals, when their innards are crushed by pure vibration. Given that this is so, it seems perfectly feasible that the UFO's flickering beams of light, or laser beams, when combined with infrasounds, could have led to many cases of contactee hypnosis.

According to McCampbell, a weapon similar to the immobilizing lights used by the UFOs may have been developed during the 1960s by the Federal Aviation Agency under the direction of Dr H.L. Reighard. The purpose of this 'high-frequency radiation' weapon was to counter aeroplane hijacking, but the device was never used because of the dangers it might present if used inside an aircraft. In the same field, John Cover, a scientist in Newport Beach, California, developed the 'taser', which is a ray gun that passes an alternating current of 30/40 milli-amps through the body, temporarily freezing the skeletal muscles with no lasting adverse affects.

While much of the laser experimentation is top-secret, it is known that as far back as the 1950s the US Air Force was watching and photographing the secret Soviet laboratory at Semipalatinsk, where the Russians were known to be developing an extremely powerful 'beam weapon' capable of destroying intercontinental missiles at almost the speed of light. It was suspected that the beam comprised atomic or sub-atomic particles - electrons, protons or ions - equivalent to billions of volts of electricity and accelerated toward the target at just under 180,000 miles per second. John Allen, senior US government scientist, stated that a weapon of this type appeared to be a distinct possibility; and both George J. Keegan, head of USAF intelligence, and Dr Willard Bennett, member of the US team that was obliged to abandon beam weapon work in 1972, believed that the Russians were well ahead of the Americans in this field.

So what, precisely, is a laser?

The acronym 'laser' is short for 'Light Amplification by Stimulated Emission of Radiation'. The laser 'stimulates' radiation when it 'pumps' energy into some material in a way that causes large numbers of its electrons to become precariously balanced at a high energy level, then drop back to their normal or 'ground' state. As each electron drops back, it gives up its excess energy by throwing out a 'packet' of radiation - a photon. The resultant energy gap between the upper, or 'balanced', and the ground, or 'normal', energy states, gives a particular frequency to the photon radiation emitted. When this particular form of radiation then falls on an energised atom, it 'stimulates' it into emitting its own photon, with each photon then stimulating more energised atoms in a perpetual chain reaction. The visual result is a beam of light formed when the 'surge' of light built up in the laser is reflected back and forth between precisely spaced mirrors. If one of the mirrors is partly transparent, an intense output beam can escape to form a visible, often dazzling laser beam.

But could secret laser research account for the affects of the 'beams of light' described by so many UFO contactees?

It is common knowledge in the West that unclassified laser technology has reached a state of advancement that once was only imagined by science fiction writers. In fact, laser technology has been on the agenda for almost four decades, with the first lasers demonstrated in 1960. Though these early demonstrations made the concept of the 'death ray' respectable, many scientists of the time refused to believe in their potential either for death-dealing or for other equally devastating applications. The laser arms race, however, accelerated at remarkable speed, producing ever more varied and powerful beams - electrical discharges, lightning flashes, neutron flux from a nuclear reactor - culminating in the most powerful of all laser weapons: carbon dioxide lasers with outputs in the megawatt range. These emit invisible infrared radiation, though the beam is highly visible as a row of sparks like tiny lightning bolts. Their capabilities are still a matter of dispute, but it is known that as far back as 1980 such laser beams could destroy a small anti-tank missile at a range of one kilometre and that other laser beams were being fired at aircraft or in orbit during top-secret tests. According to published reports those first trials produced no spectacular results, but an official British study predicted that by 1995 anti-aircraft, anti-satellite and possibly even hand-held lasers would be in 'routine' use as weapons and for other, more productive uses, such as bloodless surgery.

At the time of writing (1994), serious research is being conducted regarding the possibilities of the gamma-ray laser, or graser. According to reports, while 'known' (ie., non-secret) technology presently lacks the controlled power required to pump a gamma-ray laser, such a weapon, whether created secretly or in the future, would be: 'a true death ray, horrifyingly powerful'.

While we cannot know what is going on behind the closed doors of our top-secret research facilities, we do know that the US Space Command, for example, has for years been seriously involved in a 'Star Wars' program that views laser-equipped satellites as a viable, and vitally necessary, weapon of the future. Despite the initial doubts of certain scientists, over the past two decades the major powers, notably Great Britain, Russia (formerly the Soviet Union) and the United States, have been pursuing this technology. As long as arms negotiators cannot agree to ban anti-satellite and laser weapons, this race will continue, with startling advances being made - for good and for ill.

Certainly, at the time of writing, laser beams are being

developed not only as future weapons of war, but also for use in surgery, chemistry, biology, engineering, and nuclear fusion control. They are also being researched as potential mesmerising or immobilizing devices. It seems, then, that the laser-beam weapons reportedly used by UFOs as paralysing or more destructive weapons are not beyond the reach of the present technology. On the assumption, therefore, that the classified, or unknown, technological achievements must always be far ahead of known technology, the capabilities and characteristics of the UFOs do not place them beyond the possibility of Earthly origin.

Chapter 11

Speculations on Terrestrial UFO Bases

UFOs are often reported to appear from, and depart toward, the sea. Given the relatively limited number of people traveling by sea, it is surprising that so many reports have concerned UFOs diving into or erupting from oceans all around the world, in areas such as the Bermuda Triangle, in the West Atlantic, connecting Bermuda, Puerto Rico and the coast of Florida; the so-called 'Devil's Sea' bounded by the southeast coast of Japan, the northern tip of Luzon, in the Philippines, and Guam; the coastal waters of Argentina, particularly near Plata del Mar; and the Great Lakes of Canada - all of which are also known as areas where many aircraft and ships mysteriously disappear without trace. This has led to much speculation about the possibility of USOs (Unidentified Submarine Objects) hiding on the sea bed, or of undersea laboratories which are visited frequently by UFOs.

Of the regions mentioned above, the Bermuda Triangle is the most notorious. Its reputation as a 'Devil's Triangle' (not to be confused with the 'Devil's Sea' mentioned above) really began on 5 December 1945, with what has since become widely known as the mystery of Flight 19. Months after the end of World War II, five US Navy aircraft vanished without a trace when on a routine training mission out of Fort Lauderdale Naval Air Base. Reportedly the control tower received some very strange, panicky messages from the flight leader just before the five planes disappeared. These included the words: 'We seem to be off course, we cannot see land... we are not sure of our position... everything is wrong, strange... even the sea doesn't look as it should... it looks like we're entering...' According to legend, the voice was then cut off, the planes and their crew vanished without trace, and the mystery was only deepened when, a few hours later, an aircraft participating in the search operation also vanished without trace.

It later became clear that no such words had been received by the control tower, that the air crews were inexperienced and in error about their course, and that the five planes probably crashed, with the crews and debris swept away beyond recovery. Nevertheless, the case of Flight 19 was soon turned into a major mystery and the area gained the reputation for being responsible for hundreds of similar, inexplicable disappearances. Reportedly they were often preceded by terrified radio messages about weird fogs, an equally weird or 'different' sea or sky, pulsating lights, strange cloud formations, unaccountable loss of power in the ship or aircraft, and the aberrant behaviour of radar and other electrical equipment.

The 7th District Coast Guard has always maintained that the high degree of ship and aircraft disappearances in the Bermuda Triangle are due to three major factors: it is one of the busiest air and sea routes in the world;, the air and sea traffic includes thousands of private pilots and boat owners, many of whom are dangerously inexperienced; and the region is prone to sudden, dramatic changes in weather. The fact that many of the ships and aircraft disappear 'without a trace' is due to the Gulf Stream, which moves so fast that it can carry a disabled ship miles off course and disperse wreckage over a vast area in a very short time.

Nevertheless, if most of the disappearances can be accounted for, the area still has some unusual characteristics, including unexplained regional magnetic aberrations, shining or pulsating lights in the night sky or beneath the sea (possibly 'white water'), the often reported 'glowing fogs' and 'boiling clouds', and an unusually high incidence of UFO, or USO, sightings. Of particular interest in this respect is the fact that the 'white water' often found in the area is reported to contain unusual chemical properties, including sulphur, strontium and lithium, which have also been found in analyzed pieces of supposed UFO debris.

Charles Berlitz, author of *Without a Trace* (1978), makes an interesting connection between the Bermuda Triangle, or Devil's Triangle, and the Devil's Sea at the other side of the world: 'They both are located approximately between 20° and 35° north latitude, and the 130° east meridian runs approximately through its centre. This same meridian, when it crosses the North Pole, becomes 50° west longitude and runs through the eastern section of the Bermuda Triangle. Berlitz also points out that both areas are crossed by the Earth's agonic lines (lines with no magnetic variation, along which the magnetic needle points directly north *and* south) and suggests from this curiosity that electromagnetic forces may have much to do with the strange phenomena in both areas.

Because the Bermuda Triangle's known magnetic aberrations are combined with a high incidence of UFO or

USO sightings, there are many who believe that the missing ships, aircraft and crew members are somehow being 'abducted' by gigantic USOs that may emerge from, and return to, the sea bed. Dr Manson Valentine, former curator honoris of the Museum of Science in Miami and research associate of the Bishop Museum of Honolulu, believed that the disappearances within the Bermuda Triangle were due to fields of ionization created by the propulsion systems of UFOs, which could possibly change the molecular structure of ships, aircraft or people who strayed accidentally into their path or wake. Whether the cause of the disappearances is due to abduction or dematerialization, the widespread belief is that the Bermuda Triangle and other bodies of water like it hide USOs, or USO bases or laboratories.

Given UFO technology, this just might be possible. If such laboratories exist, they could be manned permanently by cyborgs or 'programd' human beings who would not be affected adversely, either physically or psychologically, by their undersea prison. As for the actual construction of laboratories at such depths, if, as reported, the 'mother' ships are up to a mile in diameter, they could simply settle onto the sea bed and the laboratory would then be constructed, or deposited, there with the aid of specially reinforced, remote-controlled CAMS. The UFO, or USO, would then ascend to the surface again, leaving the reinforced laboratory down there, complete with its crew.

Telechirics, or advanced man-machine manipulators, have already been used extensively on the sea bed. As far back as 1962, the Hughes Aircraft Corporation developed the Mobot, a complex 'swimming socket wrench' designed for Shell to complete the assembly of underwater oil well-heads. The Mobot had television 'eyes' and sonar 'ears' and was capable of wire-brushing surfaces and turning valves on and off at a depth of 1,000 feet. It was superseded by the even more ingenious UNOMO, a 'universal underwater mobot' that had four arms - two for work and two for hanging on to the well-head. That was nearly thirty years ago. Since then, within the *known* technology, manned descent to the deepest undersea point (35,800 feet) has been made, huge saturation diving complexes are already on the sea bed, and 'submarine homes' and 'floating islands' (contained within sea domes) have come onto the agenda. It is therefore possible, given the estimated technology of the UFOs, that they would be capable of at least exploring, or settling upon, the sea bed.

Returning to dry land, the question of UFO bases has led to much wild speculation. It is clear that a great deal of UFO activity has taken place over military establishments, such as those scattered throughout the White Sands Proving Ground, and that many people think it possible that crashed UFO debris, and possibly dead occupants, are being preserved in guarded hangars on various Air Force bases. Nevertheless, if the presence of UFOs is felt most strongly on or near military establishments, the sheer number of sightings indicates that they are being mass produced and maintained in one or more top-secret, isolated locations.

It is the belief of Renato Vesco that one of the most likely locations for a hidden UFO base is the vast, mountainous, wooded region of southwest Canada, on the boundary between British Columbia and Alberta, bordering the state of Washington on the south. One of his reasons for this belief is that A.V. Roe Canada Limited (AVRO-Canada, since closed down) in Malton, Ontario, was responsible for the saucer-shaped Avrocar, or Omega, at a time when Canada was regarded as 'the Promised Land of Aviation' (J.H. Stevens) and 'among the greatest aeronautical powers in the world' (N.S. Currey), including, apart from AVRO, its fellow giants Canadair and De Havilland. Vesco supports his theory with the factually accurate contention that in the sightings that began the modern UFO era - the Kenneth Arnold and Maury Island sightings of 1947 - the UFOs were observed over Washington State and flew away in the direction of the Canadian border. It is also a fact that analysis of the UFO wave that preceded the famous UFO 'invasion' of Washington DC in 1952 revealed that the UFOs had advanced steadily on the capital from the direction of the Canadian border. The same has been true for many of the other American sightings.

The second most likely location for man-made saucers is in a sense the most unlikely, since it is inextricably entwined with 'hollow Earth' theories. Ironically, this idea, which had been around for centuries, became concrete for contemporary UFOlogists through aerial photos released in all innocence by an official US government body.

In early 1970 the Environmental Science Service Administration of the US Department of Commerce released to the press photographs of the North Pole that had been taken by the ESSA-7 satellite on 23 November 1968. One of the photographs showed the North Pole wreathed in its customary cloud cover; the other, showing the same area without cloud cover, revealed an enormous black hole where the Pole should have been

Little did the Environmental Science Service Administration know that their routine weather reconnaissance photographs would lead to one of the most sensational and highly publicized controversies in UFO history.

In the June 1970 issue of *Flying Saucers* magazine, editor Ray Palmer reproduced the ESSA-7 satellite photographs with an accompanying article that claimed that the enormous hole shown on one of the photographs was real.

It had long been the belief of Ray Palmer and a great many other UFOlogists that the Earth is hollow, and that the UFOs emerge from and return to a civilization of superior beings that is hidden in the Earth's unexplored interior. Now, with an 'official' photograph of an enormous black hole at the North Pole, Palmer was able to assert that his subterranean super race probably existed and could most likely be reached through the holes at the North and South Poles.

According to Palmer, the ESSA-7 satellite photographs were proof that an enormous hole existed at least at the North Pole; and in subsequent issues of *Flying Saucers* he strengthened his case by resurrecting another long-standing 'hollow Earth' controversy: the famous expeditions of Rear-Admiral Richard E. Byrd to the North and South Poles.

Rear-Admiral Richard E. Byrd (1888-1957) of the US Navy was a distinguished pioneer aviator and polar explorer who flew over the North Pole on 9 May 1926, and then led numerous exploratory expeditions to the Antarctic, including a flight over the South Pole on 29 November 1929. From 1946 to 1947, he led the full-scale Operation Highjump, which was reported to have discovered and mapped 537,000 square miles (1,390,000 kilometres) of Antarctic territory. Just before his death, in 1957, he directed the 1955-1958 Antarctic expedition as a contribution to the International Geophysical Year.

Byrd's most famous polar expeditions were first drawn into the hollow Earth controversy when numerous articles and books - notably *Worlds Beyond the Poles* (1959) by Amadeo Giannini and *The Hollow Earth* (1969) by Dr Raymond Bernard - claimed that Byrd had actually flown, not *across* the North and South Poles, but *down* into the great hollows that led into the Earth's interior. Ray Palmer, quoting extensively from Giannini's book (as, subsequently, did Dr Bernard), introduced this theory in the December 1959 issue of *Flying Saucers* and thereafter ran a voluminous correspondence on the subject.

According to Giannini, Bernard and Palmer, Rear-Admiral Byrd announced in February 1947, prior to a supposed flight of 1,700 miles (2,750 kilometres) beyond the North Pole: 'I'd like to see that *land beyond the Pole*. That area beyond the Pole is the centre of the *Great Unknown*.' Giannini, Bernard and Palmer also claimed that during Byrd's supposed flight over the North Pole in February 1947, he reported by radio that he saw below him, not ice and snow, but land areas consisting of mountains, forests, green vegetation, lakes and rivers; and, in the undergrowth, a strange animal that resembled a mammoth.

Also, according to Giannini, Bernard and Palmer, in January 1956, after leading another expedition to the Antarctic, Byrd claimed that his expedition had there penetrated to a land extent of 2,300 miles (3,700 kilometres) *beyond* the South Pole. Last but not least, they claimed that just before his death in 1957, Byrd had called the land beyond the Pole 'that enchanted continent in the sky, land of everlasting mystery'. That land, according to other hollow Earth theorists, was actually the legendary Rainbow City, home of a fabulous lost civilization.

For Giannini, Bernard and Palmer, Rear-Admiral Byrd's reported comments merely confirmed what they had suspected all along: that the Earth is shaped 'strangely' at both Poles, something like a doughnut, with a depression that either goes down an enormous distance into the bowels of the Earth or forms a giant hole that runs right through the Earth's core, from one Pole to the other. Since geographically speaking it would be impossible to fly 1,700 miles (2,750 kilometres) beyond the North Pole or 2,300 miles (3,700 kilometres) beyond the South Pole without seeing water, it stands to reason that Rear-Admiral Byrd must have flown *down* into the enormous convex depressions at the Poles, into the 'Great Unknown' of the Earth's interior, and that, had he flown farther, he would have arrived eventually at the secret base of the UFOs belonging to the hidden super race - perhaps the legendary Rainbow City that Byrd had possibly seen reflected in the Antarctic sky.

Thus, when in June 1970 Ray Palmer was able to publish an official satellite photograph that showed what appeared to be an enormous black hole at the North Pole, hollow Earth theorists all over the world were confirmed in their beliefs - and the controversy began.

But is the Earth really hollow? And do the holes in the Poles actually exist? The short answer is, 'No.'

The most extensive research has produced no confirmation for any of the extraordinary statements attributed to Rear-Admiral Byrd - nor for his reported flight over the North Pole in February 1947. (Byrd flew over the *South* Pole on 16 February 1947, during his extensive Operation Highjump.) Even accepting that Byrd *did* make such comments, it is more reasonable to assume that 'the land beyond the Pole' and the 'Great Unknown' were merely descriptive phrases for hitherto unexplored regions, rather than for unknown continents hidden in a hollow Earth - and that the 'enchanted continent in the sky' was no more than a description of a phenomenon common in Antarctic conditions: the mirage-like reflection of the land below.

But what, precisely, did Rear-Admiral Byrd say? In extracts from his journal, published in the *National Geographic* magazine of October 1947, he wrote: 'As I write this, we are circling the South Pole... The Pole is approximately 2,500 feet (760 metres) below us. On the other side of the Pole we are looking into that vast unknown area we have struggled so hard to reach.'

Did Byrd claim to have flown 1,700 (2,750 kilometres) beyond the North Pole in February 1947? No. Describing his flight beyond the *South* Pole on 16 February 1947, he wrote: 'We flew to approximately latitude 88° 30 south, an estimated 100 miles (160 kilometres). Then we made approximately a right-angle turn eastward until we reached the 45th east meridian, when we turned again, this time on the way back to Little America.'

Did Byrd report seeing on his journey, not ice and snow, but land areas consisting of mountains, forests, green vegetation, lakes and rivers; and, in the undergrowth, a strange animal that resembled a mammoth? No. According to his journal: 'Altogether we had surveyed nearly 10,000 square miles (25,900 square kilometres) of "the country beyond the Pole". As was to be expected, although it is somewhat disappointing to report, there was no observable feature of any significance beyond the Pole. There was only the rolling white desert from horizon to horizon.'

The fabled Rainbow City is almost certainly no more than a romanticized rewrite of Rear-Admiral Byrd's original description of his flight back from the South Pole in February 1947, over hitherto unexplored country between the Beardmore and Wade Glaciers. 'It might have been called the Avenue of Frozen Rainbows,' Byrd wrote. 'To east and west towered great mountains. Some were free of ice - coal black and brick red. Others were completely ice-covered. These looked like titanic waterfalls. Where the sun struck their peaks and slopes the light was reflected from them in an indescribable complex of colours. There were blends of blue, purple, and green such as man seldom has seen.'

Thus, given Byrd's actual words as distinct from those attributed to him, we can see that neither lush green lands nor living mammoths were observed beyond the South Pole; that the quoted figure of 1,700 miles (2,750 kilometres) beyond the Pole, even if not invented, was probably extrapolated from an original figure given in square miles; that Rainbow City has no substance other than as Byrd's descriptive 'Avenue of Frozen Rainbows' - a normal atmospheric phenomenon in the Antarctic - and that 'the land beyond the Pole' and the 'Great Unknown' were actually, in Byrd's words, 'the vastest unknown which remains in the world'.

Nonetheless, could the Earth still be hollow? Again, the answer has to be negative. Contrary to the assertions of the hollow Earth theorists, the physical properties and structure of the Earth's interior can now be accurately measured with seismometers and electronic computers. Far from being hollow, the Earth is composed of three principal layers: the crust, the mantle and the core. The crust of granite and basalt rock is up to twenty-five miles (forty kilometres) thick (much thinner beneath the deep oceanic basins). Below the crust is the mantle, extending downwards for about 1,800 miles (2,900 kilometres), solid and composed of magnesium silicates, iron, calcium and aluminium. And below that is the core, believed to be predominantly composed of metallic iron in the molten state. Finally, at a depth of about 3,160 miles (5,090 kilometres), is the boundary of the inner core, which may be solid as the result of the freezing under the extraordinary pressure of about 3,200,000 atmospheres. Certainly, then, the Earth is not hollow.

So what about the enormous hole apparently shown on the ESSA-7 satellite photograph of the Arctic regions? The photograph is actually a mosaic of television images gathered by the onboard vidicon camera system of the satellite over 24 hours, showing the Earth from many angles. The images were processed by a ground computer and reassembled to form a single composite view of the Earth as if observed from a single point directly over the Pole. During the 24 hours, every point in the middle and equatorial latitudes received sunlight for a period, and so appears on the composite picture. But regions near the Pole were experiencing the continuous darkness of the northern winter. Hence an unlit area occupies the centre of the picture.

Similar pictures made during the northern summer show the polar ice-cap. So do pictures made at any time of year using infrared (heat) wavelengths, since the Earth sends out heat radiation during both night and day.

In short, there are no holes at the Poles - and the Earth is not hollow.

Although the Antarctic is an inhospitable continent known as the White Desert and Home of the Blizzard, where snow and ice form 95 per cent of the surface terrain, it does have many ice free areas, such as the Taylor, Wright and Victoria valleys near McMurdo Sound. Other, lesser known ice free areas are hidden at the base of mountains or under the vast ice sheets that reach heights of 11,500 feet. Contrary to popular belief, Antarctica also has rivers, lakes, about 800 species of cold-tolerant land plants, mosses, linchens, liverworts, molds, yeasts, other fungi, and varied flora and fauna. As the *Encyclopaedia Britannica* tells us: 'The continent was ice free during most of its lengthy geological history, and there is no reason to believe it will not become so again in the probably distant future.'

It is not yet known just what lies concealed in buried mountain ranges, such as the recently found Gamburtsev

Mountains. The extraordinarily thick cover (average thickness of 6,500 feet), the extreme difficulty of the working conditions, and the great expense of mounting expeditions into remote areas have 'long left geological knowledge of Antarctica far behind that of other continents'. In other words, while Antarctica is a place that can be inhabited by man, the greater portion of it remains relatively unexplored, therefore unknown.

While the Englishman Edward Bransfield, the American Nathaniel Palmer, and the Russian Fabian Gottlieb von Bellingshausen all claim first sightings of the continent in 1820, the first actual sighting is now believed to have been by the latter. Exploitation of the rich Antarctic and sub-Antarctic seas, particularly along Scotia Ridge, took place from the 1760s to about 1900, with the hunting of seal and whales by US, British, Argentine, Australian, New Zealand, German, and Norwegian vessels. Bellingshausen, commanding the Russian ships *Vostok* and *Mirny*, made the first circumnavigation of the continent in 1819-21; a British expedition led by Branson charted part of the Antarctic peninsula in 1819-20; the French expedition of 1837-40, commanded by Dumont d'Urville, led to the discovery of Adélie Land, which the French claimed; the US Naval expedition led by Charles Wilkes explored a large section of the East Antarctic coast in 1838-42; and during the British expedition of 1839-43, James Clark Ross discovered the Ross Sea and Ross Ice Barrier (now the Ross Ice Shelf), as well as the coast of Victoria Land.

The great era of land exploration began in the period 1901-13 when the Englishmen Robert F. Scott and Ernest

Henry Shackleton led three expeditions into the interior, making important geological, glaciological, and meteorological discoveries that laid the foundations for the present-day scientific program. Even deeper probes into the continent were made by Scott and Shackleton in later years, both launched from base camps on Ross Island, with the latter reaching a point within ninety-seven miles of the South Pole on 9 January 1909. Scott eventually reached the Pole itself on `7 January 1912.

By this time Shackleton had presaged the mechanical age in Antarctica with the use of a motor car at Cape Royds, and Scott had presaged the aerial age by using a captive balloon for aerial reconnaissance. However, the true beginning of the mechanical, particularly the aerial, exploration of the continent began in the period between World Wars 1 and II, when motor transport, aircraft, aerial cameras and radios came into their own. The first Antarctic heavier-than-air flight was made on 16 November 1928 by Alaskan bush pilot C.B. Eielson and George Herbert Wilkins in a Lockheed Vega monoplane. Rear-Admiral Richard E. Byrd was first to fly over the South Pole, which he did on 29 November 1929. He followed this great achievement with his four famous air-supported expeditions, which took place between 1928 and 1947, leading to the increasing use of skiplanes and aerial photography.

The south geomagnetic pole, the theoretical pole of the Earth's magnetic field, was reached by a Soviet IGY (International Geophysical Year of 1957-58) tractor traverse on 16 December 1957; and the pole of relative inaccessibility, the point most remote from all coasts, was reached, again by the Soviets, on 14 December 1958. After various set-backs, the dream of an overland crossing of the continent came true when, on 24 November 1957, using tracked vehicles and aided by aerial flights, the British Commonwealth Trans-Antarctic Expedition led by Vivian Fuchs left Shackleton Base on Filchner Ice Shelf and, by way of the South Pole, reached the New Zealand Scott Base on Ross Island on 2 March 1958.

By this time, territorial claims were being made by the various nations involved in exploration. Between 1908 and 1942, seven nations decreed sovereignty over certain sectors of the continent. While the US refused to recognize any claims of sovereignty as valid, Chile claimed Ellsworth Land, Australia claimed the American Highland near Amery Ice Shelf of East Antarctica, Nazi Germany claimed Queen Maud Land even though it was claimed by Norway, the French claimed Adélie Land, and though the British initially claimed Victoria Land, it was later claimed by New Zealand. In January 1943, in the middle of World War II, the British ignored Argentine's claim to Deception Island and established a base there. Britain, Argentina and Chile squabbled over various claims to the Antarctic Peninsula, with violence flaring up on occasion. By the early 1950s, with the US still refusing to recognize any claims of sovereignty as valid and the Soviet Union taking the same stand regarding claims made without its participation, a profusion of British, Argentine and Chilean bases was cluttering the Peninsula and nearby islands, while France, Norway, Sweden, South Africa, and Australia had raised their flags defiantly over other areas.

Notably absent from this collection was Germany, so recently defeated in war. This is ironic in that Nazi Germany had a particular interest in the Antarctic; and by the early 1950s, studies of the non-military aspects of Nazi philosophy were revealing just why this was so.

The Third Reich was born from a dangerous *völkish* mysticism: the Cosmic Circle of Munich; the Anthroposophy of Rudolph Steiner; the Theosophy and Rosicrucianism of Vienna and Prague; the Luminous Lodge and the Thule Group; the ancient dreams of Atlantis and Lemuria and the true 'Nordic' German. Central to this was the bizarre 'World Ice' theory of the unorthodox cosmologist, Hans Hörbiger, who preached that the universe had come into being because of, and was maintained by, an eternal struggle between ice and fire. According to Hörbiger, the original 'free' matter in the universe was in the form of frozen ice. Chunks of the ice often fell into stars, and the debris from the resulting, immense explosion formed our planetary system. As this theory could be used to discredit the Theory of Relativity put forward by Dr Albert Einstein, an eminent Jew, it was taken up enthusiastically by many Nazis, including the party philosopher, Alfred Rosenberg, and the mystically inclined Heinrich Himmler and Rudolf Hess. The last two named also believed in Thule, which actually lies off the coast of Greenland, but which legend has it was a long vanished civilization, like Atlantis, consisting of a pure Aryan, or 'Nordic' peoples.

This vision of a 'pure' Aryan race, or 'Master Race', became inextricably entwined with the belief that the lost Thule was not the 'Thule' located in Greenland, but another place altogether, which had not been lost but merely moved elsewhere, either by the shifting of land masses or by one of the many 'cosmic' catastrophes described by Hörbiger. Last but not least, since part of Hörbiger's theory, as well as the so-called 'secret doctrine', has it that mankind lives on the inside surface of a hollow Earth, certain Nazis, including Himmler and Hess, began thinking of the resurrection of the Master Race in terms of isolated colonies, located in Nordic, or icy, areas where the 'impurities' of German youth could be breeded out and the 'pure' Aryan 'Master Race' be recreated through the process of selective breeding and monastic, military discipline.

To this end, the Nazi hierarchy created Himmler's Death's Head SS troops, practised the sterilization or extermination of 'inferior' races, researched racial characteristics through the *Ahnenerbe* (Institute for Research into Heredity), including the ghastly 'anthropological' experiments undertaken in the concentration camps, and established 'breeding colonies' in the shape of the ghastly *Lebensborn* organization which, under the guise of a national maternity home and hostel for nursing mothers, was actually a collection of stud farms for the elite of the SS. The Nazis also raced to invent highly advanced 'secret weapons' and find the great spaces (hopefully underground, or well hidden, like the many immense rocket sites) before the war ended with their defeat.

This much is known. Toward the end of 1938, Hitler, anxious for a foothold in the Antarctic, sent an expedition commanded by Captain Alfred Rischter to the South Atlantic Ocean coastal region of Antarctica. The expedition arrived there in early 1939. Daily for three weeks two seaplanes were catapulted from the deck of the German aircraft carrier, *Schwabenland*, with orders to fly back and forth across the territory that previous Norwegian explorers had named Queen Maud Land. According to the *Encyclopaedia Britannica*: 'The German Antarctic Expedition of 1939 aerially photographed an extensive segment of Princess Astrid and Princess Martha coasts of western Queen Maud Land and, dropping metal swastikas over the region, claimed it for the Hitler government (the area is now claimed by Norway)'. The Germans called this territory Neu Schwabenland.

Throughout the war, German ships and U-boats continued to prowl the South Atlantic Ocean along the coastline of Antarctica, thus blocking any possible incursions into Neu Schwabenland. In 1941 a couple of large Norwegian whaling ships were seized by boarding parties from the German raider *Pinguin* as they rested at anchor in their own territorial waters just off Queen Maud Land. Within hours of that incident, a Norwegian supply ship and most of the nearby whaling convoy suffered the same fate. Not long after, in May 1941, HMS *Cornwall* located and sank the *Pinguin*, but not before the latter had captured a whole string of Allied merchant ships totalling more than 135,000 tons. What is also historical fact is that *Pinguin's* sister ships, appropriately named *Komet* and *Atlantis*, continued to prowl the Antarctic shores until the end of the war.

In London there was growing concern that a 'pro-

German Argentine government' might take control of the vital Drake Passage. Thus, in 1944, the British established a permanent base on Deception Island.

On 25 April 1945 the German submarine *U-977*, commanded by Captain Heinz Schaeffer, put out of Kiel Harbour in the Baltic. That submarine stopped in at Christiansand South on 26 April, departed the following day, and was not seen again until it surfaced at Mar del Plata, Argentina, on 17 August - a period of nearly four months.

Where was the submarine all that time? According to Captain Schaeffer, he had left with the intention of patrolling the South Atlantic Ocean, had docked for fuel at Christiansand South the following day, and had then, several days later, heard over the radio the news that the war was over. Convinced that they would not be treated too kindly by the Allied Command, Schaeffer gave his crew the option of being put off along the coast of Norway or instead traveling on with him to what he assumed would be a friendly Argentina. Since some of the crew preferred to return to Germany, the next few days were spent in hugging the Norwegian coastline, until, on 10 May, some of the men were dropped off on the mountain coast not far from Bergen. This done, according to Schaeffer, he and the remaining crew embarked upon what surely must have been one of the most remarkable naval feats of the war: a journey through the North Sea and English Channel, past Gibraltar and along the coast of Africa, to finally surface, all of sixty-six days later, in the middle of the South Atlantic Ocean. During the next month they alternated between floating on the surface and diving back to the depths, once even surfacing off the Cape Verde Islands and going ashore on Branca Island; another time going so far as to 'disguise' the submarine when it was on the surface by rigging up false sails and funnel to make it more like a cargo steamer.

Finally, when close to Rio de Janeiro, they heard over their radio that another fleeing German submarine, *U-530*, had put into the River Plate and that its crew had been handed over to the United States as prisoners of war. Disturbed by this news, Schaeffer nonetheless put into Mar del Plata on 17 August 1945 - nearly four months after he had put out from Kiel harbour.

Since this is an unusually, even remarkably, long time for a submarine such as the *U-977* to be at sea, Captain Schaeffer, when he docked at Mar del Plata, was interrogated by the Argentine authorities regarding why he had arrived in Argentina so long after the war had ended. He was also asked if *U-977* had carried anyone of 'political importance' during its voyage to Argentina. He explained his late arrival in Argentina with the fantastic story recounted above, and stated that no-one of political importance had ever been aboard *U-977*.

Even more intriguing is that a few weeks later, an Anglo-American commission, composed of high-ranking officers flown especially to Argentina to investigate the 'mysterious case' of *U-977*, spent a great deal of time interrogating Schaeffer regarding the possibility that he might have taken Hitler and Martin Bormann aboard his U-boat, first to Patagonia, then on to a secret Nazi base in the Antarctic. Indeed, they were so insistent on this that they subsequently flew Schaeffer and his crew - *and* Otto

Wehrmut, commander of *U-530* - back to a prisoner-of-war camp near Washington DC, where for months they continued their interrogations. The fate of Wehrmut remains unknown, but according to Schaeffer, he repeatedly denied having shipped anyone anywhere. Nonetheless, he was then handed over to the British in Antwerp, Belgium, and *again* interrogated for many months. Oddly, since Schaeffer stuck to his story and reportedly the Allies found nothing unusual in *U-977*, the submarine was taken to the United States where, under direct orders from the US War Department, it was blown to pieces.

As for Schaeffer, whether telling the truth or not, he was shipped back to Germany, did not feel comfortable under Allied rule, and so went back to join other expatriate German officers in Argentina - which was, and remains, the last major stop before the South Atlantic coastline of Antarctica.

This much is known, also. The International Geophysical Year (IGY) of 1957-58 was created to allow the nations of the world to 'take advantage of increasing technological developments, interest in polar regions, and, not the least, the maximum sunspot activity expected in 1957-58. It was adopted by the International Council of Scientific Unions (ICSU) and coordinated by the Comité Spécial de l'Année Géophysique Internationale (CSAGI) and eventually, with 67 nations joining, plans were laid for simultaneous observations of the sun, the aurora, the magnetic field, the ionosphere, and cosmic rays. Twelve nations taking part established more than fifty overtime winter stations on the continent. Massive tractor runs and airlifts enabled inland stations to be established: Byrd Station in West Antarctica for the US; Amundsen-Scott Station at the South Pole, also for the US; and Vostok Station at the geomagnetic pole for the USSR and at the pole of inaccessibility, also for the USSR. Many coastal bases were also established.

This was the greatest scientific program ever launched in the history of Mankind - and its main concentration was on two areas: outer space and Antarctica. For eighteen months, from 1 July 1957 to 31 December 1958, there was a frenzy of scientific activity, resulting in a vast collection of data on cosmic rays, the aurora and airglow, geomagnetism, gravity measurement, ionospheric physics, meteorology, oceanography, and seismology. Even more startling, in recollection, is that this wealth of information was gathered by satellites launched by the United States and the Soviet Union. It was then, through World Data Centres established to collect all observations, made freely available for analysis to scientists of *any* nation.

Even as this unprecedented act of international cooperation was taking place, notably in Antarctica, worldwide UFO sightings were reaching their peak and, simultaneously, a blanket of disinformation and secrecy was falling over what was now being termed officially: ‘the UFO problem’.

Chapter 12

Disinformation and the International Cover-Up

US Air Force involvement in official UFO investigations began as far back as 1947 at the Intelligence Division of the Air Force's Air Material Command, based at Wright Field (now Wright-Patterson AFB) in Dayton, Ohio. Contrary to its public debunking of civilian UFO sightings, the Air Force was actually in a state of near panic because of a wave of sightings, first over Maxwell Air Force Base in Montgomery Alabama, then, to the horror of the top brass, over the White Sands Proving Ground - right in the middle of their Atom bomb territory. Finally, after a whole series of sightings on 8 July 1947, over Muroc Air Base (now Edwards AFB) - their top-secret Air Force test centre in the Mojave Desert, California - they decided to do something about it.

General Nathan Twining, commander of the Air Materiel Command, wrote to the commanding general of the Army-Air Force stating that the phenomenon was something real, that it was not 'visionary or fictitious', and that the objects were disk-shaped, as large as aircraft, and *controlled*. Shortly after, on 22 January 1948, a UFO investigation program, Project Sign, was established, given a 2A classification, and placed under the jurisdiction of the Intelligence Division of the Air Force's Air Material Command at Wright Field. Later renamed the Air

Technical Intelligence Centre, or ATIC, its function was to 'collect, collate, evaluate and distribute to interested government agencies and contractors all information concerning sightings and phenomena in the atmosphere which can be construed to be of concern to the national security'.

The UFO-related death of Air Force pilot Captain Thomas F. Mantell over Godman AFB, Kentucky, on 7 January 1948, combined with the 'classic' UFO sighting made by Eastern Airlines Captain Charles S. Chiles and co-pilot John B. Whitted near Montgomery, Alabama, on the evening of 24 July the same year, prompted Project Sign to write an official, top-secret Estimate of the Situation. That Estimate outlined the whole history of UFO sightings, including the fireballs, Scandinavian 'ghost rockets' and American sightings before 1947, then concluded that the UFOs were of extraterrestrial origin. Classified as top secret and issued in July 1948, the Estimate was sent through channels, all the way to Chief of Staff, General Hoyt S. Vandenberg; but to the surprise of all concerned, the general rejected it on the grounds that it 'lacked proof'.

Possibly it was fear of further offending the powerful general that led to a whole new policy at Project Sign: in the future, Sign personnel were to assume that *all* UFO reports were hoaxes. Not only that, but they had to check with FBI officers, and with the criminal and subversive files of police departments, looking into the private lives of the witnesses to see if they were 'reliable'. Most of the Project Sign team took this as fair warning that it was not particularly wise to raise the subject of UFO sightings - and as if to prove them right, the Sign Estimate was later incinerated, reportedly on the orders of General Vandenberg.

On 11 February 1949, Project Sign was renamed Project Grudge. While the Air Force claimed that this was because the classified name 'Sign' had been compromised, there were those who took it as another indication of General Vandenberg's displeasure with their findings. Certainly, the new, lowlier status of Project Grudge was indicated in the recommendation made in Project Sign's final report: 'Future activity on this project should be carried on at the *minimum* level (author's emphasis) necessary to record, summarize and evaluate the data received on future reports and to complete the specialized investigations now in progress.'

It now became the function of Project Grudge to shift the investigations away from the actual UFOs and on to those who reported them - but since a good twenty-three per cent of their reports were still classified as unknowns, this wasn't that easy. Nevertheless, Project Grudge launched a public relations campaign designed to convince the American public that UFOs did not represent 'anything unusual or extraordinary'. As part of their 'debunking' effort, they encouraged the *Saturday Evening Post* journalist Sidney Shallet to write a two-part article exposing UFOs as a waste of time; but when that backfired by increasing public interest rather than diminishing it, the Air Force tried to counteract by stating officially that UFOs were either misidentifications of natural phenomenon or the products of mass hallucination.

Project Grudge issued its final report in August 1949 - only six months after its inception. Put simply, its conclusion was that while 23 per cent of the UFO reports were still classified as unknowns, most had 'psychological explanations' and the investigation was therefore a waste of time and should be downgraded even further. On 27 December the Air Force announced the termination of the project. Shortly after, the Project Grudge records were stored and most of its personnel were widely scattered.

The most famous, and certainly the most respected, head of the Air Force's UFO research project was Captain Edward J. Ruppelt, who was assigned to the Air Technical Intelligence Centre in January 1951, working as project director under General Lieutenant Jerry Cummings. Prior to moving to ATIC, Ruppelt had no particular interest in UFOs, but what he found in the ATIC files intrigued him.

He was particularly impressed by the reports on the two movies taken in 1950 by Air Force technicians at the White Sands Proving Ground (not to be confused with the cinetheodolite photos taken earlier by Navy Commander R.B. McLaughlin), which was fully instrumented to track high-altitude, fast-moving objects - usually the guided missiles - and had camera stations equipped with cinetheodolite cameras located all over the area. In June of that year two UFOs had been shot by two different cameras. By putting a correction factor in the data gathered by the two cameras, the Photo Laboratory at White Sands was able to arrive at a 'rough' estimation of the objects' size, altitude and speed. According to their report, the UFOs were over 300 feet in diameter, higher than 40,000 feet, and traveling at over 2,000 mph.

On 25 August 1951 the famous UFO sightings at

Lubbock, Texas, caused an enormous stir with the American public. When those sightings were followed by the Fort Monmouth sightings of 12 September 1951 - which were clearly seen by a lot of visiting top brass - the Air Force was galvanized back into action and, in March 1952, Project Grudge was upgraded from 'a project within a group' to a separate organization. Renamed Project Blue Book, it was based at ATIC in Wright-Patterson AFB, Dayton, Ohio, with Captain Ruppelt as its chief.

Ruppelt took the UFO sightings seriously, but after the debacle of the Washington UFO 'invasion' of July, 1952, when he was hampered from doing his job and so many witnesses contradicted their original statements, he became convinced that pilots reporting UFOs were being intimidated into changing their reports or simply remaining silent, that a lot of information was being withheld from Blue Book, and that the CIA were stepping into the picture for unexplained reasons.

The person who most worried Ruppelt was Chief of Staff, General Hoyt S. Vandenberg. It was Vandenberg who had buried the original Project Sign Estimate, caused its incineration, and had the project renamed Project Grudge. It is not clear just *how much* Vandenberg was influencing either the Air Force or the CIA, but he had been head of the Central Intelligence Group (later the CIA) from June 1946 to May 1947 and his uncle had been chairman of the Foreign Relations Committee, then the most powerful committee in the Senate. Clearly, Vandenberg still had great influence in those areas - and according to Ruppelt, pressure was always coming from them to suppress the results of official UFO investigations.

Ruppelt was therefore not surprised when he was informed that the CIA and some high-ranking officers, including Generals Vandenberg and Samford, were, against the objections of the Batelle Memorial Institute (a private research group used by the Air Force to carry out statistical studies of UFO characteristics), convening a panel of scientists to analyze all the Blue Book data. Nor was he surprised to discover that this panel was to be headed by Dr H.P. Robertson, director of the Weapons System Evaluation Group in the Office of the Secretary of Defence - and a CIA classified employee.

The Robertson Panel was convened in great secrecy in Washington DC during January 1953. While some insist that it opened on 12 January, the dates on the group's final report state 14- 18 January. Apart from Robertson, the group's panel consisted of physicist and Nobel Prize-winner Luis W. Alvarez; geophysicist and radar specialist Lloyd V. Berkner, and physicist Samuel Goudsmit, both of the Brookhaven National Laboratories; and astronomer and astrophysicist Thornton Page, Deputy Director of the John Hopkins Operations Research Office. Other participants included J. Allen Hynek, then a consultant to the United States Air Force; Frederick C. Durant, an army ordnance test station director; William M. Garland, the Commanding General of the Air Technical Intelligence Centre (ATIC); ATIC's Pentagon liaison officer, Major Dewey Fournet; Project Blue Book chief, Captain Ruppelt; two officers from the Navy Photo Interpretation Laboratory; and three high-ranking CIA representatives.

The seriousness with which the subject was supposed

to be treated is best illustrated not only by the calibre of the men involved, but also by the fact that the group's report was to be given to the National Security Council (NSC) and then, if the decision was that the UFOs were of extraterrestrial origin, to the President himself. This may have been so much cotton wool.

For the first two days of the session, Captain Ruppelt reviewed the Blue Book findings for the scientists. First, he pointed out that Blue Book received reports of only 10 per cent of the UFO sightings made in the United States, which meant that in five and a half years about 44,000 sightings had been made. He then broke the sightings down into the percentage that was composed of balloons, aircraft, astronomical bodies, and other misinterpretations, such as birds, blowing paper, noctilucent and lenticular clouds, temperature inversions, reflections, and so forth, and pointed out that this still left 429 as definite 'unknowns'. Of those unknowns, it was clear that the most reported shape was elliptical, the most often reported colour was white or metallic, the same number of UFOs were reported as being seen in daylight as at night, and the direction of travel equally covered the sixteen cardinal points of the compass. 70 per cent of those unknowns had been seen visually from the air - in other words, by experienced pilots and navigators; 12 per cent had been seen visually from the ground; 10 per cent had been picked up by airborne and ground radar; and 8 per cent were combination visual-radar sightings. Ruppelt also confirmed that many UFO reports came from top-secret military establishments, such as atomic energy and missile-testing installations, plus harbours and manufacturing areas.

Ruppelt and Major Dewey Fournet had completed an analysis of the motions of the reported unknowns as a means of determining if they were intelligently controlled. Regarding this, Major Fournet told the panel of how, by eliminating every possibility of balloons, aeroplanes, astronomical bodies, and so forth, from the hundreds of reports studied, and by then analyzing the motions of the UFOs in the remaining unknown category, his study group had been forced to conclude that the UFOs were, in the words of the group report: 'intelligently controlled by persons with brains equal to, or far surpassing, ours'. The next step in the study, Fournet explained, had been to find out where those beings came from; and since it seemed unlikely that their machines could have been built in secret, the answer was that the beings were from outer space.

The morning after Fournet's summary, the panel was shown four strips of movie film that had been assessed as falling into the 'definite unknown' category. These were the cinetheodolite movies taken by Air Force technicians at the White Sands Proving Ground on 27 April 1950 and approximately a month later; the 'Montana' movie taken on 15 August 1950 by the manager of the Great Falls baseball team; and the 'Tremonton' movie taken on 2 July 1952 by Navy Chief Photographer, Warrant Officer Delbert C. Newhouse.

One of the White Sands movies showed 'a dark smudgy object' which proved only, in the words of Ruppelt, 'that something had been in the air and, whatever it was, it had been *moving*'. The second movie had been analyzed by the Data Reduction Group at Wright-Patterson AFB, with results indicating that the object had been approximately higher than 40,000 feet, traveling over 2,000 mph, and was over 300 feet in diameter. The Montana movie showed two large, bright lights flying across the blue sky in an echelon formation; the lights did not show any detail, but they appeared to be large, circular objects. The Tremonton movie showed about a dozen shiny, disk-like objects fading in and out constantly, performing extraordinary aerial manoeuvres, and darting in and out and circling one another in a cloudless blue sky. Any possibility that the objects might have been astronomical phenomena was dispelled when the film clearly showed them heading in the same tight cluster toward the western horizon and, more specifically, when one of them left the main group and shot off to the east.

The Montana movie had been subjected to thousands of hours of analysis in the Air Force laboratory at Wright Field and the results proved conclusively that the objects were not birds, balloons, aircraft, meteors, clouds, or reflections - in short, they were unknowns. As for the Tremonton movie, it had been studied for two solid months by the Navy Laboratory in Anacostia, Maryland, and their conclusion was that the unidentifieds were not birds or aeroplanes, were probably traveling at several thousands of miles an hour, and were, judging by their extraordinary manoeuvres, intelligently controlled vehicles.

In the view of Ruppelt and Fournet, the evidence seemed conclusive - yet the Robertson Panel still managed to reject it. After going over the evidence for two days, the panel concluded in its report that the evidence was *not* substantial, that the continued emphasis on the reporting of the phenomenon was resulting in 'a threat to the orderly functioning of the protective organs of the body politic', and that the reports clogged military channels, could possibly precipitate mass hysteria, and might encourage defence personnel to misidentify or ignore actual enemy aircraft. In other words: the real problem was not the UFOs - it was the UFO *reports*.

Based on this assessment, the Robertson Panel made some unexpected, even startling, recommendations. First, it recommended that the two major private UFO organizations - the Aerial Phenomena Research Organization (APRO) and the Civilian Saucer Intelligence (CSI) - be watched because of what was described as their 'potentially great influence on mass thinking' in the event of widespread sightings. Included in this recommendation was the statement: 'The apparent irresponsibility and the possible use of such groups for subversive purposes should be kept in mind.' Next, it recommended that the national security agencies take immediate steps to strip the UFO phenomenon of its importance and eliminate the 'aura of mystery' it had acquired, the means being a 'public education program'. Finally, the panel outlined a program of 'public education' with two purposes: training and debunking. The former would help people identify known objects and thus reduce the mass of reports caused by misidentification; the latter would reduce public interest in UFOs and thereby decrease or eliminate UFO reports.

As a means of pursuing this 'education' program, the panel suggested that the government hire psychologists familiar with mass psychology, military training film companies, Walt Disney Productions, and popular personalities such as Arthur Godfrey to subtly convey this new thinking to the masses. Also, contrary to what the CIA were later to tell Ruppelt, it was decided *not* to declassify the sighting reports and, instead, to tighten security even more and continue to deny 'non-military personnel' access to UFO files.

It was clear then, certainly to Captain Ruppelt and other members of Project Blue Book, that the whole purpose of the Robertson Panel was to enable the Air Force to state for the next decade or so that an *impartial* body had examined the UFO data and found no evidence for anything unusual in the skies. While this was an obvious distortion of fact, it *did* mean that the Air Force could now avoid discussing the nature of the objects and instead concentrate on the public relations campaign to eliminate the UFO reports totally.

Given the nature of the Robertson Panel's recommendations, there can be little doubt that they were directly responsible for the policy of ridicule and denial that has inhibited an effective study of the phenomenon ever since.

In December 1952, when it became obvious that the CIA and Air Force intelligence were between them trying to severely limit the investigations of Project Blue Book, Captain Ruppelt asked for a transfer. By the following February, when he was due to leave, no replacement for him had arrived; nor were there any replacements when Lieutenant Flues was transferred to the Alaskan Air Command, when Lieutenant Rothstein's tour of active duty ended, or when others on the staff left or were transferred out. Thus, when Ruppelt was transferred out in February, he left a drastically reduced Blue Book staff. By the time he returned, in July, he found that the Air Force had reassigned most of the remaining staff, that they had sent no replacements for them, and that his Blue Book now consisted of only himself and a mere two assistants. Project Blue Book had virtually been closed down.

In August 1953 Ruppelt left the Air Force... and the Pentagon issued the notorious Air Force Regulation 200-2. This was drafted purely as a public relations weapon in that it prohibited the release of *any* information about a sighting to the public or media, except when it was *positively* identified as natural phenomena. In addition, whereas AFR 200-5, the previous classification, had stated that sightings should not be classified higher than restricted, the new regulation ensured that *all* sightings would be classified as restricted. Then, much worse, in December 1953 the Joint Chiefs of Staff followed AFR 200-2 with Joint-Army-Navy-Air Force Publication 146. This made the releasing of *any* information to the public a crime under the Espionage Act, punishable by a one to ten year prison term or a fine of $10,000. And the most ominous aspect of JANAP 146 was that it applied to anyone who knew it existed, including commercial airline pilots.

Needless to say, this new regulation effectively put a stop to the flow of information to the public.

By the end of that year, the investigating authority of the decimated Project Blue Book had been handed over to the inexperienced 402d Air Intelligence Squadron and most of its operations had been cut off by a drastic reduction in funding. Ruppelt, Fournet and the other original members of the team were no longer involved; and General Garland, once a strong Ruppelt supporter, never again raised his voice in defence of any UFO investigation.

To all intents and purposes, and contrary to official Air Force pronouncements, the UFO project had been plunged into secrecy.

Why?

By 1953 the US was fighting the war in Korea, the Soviets had dropped their first hydrogen bomb, and the cold war was in its chilliest phase. This was good enough reason for the Robert Panel to claim that the UFO reports were a threat to national security: first, because a deliberately confused American public might think attacking enemy bombers were merely UFOs; second, because a foreign power could exploit the UFO craze to make the public doubt official Air Force statements about UFOs and thereby undermine public confidence in the military; and third, because in terms of psychological warfare, the communications lines of the whole country could be saturated by a few hundred phone calls; and such calls (which always came after a rash of UFO sightings) were putting the defence network in jeopardy.

Those were the reasons given for the recommended program of 'public education', or, in layman's terms, the suppression of information.

If it is true that national security was the issue, then the suppression of information had a certain amount of logic behind it. However, if national security was the *only* concern, why was the Air Force humiliating so many UFO witnesses, harassing its own ground and air crews into remaining silent, and even threatening civilian airline pilots with enormous fines or jail sentences? The only explanation is that the higher echelons of the Air Force were more concerned about the phenomenon that they were willing to admit, that they possibly knew more about it than they were willing to say, and that for reasons of their own, they were actively discouraging their most competent personnel, such as Captain Ruppelt, from investigating or reporting on the subject.

In September 1952, approximately four months before the convening of the Robertson Panel, Ruppelt had investigated the UFO sightings over the NATO fleet during Operation Mainbrace and assessed all the sightings as unknowns. This encouraged him to imagine that he could now pin down the UFOs for good - and it was this very enthusiasm that led to the destruction of the most important system ever devised for UFO research.

For a long time Ruppelt and Brigadier General Garland, then chief at ATIC, had been looking for a way of getting concrete information about the UFOs. What they eventually came up with was a plan for visual spotting stations to be established all over northern Mexico - the area that had consistently produced more UFO reports than any other place in America. The visual spotting stations would be equipped with specially designed sighting devices, all of which would be linked with an instantaneous interphone system; any two stations could then track the same object and, from their separate readings, compute the UFO's altitude, speed and characteristics. Also at each visual spotting station would be instruments to measure the passage of any body that was giving off heat, any disturbance in Earth's magnetic field, and any increase in nuclear radiation at the time of the sighting.

This was the first time that a proper, scientific system had been designed and submitted to the Air Force. According to Ruppelt, it was virtually foolproof and had it been adopted, it would have been possible to track, photograph and measure UFOs with unprecedented precision - yet nothing came of it.

There is no proof that the Air Force deliberately killed it off, but these are the facts as reported by Ruppelt...

In December 1952, when Ruppelt's plans went to Washington DC for approval, the US Navy were preparing to shoot their first H-bomb during Project Ivy and some officers in the Pentagon, recalling the unidentifieds seen over Operation Mainbrace, directed Ruppelt to fly out to the test area and organize a UFO reporting team. That order actually came down in November, but Ruppelt's plans for the visual-radar sighting network were received in Washington DC the following month... and a few days later, for reasons never explained, Ruppelt's trip to Project Ivy was cancelled. A month later, in January 1953, came the Robertson Panel and its consequences. By August of that year, Ruppelt had left the Air Force - and the activities of Project Blue Book were wound down.

After leaving the Air Force, Ruppelt went to work for the Northrop Aircraft Company and, in his spare time, wrote *The Report on Unidentified Flying Objects* (1956), in which he stated his belief that UFOs were a genuine phenomenon and probably of extraterrestrial origin. Three years later, however, he inexplicably revised the book, adding three chapters in which he completely reversed his previous opinions. Many believe that this was due to pressure from official quarters; others are equally convinced that it was his response to the wilder claims of UFO contactees.

Since Ruppelt died unexpectedly of a heart attack in 1960, shortly after revising his book, the truth will probably never be known.

Throughout the UFO controversy, the scientists had remained silent, but in 1965, after a fresh, spectacular wave of sightings over Texas had caused nationwide concern and a revival of press interest, the US Air Force in particular came under fire for supposedly not telling the truth about UFOs. Knowing of the Air Force's concern, Dr J. Allen Hynek suggested that they set up a 'panel of civilian scientists' to review the situation once and for all, and the Air Force, agreeing, turned the program over to the Public Information Office. This led to the formation of the Ad Hoc Committee to Review Project Blue Book. It was headed by Dr Brian O'Brien, and the rest of the team, excepting Dr Carl Sagan, were members of the Air Force's scientific advisory board. The committee met for one day in February 1966, reviewed the Robertson report, and decided that while the UFOs did not threaten the national security, they *did* warrant further investigation. Their main recommendation was that the Air Force negotiate contracts with a few selected universities to provide teams of specialists who could investigate 'promptly and in depth' selected sightings of UFOs.

On 20 March 1966, eighty-seven women and a civil defence director at Hillsdale College, Michigan, saw a 'football-shaped, glowing object hovering over a swampy area a few hundred yards from the woman's dormitory'. The object flew repeatedly at, and retreated from, the dormitory, dodged an airport beacon light, dimmed and brightened, and was observed by the witnesses for four hours. The next day, five people, including two police officers, in Dexter, Michigan, saw a similar object rising from a swampy area on a farm. It hovered for a few minutes at about 1,000 feet, then left the area. Over a hundred other reports of similar sightings were received in those two nights in those two cities sixty-three miles apart.

The sightings led to an extraordinary press conference, held in the Detroit Press Club. Representing the Air Force, Dr J. Allen Hynek suggested to the clamouring journalists that the UFOs, or lights, could have been the result of decaying vegetation that spontaneously ignited, creating a faint glow - in other words, swamp gas. His tentative suggestion was blown out of all proportion by the press, leading to accusations that the Air Force was engaged in a cover-up. There were also demands in the media for a proper, scientific investigation to be mounted. So great was the uproar that House Republican minority leader (later US President) Gerald R. Ford and Weston E. Vivian, Democratic congressman for Michigan, formally called for congressional hearings. Thus, on 5 April 1966, for the first time in the history of the UFO controversy, Congress held an open hearing on the subject. This led to the O'Brien committee recommendations being implemented - which in turn led to what many would consider to be the biggest Air Force cover-up of them all: the Condon committee report.

A Gallup Poll undertaken in May 1966 indicated that

96 per cent of the American people had heard or read about UFOs and that approximately *nine million* of them were convinced that they had actually seen one. That same month, a besieged Air Force disclosed publicly that it was going to contract with scientists for a UFO investigation. Five months later, on 7 October 1966, the Air Force announced that the University of Colorado had accepted the UFO project and that Dr Edward U. Condon, internationally known physicist and former head of the National Bureau of Standards, would be in charge. Working with Condon on the project would be Robert Low (Assistant Dean of the Graduate School) as project coordinator, and psychologists Stuart Cook and Franklin Roach as principal investigators.

In October 1966 the Condon committee got off to a bad start and went inexorably downhill thereafter. Within days of its formation, Condon was making it publicly clear that he did not believe in extraterrestrials or flying saucers, but *did* believe that the Air Force had been doing a good job of investigating the phenomenon. He also stated that there was 'an appalling lack of understanding' of 'ordinary phenomena' that could resemble UFOs, and that he hoped to 'reduce the number of UFO reports' through 'approved teaching about these things'. By 25 January 1967 Condon was informing the Corning Section of the American Chemical Society that his personal inclination was to 'recommend that the government get out of this business' and that in general he thought there was 'nothing to it'.

By this time it had become clear to dismayed observers that Condon had already decided to concentrate on only two facets of the phenomenon: 'misinterpretations of natural phenomena, and the psychological bases for UFO reports'. At roughly the same time, John Lear, science editor of the *Saturday Review*, publicly disclosed that the CIA had severely edited, or censored, the unclassified Robertson report, leaving out the names of the participants and many of their recommendations. Public concern over the actual contents of the report was only increased when Dr James E. McDonald, senior physicist at the University of Arizona's Department of Atmospheric Sciences, revealed that he had read the classified Robert report and could confirm that the CIA had ordered the Air Force to debunk UFOs and those who reported them.

In view of Condon's widely reported negativity about the phenomenon, McDonald's revelations only increased cynicism about the motives and findings of the Condon committee. The committee staff included psychologists, a chemist, and an astronomer, and was backed up with project members of the calibre of Dr J. Allen Hynek, computer scientist Jacques Vallee, USAF Major Hector Quintanilla, the head of Project Blue Book, and Donald E. Keyhoe, director of the National Investigations Committee on Aerial Phenomena (NICAP), and his assistant director, Richard Hall. Nonetheless, it soon degenerated into a disturbing series of internal disagreements and personality clashes, most of them caused by the increasingly blatant cynicism of Condon and his project coordinator, Robert Low, both of whom showed a distinct partiality to absurd contactee-like claims and tried to block the inclusion of more reliable reports from military observers and civilian pilots.

These conflicts burst into the open when, in February

1968, Dr James E. McDonald revealed the contents of a memorandum submitted by Low in August 1966 to the administrators of the University of Colorado, in order to explain his views on the UFO phenomenon and the attitude which he felt the Condon committee should adopt. Low's views, as expressed in the memorandum, were that the UFO phenomenon had 'no physical reality', that the staff of the Condon committee should be composed of 'nonbelievers', and that the best way to bolster a healthily negative attitude about UFOs would be to focus on the psychology and backgrounds of those who report them.

'The trick,' Low wrote, 'would be to describe the project so that, to the public, it would appear a totally objective study but, to the scientific community, would present the image of a group of nonbelievers trying their best to be objective but having an almost zero expectation of finding a saucer.'

The revealed contents of the Low memorandum nearly blew the Condon committee apart. An outraged Condon fired committee members David Saunders and Norman Levine, who had been instrumental in getting the report to Keyhoe and McDonald. The dismissal of these key members led to the resignation of Condon's administrative assistant, Mary Lou Armstrong. With Armstrong gone, others lost faith in Condon and left also, until eventually, out of the original staff, only Low and two other full-time staff members remained. NICAP then withdrew its support from the committee.

Saunders and Levine attacked Condon for his 'unscientific approach' to the subject. The same criticisms were levelled against Condon in Congress, which led to another Congressional hearing. This took place on 29 July 1968, under the auspices of the House Science and Astronautics Committee. Participants included Drs McDonald and Hynek, famed astronomer and writer Carl Sagan, sociologist Robert L. Hall, professor of civil engineering, James A. Harder, and astronautics engineer Robert M. Baker. These participants were prohibited from criticizing the Condon committee openly; nonetheless, the criticism was implied when they all recommended that the scientific investigation of UFOs be continued.

The Condon report was published in January 1969 with the seal of approval of the National Academy of Science (NAS). Its conclusion was that nothing of scientific value could come from the study of UFOs, that further study of the subject could therefore not be justified, and that Project Blue Book should be closed down. In order to reach this conclusion, Condon devoted most space to the 'identified' reports, carefully buried those considered to be genuine 'unidentifieds', wilfully ignored many of the conclusions reached by other contributors, and emphasized in his summary (which he placed at the beginning of the report instead of the end) the negative views he had been proclaiming publicly throughout the eighteen months of the Condon committee investigations.

In *The UFO Controversy in America*, David Michael Jacobs describes the Condon report as 'a rather unorganised compilation of independent articles on disparate subjects, a minority of which dealt with UFOs'. Others were not so generous. On 11 January 1969, a few days after the report appeared, McDonald, Keyhoe and Saunders held a press conference to denounce it as a waste of money, pointing out that Condon had revealed his bias and the committee had failed to investigate the vast majority of 'significant' UFO reports. Later, on behalf of NICAP, Donald E. Keyhoe accused Condon of trying to discredit some witnesses, as well as concentrating on 'kook cases'. The Aerial Phenomena Research Organization (APRO) charged that Condon had not investigated enough cases, but added that his selected cases had been investigated inadequately, that the report was filled with inconsistencies and unsubstantiated conclusions, and that it should be 'dismissed and/or discredited'. James E. McDonald, J. Allen Hynek, and many others also offered extensive, valid criticism, much of which implied that Condon had been used by the Air Force to discredit the UFO phenomenon and give it an excuse to close down the UFO project once and for all.

This is did. On 17 December 1969, Secretary of the Air Force, Robert C. Seamans, announced the official termination of the Air Force's twenty-two year study of UFOs. The files of Project Blue Book were then placed in storage in Maxwell Air Force Base, Montgomery, Alabama.

As the Air Force had anticipated, the official closing of Project Blue Book dramatically reduced public interest in the UFO phenomenon. As a result of this, Dr J. Allen Hynek was no longer required and returned to teaching at Northwestern University. Membership of the National Investigations Committee on Aerial Phenomena (NICAP) was soon reduced from 12,000 to 4,000. The Aerial Phenomena Research Organization (APRO) had the same problem and Donald Keyhoe, after twelve years as director, was eventually forced to step down. By 1970, the 'UFO problem' was practically a forgotten issue in the press, though the ridicule attached to the study of the subject had greatly increased.

In 1971, Dr James E. McDonald, a loudly vocal opponent to the Condon report, had that ridicule used against him to discredit his professional credibility. As the scientist who had discovered that supersonic transport (SST) aircraft would reduce the ozone layer and lead to thousands of more cases of skin cancer in the United States, he was called to testify before the House Committee on Appropriations. Throughout his testimony he was relentlessly mocked about his belief in 'flying saucers' and 'little men flying around the sky', while his perfectly accurate warnings about ozone depletion were ignored. With similar humiliations heaped upon him in the following months, both in and out of Congress, McDonald began suffering from depression, his marriage broke up, and in June of that year, at fifty-one years old, he committed suicide.

By the end of 1972, public interest in UFOs had been nullified, humiliation had ensured that new reports were relatively few, and the US Air Force, formerly compelled to give answers, could retain a comfortable silence. That official silence has been maintained to this day.

Howard Blum is an award-winning former *New York Times* journalist whose work has twice been nominated by the editors of that paper for the Pulitzer Prize in Investigative Journalism. The publication of his book *Wanted! The*

Search for Nazis in America initially led to ridicule being heaped upon him from various official quarters, but finally resulted in Congressional hearings, the creation of a Justice Department War Crimes Task-force, and the deportation of thirty-seven people accused of war crimes.

Blum had no interest in UFOs whatsoever until, in 1987, when investigating the notorious John Walker spy family, he received a call from a senior official at the National Security Agency (NSA), asking for a clandestine meeting. During the subsequent meeting that official told Blum that 'a lot of strange things' were happening in space and, as a result, the government had formed a top-secret panel of 'hot-shots' to look into the UFO phenomenon.

That single meeting led Blum into a two-year investigation of what turned out to be a massive cover-up by the government regarding the UFO problem. By the end of his search, during which he talked to top officials in secret military bases, laboratories, aeronautical establishments, the Pentagon, the White House and even CIA Headquarters, Langley, Virginia, Blum had discovered that in the winter of 1987 the government, disturbed by 'unexplained intrusions into our planetary space', had summoned seventeen members of the US intelligence community to the Pentagon. Formed into a top-secret UFO Working Group, those seventeen men, including members of the NSA and the CIA, had since been meeting once a month in 'the Tank' - the innermost sanctum of the Pentagon - to assess reports of UFOs that were being constantly monitored by the US Space Command's Space Surveillance Centre. Blum also discovered that the Pentagon, while insisting that it had no interest in UFOs, was involved in a 'dirty tricks' campaign to ensure that anyone delving too deeply into the UFO mystery ended up a laughing stock and that infiltration of UFO groups and the spreading of misinformation were being used to protect the Pentagon's own UFO investigations from public scrutiny.

Impressed by the contents of the MJ-12 documents first discovered by the widely respected British UFO research and author, Timothy Good (classified reports of the recovery in 1948 of the crashed flying saucer at Roswell, New Mexico, and the dead bodies of its supposedly extraterrestrial four-man crew) and by what he had been told by various interviewees, Blum naturally accepted that the secret working group was concerned with extraterrestrial intervention. However, when Blum published his findings in a book, *Out There: The Government's Secret Quest for Extraterrestrials* (1990), he received the expected flak from the government. The US Space Command dismissed Blum's claim that the UFO Working Group had been formed after a UFO penetrated America's defence perimeter in December 1986 and insisted that the 'tripping' of the electronic fence in space had been caused by 'an explosion of a rocket body broken up into 400 pieces'. The Pentagon categorically denied that the UFO Working Group existed and insisted that there was no such person as Colonel Harold Phillips, named in Blum's book as chairman of the group. The CIA denied all knowledge of the UFO Working Group and insisted that the agency had not been involved with UFOs since the Robertson Panel Report was issued in 1953. The Department of Defence stated that there was no record of any committee, either official or unofficial, called the UFO Working Group, and that since the conclusion of Project Blue Book in 1969 there had been no official or unofficial investigation, study, or involvement in the matter of UFOs by any branch of the Armed Forces or the Defence Intelligence Agency.

Blum responded by pointing out that the existence of the group had been confirmed to him by four separate sources and that he had found support for their assertions in classified military documents seen by him. He then pointed out that the government had responded in exactly the same way - with ridicule - to his book about Nazis living in America... until the subsequent Congressional hearings had proved him right. He also said that he hoped his book would ‘break the taboo about writing on UFOs’ and that he thought there was ‘a chance of getting Congressional hearings on why this work is being kept secret’.

There was, of course, a good reason for that secrecy. The US Air Force had insisted that UFOs did not exist, yet made the release of information about UFOs a crime under the Espionage Act. It claimed that national security was its only concern, yet ensured at the same time that its own air and ground crews would *not* report unidentified flying objects. And since killing off Project Blue Book in a gale of publicity, it has possibly convened, in the strictest secrecy, a UFO Working Group that meets once a month in the Pentagon to monitor UFO reports.

Clearly, since national security is not the issue, the US government was, and still is, protecting some secret knowledge: the reality of the man-made flying saucers.

Chapter 13

The Case Summed Up

If we go back to the first UFO sightings in the US, we can see that the technology of the late nineteenth century supports the contention that the Great Airship Scare of 1896-7 was caused by one or more genuine airships of advanced design, constructed secretly somewhere in the United States. The identity of the genius who designed them may never be known.

In the 1930s the first liquid-fuel rockets were constructed and flown by another American genius, Robert H. Goddard, in Roswell, New Mexico. Goddard's work was initially ignored by the US government, but adapted enthusiastically by the rocket scientists of Nazi Germany. Thus that country was soon leading the world in rocket technology and investing more than any other nation in advanced technology experimentation of all kinds. The existence of a Nazi 'flying saucer' program, Projekt Saucer, has now been proven. Press cuttings from the Imperial War Museum, London, and news agencies worldwide confirm that the 1945 reports of 'foo fighters' and 'balls of fire', were about a real, physical object which we now know to have been the German saucer-shaped anti-radar device, the *Feuerball*. Rudolph Schriever, Walter Miethe, and Georg Klein insisted separately that a larger, piloted version of the *Feuerball*, possibly named the *Kugelblitz*, was tested over Kahla, in Thuringia, which is in the immediate vicinity of Werner von Braun's underground V-1 and V-2 rocket establishment at Nordhausen. At the end of World War II, Schriever escaped and made his way back home to Bramerhaven where he insisted, to the day he died, that he had been involved in the German flying saucer project; Habermohl was captured by the Russians and taken back to work with other captured rocket scientists in the Soviet Union; and Miethe went with Werner von Braun to work for NASA, in the United States, but ended up working for A.V. Roe Canada (AVRO Canada).

The Soviets were the first to send a man into space, NASA was first at landing a man on the moon, and the first (known) man-made, completely saucer-shaped aircraft was the Avrocar developed by AVRO-Canada.

In the immediate post-war years Canada was one the greatest aeronautical nations in the world. The first US-Canadian flying saucers were constructed at AVRO-Canada in Malton, Ontario. The first post-war UFO sightings, inaugurating the 'flying saucer' age, were made over the Cascade mountain range in Washington State, near the border of Canada, and the UFOs appeared to fly back in the direction of Canada (as was the case with the UFOs involved in the Washington DC 'invasion' of 1952). Because of this, Renato Vesco and others believe that there are hidden UFO bases in the vast, mountainous, wooded regions of southwest Canada, between British Columbia and Alberta, and that many of those UFOs land regularly, secretly on US military bases.

This may well be true, but another possibility, presents itself. The unworkable, unsigned flying saucer designs reproduced in *Brisant* magazine (see Foreword) were used to illustrate an unsigned article about Nazi flying saucers. The thrust of the article was this: the Captain Rischter naval expedition of 1938 had been for the purpose of finding a suitable ice-free area in Antarctic to be used as a hidden Nazi base after the war. This he found in a part of Queen Maud Land, which he claimed for Germany and renamed Neu Schwabenland. Throughout the war, the Germans sent ships and aircraft to Neu Schwabenland with enough equipment and manpower (much of it slave labour from the concentration camps) to build massive complexes under the ice or in well hidden ice-free areas. At the close of the war selected Nazi scientists and SS troops fled to Antarctica (this accounts for the Hitler and Martin Bormann 'escape' rumour), taking with them the technology required to complete the aborted Projekt Saucer. The Allies learned about this when a German U-boat surfaced at Mar del Plata four months after the war and its captain and crew were interrogated by Allied intelligence.

About a year after this, the Americans launched the biggest Antarctic expedition in history, Operation Highjump, led by the famous US explorer and naval officer, Rear-Admiral Richard E. Byrd. As Byrd's resources included thirteen ships, at least two sea-plane tenders, an aircraft carrier, six two-engine R4D transports, six Martin PBM flying boats, six helicopters, and a staggering total of 4,000 men, it was widely believed that the expedition was designed more as an assault force than as a simple exploratory expedition. It also seemed odd that when this virtual assault force reached the Antarctic coast, it not only docked, on 12 January 1947, near the German-claimed territory of Neu Schwabenland, but then divided up into three separate task forces. When the expedition ended, in February the same year, reportedly much earlier than anticipated, there were numerous stories in the press about Rear-Admiral Byrd's references to 'enemy fighters which came from the Polar regions' and could 'fly from one Pole to the other with incredible speed'. The United States then withdrew from Antarctica for a decade.

During that decade, while the United States was keeping out of Antarctica, the US-Canada flying saucers came to light; and by 1954 the US press was informing the public that the Avrocar, or Omega, had been designed by John Frost for use in 'subarctic and polar regions'. This was followed, on 22 October 1955, by US Air Force Secretary Donald Quarles' references to 'aircraft of unusual characteristics' that would be used for 'the common defence of the subarctic area of the continent'.

The US finally returned to the Antarctic as part of the International Geophysical Year (IGY) of 1957-58, when it was inexplicably supported by the combined might of the USSR, Great Britain, and many other nations of the free world. After that, the US government announced that they were dropping their flying saucer projects; and eventually they also announced the termination of their UFO investigations program.

The same issue of *Brisant* contained another article, also without a byline, which insisted that Germany should claim back their rights to Neu Schwabenland, originally part of Queen Maud Land, still claimed by Norway.

The implication contained in these twinned articles

was that at the close of the war certain Nazi scientists and troops fled to the Antarctic, via a friendly Argentina (as Hitler and Martin Bormann were rumoured to have done) to establish a secret UFO base hidden under the ice. The US, the Soviet Union, and other nations know about them and, having failed to dislodge them with Operation Highjump, are either cooperating secretly with them to share in their technology, or trying to defeat them by gradually taking over the Antarctic with the combined scientific might of the major powers and their allies.

Much of this theory can be traced back to a neo-Nazi group located in Canada. Taking note of the National Socialist leanings of the articles in *Brisant*, I checked the origins of the magazine and learned that it had been published in West Germany by a company that has long since disappeared from its only known address: Lintec, GmbH, Jungfrauenthal 22, D-200, Hamburg 13. The company was not listed with any of the West German press organizations, nor with any public relations bureau.

None of the articles in *Brisant* carried bylines, but most of the information contained in them was originally published in the books, *UFO: Nazi Secret Weapons?* by Mattern Friedrich and *Secret Nazi Polar Expeditions* by Christof Friedrich. Neither book contains a copyright date, but both are published by Samisdat Publishers Limited, located at 206 Carlton Street, M5A 2L1, Toronto, Canada.

'Mattern Friedrich' and 'Christof Friedrich' are pseudonyms for one Ernst Zundl, an active neo-Nazi who appears to have many links with surviving Nazis in Argentina and elsewhere. He was once deported from the United States, and now runs Samisdat Publishers Limited as a mouthpiece of neo-Nazi propaganda and commercial enterprise, specialising in the sale of Nazi books, record albums, tape-recordings, photographs, medals, and other Nazi memorabilia.

Zundl's Antarctic-Nazi-UFO theories appear to have been culled from a variety of fanciful sources, most of them related to Vril (a secret society founded by a group of Berlin Rosicrucians and fiercely anti-Christian) and Thule mythology. However, his main source of inspiration may well have been Wilhelm Landig's *Götzen gegen Thule* (1971), described as 'a fiction full of facts' and promising the reader a wealth of information on 'secret military technology'. The similarities between this novel and Zundl's so-called 'factual' books are obvious.

The definitive analysis of the literary roots of Nazi-Antarctic-UFO theories can be found in *Arkto: The Polar Myth in Science, Symbolism, and Nazi Survival* (Thames & Hudson, London, 1993) by Joscelyn Godwin. In this seminal work *Götzen gegen Thule* is described as the story of two German airmen who are sent, near the end of World War II, to a secret base named Point 103, located in the most remote region of Arctic Canada. Though the existence of the base is not known to either the Allies or most German authorities, it is an immense underground complex supported by a technology far superior to anything else in the world. Travel in and out of the base is by the V7 - a vertical take-off aircraft shaped like a sphere, surmounted with a glass dome and propelled by a rotating ring of turbine blades. (Reportedly, a few prototypes of this very craft were actually constructed in German and Czech factories towards the end of the war, but never put into production.) In the secret Arctic base, the two airmen are taken under the wing of a Waffen-SS officer who, becoming their guide and 'philosophical instructor', tells them about Thule, that original Aryan paradise located at the North Pole, not far from their secret base, Point 103. Apart from being racial supremacists, Thuleans are aware of an 'esoteric world-centre' of 'ethically positive forces' which manifests itself through phenomena known as Manisolas. Unlike the German 'disk-planes', the Manisolas are 'bio-machines' that materialise as 'disks' which, by night, 'shine in glowing or glossy colours, showing on occasion long flames at the edges and red and blue sparks, which can grow so strong as to wreathe them in fire'; by day they 'display an extremely bright gold or silver luminescence, sometimes with traces of rose-coloured smoke which then often condense into greyish-white trails'.

The rest of Landig's novel is taken up with the heroes' physical and philosophical adventures as they leave the underground polar base to travel the world and spread the Aryan gospel of Thule. In the course of this epic saga, Landig concocts a battle between Thule and Israel - between the 'white' Aryans and the 'dark' Jews - while also constructing an intricate whitewashing of the Nazis. These include the now familiar claim that the shocking pictures of piled-up, emaciated bodies in concentration camps were actually the stripped victims of Allied bombing raids being used for Allied propaganda purposes.

The combination of flying saucers and Aryan supremacy are not the only common denominators between the two authors. In Landig's 'Aryan' novel, his two German airmen are tasked with preventing the V7 flying saucer and its technology from falling into Russian or American hands in the face of the Allied advance. In Zundl's supposedly factual books, he has the German flying saucers destroyed in the BMW plant at Prague just before the plant was captured by the Russians.

In fact, the only real difference between the plot of Landig's novel and Zundl's Nazi-Antarctic UFO books is that Zundl changes his location from the North Pole to the Antarctic.

Like Landig, Zundl uses the Antarctic-Nazi-UFO fantasy to exaggerate the Nazi 'genius' in all things military and technological whilst simultaneously denying the true horrors of the Nazis' supposed great achievements during World War II. Zundl, however, also uses information culled from a wide variety of articles published in European and South American magazines. These articles are, in turn, based on some rather intriguing facts relating to Nazis, Argentina, and the Antarctic in the immediate post-war months.

Submarine *U-977*, under the command of Captain Hans Schaeffer, certainly put out of Kiel harbour in the Baltic Sea on 25 April 1945, stopped in at Christiansand South on 26 April, left there the following day, and was not seen again until it surfaced at Mar Del Plata, Argentina, on 17 August - a period of nearly four months. We will now never know whether or not Schaeffer carried someone of 'political importance' in his submarine; nor will we ever find out why Allied Intelligence were so concerned about what the submarine might have been carrying or why they crewed it all the way back to the United States, only to blow it to smithereens. However, regarding that particular, epic voyage, it is certainly worth noting that Schaeffer had spent much of his career as submarine captain protecting the rocket research centres at Regen and Peenemünde, that he was particularly experienced at patrolling the South Atlantic and polar regions, and that he was one of a select group of naval officers who had been sent to the Harz Mountains to study the highly advanced XX1 electric submarines. (While there, he heard many rumours about imminent 'death rays' and other Nazi secret weapons.) In other words, Schaeffer was not only a man familiar with the secret projects of the Harz Mountains and Thuringia, but also one ideally suited to make the voyage to Antarctica.

Could Nazi scientists, soldiers, even slave-labour and valuable equipment have been taken to Antarctica in German submarines of that period? They could: a great number of passengers and a considerable amount of equipment could have been shipped in many submarines, in the course of many voyages, over a period of years, throughout World War II, when other Nazi boats and submarines were protecting the South Atlantic coastline of Antarctica. It is also worth noting that the normal U-boat could cover 7,000 miles on each operational cruise. Also, the Germans had submarine tankers spread across the South Atlantic Ocean at least as far as south of South Africa, and any one of those tankers, which had a displacement of 2,000 tons, could have supplied ten U-boats with fuel and stores, thus trebling the time that those submarines could stay at sea.

It would also have been possible for the Germans to

build self-sufficient underground research factories in Neu Schwabenland or other areas of Antarctica, as the Antarctic continent has many unexplored, ice-free areas, many of which are well hidden from view by vast ice sheets and mountains. Given the German genius for the construction of immense underground production plants and factories, it is not inconceivable that they could have done so in the Antarctic, using their own architects, builders, troops and captured labour. Indeed, most of the underground research centres of Nazi Germany were gigantic feats of construction, containing air-shafts, wind-tunnels, machine-shops, assembly plants, launching pads, supply dumps, accommodation for all who worked there, and adjoining camps for the slave workers - yet few German civilians knew that they existed.

As an example of the immensity of some of those hidden factories, Philip Henshall informs us, in *Hitler's Rocket Sites* (1985) that the wind tunnel at Peenemünde was then the most advanced in the world, containing its own research department, instrumentation laboratory, workshops and design office. Though the wind tunnel was undoubtedly the showpiece of the research complex, the full enormity of Peenemünde can only be gauged from the fact that apart from the wind tunnel, it also had 'its own power station, docks, oxygen plant, airfield, POW camp for specially selected prisoners who provided cheap labour, and social and medical facilities associated with a town of 20,000 inhabitants'. It was, therefore, the prototype for the even larger, mostly underground, factories to be built secretly in the mountainous ranges of Germany and Austria, notably at Nordhausen in the southern Harz mountain range of Thuringia.

This immense facility consisted of a series of linked tunnels carved out of the Kohnstein Mountain near the town of Nordhausen. The parallel tunnels were 1,800 metres long. Leading off them were fifty side-chambers, a main work area of 125,000 square metres, and twelve ventilation shafts which had been bored down from the peak of the mountain. Work at converting the tunnels into a mass-production facility for rockets began in September 1943 with the use of 2000 engineers and 15,000 inmates from the nearby concentration camps. The slaves were kept in a separate camp located in a hidden mountain valley, less than a kilometre from the entrance to the tunnel. A new underground complex, to be linked to Nordhausen by another network of tunnels, was in the process of being built underground near the town of Bleicherode, twenty kilometres away, though it was not completed by the end of the war.

Known as the Nordhausen Central Works, the facility was placed under the command of Brigadier Hans Kammler, then head of building construction for the SS and later to be placed in charge of the V-2 rocket launchings against London. Similar large underground production plants were created at Wittringen, in the Saar, and near Liège.

Between them, Nordhausen and Bleicherode constituted the first of the SS underground factories - virtually living towns -and what the Nazis were doing there, under the earth, they also hoped to do elsewhere, including Antarctica.

Could the Germans have built such enduring structures

underground? Almost certainly. A measure of their ability to do so may be gleaned from a glance at the statistics regarding the V-2 rocket launching site found near the forest of Eperlecques, three miles north of the village of Watten, on the canal network between the sea and the Belgium border. The reception area was housed in a gigantic concrete bunker that contained offices and accommodation for staff. The railway station had a five-foot thick roof. The launch-control tower for the rockets was approximately sixty-three feet by seventy-three feet and fifteen feet high. The enormous main building had been constructed from reinforced concrete and was 300 feet long, 138 feet wide, and had work levels 260 feet below ground; its roof was eighty feet high and made from twenty-three-foot-thick reinforced concrete. Theoretically speaking, to pierce it would have required a bomb weighing about twelve tons and striking the ceiling at a speed of Mach 1, the speed of sound. In order to construct this towering, bomb-proof edifice, the Germans needed 49,000 tons of steel and concrete for the roof alone. Hundreds of jacks were used to raise the roof slowly, inches at a time, with the walls being built up beneath it, as it was raised. The enormous amounts of steel, cement, sand and gravel needed were brought in from Watten on a standard gauge railway. The site took six months to construct and used about 35,000 slave workers, who came from the two prison camps located about a mile-and-a-half away. At any one time there were always 3000-4000 men at work. The work went on around the clock in twelve-hour shifts, and the slave labour, or *Sklavenarbeiter*, were controlled by armed members of the black-shirted SS

Totenkopfverbande, who had no hesitation in executing anyone too ill or exhausted to work.

It is clear from these examples that the Nazis were well skilled in constructing enormous structures, many located underground, with the help of slave labour. It is therefore possible that men and materials were shipped to the Antarctic throughout the war years; that during the same period the Germans could have been engaged in the building of enormous underground complexes in Neu Schwabenland similar to those in the southern Harz mountain range of Thuringia; and that the Soviet, US and British 'cover-up' regarding saucer sightings could be due to the fact that the Germans are still entrenched there in a master-slave colony devoted to highly advanced, aggressive technology.

The hypothesis of a hidden colony of the elite of Himmler's SS defying the combined might of Russia, the US, and other countries that have political and scientific interests in the Antarctic is interesting, but not the only possibility. While it is true that the Germans were involved in flying saucer construction programs during World War II, it is also a fact that the Canadians and Americans (despite official denials), perhaps with the support of the British, were engaged in similar projects, based on the captured German technology, with the aid of German scientists and engineers.

We know that at the completion of Rear-Admiral Byrd's Operation Highjump, the US inexplicably stayed out of Antarctica for a decade. We also know that during this period the US-Canada flying saucer construction projects came to light and were being considered for use in sub-arctic and polar regions. We know, further, that despite the so-called 'Cold War', the US, the USSR, and many other nations worked together, for a common cause, during the International Geophysical Year (NYG) of 1957-58. During that period of unprecedented, international, scientific cooperation, the main focus was on Antarctica and outer space, including the study of the magnetic field and the ionosphere.

These facts raise the possibility that the unique international cooperation still extant in Antarctica (and possibly elsewhere) is due to the need to protect an ongoing technology that has already moved well beyond an ethically acceptable state of advancement. As we have seen, the Nazis paved the way for morally unimpeded physical experimentation on human beings; and modern science, in the shape of bio-cybernetic and genetic engineering experimentation, has shown itself willing and able to continue down this nightmarish path. If the desire for such experimentation is so great that legal, ethical and religious restraints must be ignored, that work would have to be, and could be, carried out in secret, in Antarctic, Siberia, the White Sands Proving Ground, or even in establishments hidden in the wilds of Canada.

It is to be assumed that a technology capable of creating the UFOs would also be highly advanced in other areas of experimentation, including bio-engineering and similar sciences of a nightmarish nature. If this is the case, there would be very good reason for keeping the results of such work, both scientific and medical, well hidden from the eyes of the world.

Russia (formerly part of the Soviet Union) has many defence and scientific establishments hidden underground, such as the immense laboratory at Semipalatinsk and others located in the desolate wastes of Siberia. The North American Air Defence Command (NORAD) is a top-secret complex of awesome proportions hidden inside the snowcapped Cheyenne Mountain near Colorado Springs, with parts of it a half-mile below the ground. During the war against Iraq in 1990 we learnt that beneath the streets of Baghdad are cavernous nuclear bunkers and enough command shelters and barracks to house thousands of Saddam Hussein's imperial guards. US Intelligence believes that the tunnels between the various complexes run for miles. Each complex is capable of holding 1200 people and has command posts, sick bays, sleeping accommodations, decontamination units, armouries, kitchens, and stores for dried food and water. Theoretically, there is enough space for nearly 50,000 people and the bunkers are covered, like the World War II German bunkers and underground factories, by enormously thick reinforced detonator slabs capable of withstanding the blast of 500lb bombs. Clearly, then, the construction of such complexes underground, in Antarctica or elsewhere, would present no major obstacles in this day and age.

Since the end of World War II, the *known* science and technology has made advances so astonishing that it is virtually in the realms of science fiction. If saucer-shaped aircraft were being developed that long ago and have continued to be developed in secret, behind closed doors, or underground, right up to the present day, they could now be extraordinarily advanced machines, being constructed, maintained and supported in hidden locations by a mixture of human scientists, cyborgs, and other highly advanced man-machine products of a morally unrestrained, nightmarish technology.

Could such a massive undertaking be kept hidden for so long? The short answer is: 'Yes'. There has been no attempt to keep the flying saucers secret - only to keep the *technology* a mystery... and to humiliate, confuse, or terrify into silence those who have reported seeing the UFOs. Also, one can point to the fact that some of science's most startling discoveries were kept under wraps for as long as fifty years. Antibiotics were discovered in 1910, but not applied until 1940. Likewise, nuclear energy was discovered in 1919, but the general public was not informed about it until 1965. In short, no matter how big the secret, it could be protected for years.

We have only to think of the extraordinary innovations in today's science and technology, then recall that such miracles are merely the tip of the iceberg and that what goes on behind the guarded fences of our top-secret establishments is probably decades ahead of what we know about from official statements. Given this, the speed and capability of the UFOs are not beyond the bounds of possibility. Nor is it beyond reason that the UFOs rumoured to have landed on various military bases, both here and abroad, are the products of military-scientific projects so secret that only the personnel involved know about them.

The technology that began with the liquid-fuelled

rockets of Robert H. Goddard in the 1930s, was adapted by the Nazis during World War II, and became the foundation of aerospace travel. It still continues and will not be stopped. The known capabilities of the F-117a Stealth night-fighter and the estimated capabilities of its likely successor, the Aurora, suggest that man-made craft are now the equal of those once reported only as UFOs. Parallel with this are the advances being made in transplant operations, plastic surgery, cloning and other forms of genetic engineering.

Most of this work takes place behind closed doors, but as all scientific, surgical and technological achievements are superseded and made public eventually, we might, in time, learn the truth.

Afterword

The here and now...

The technology described in the original *Projekt UFO*, much of it black technology, is still ongoing behind closed doors and cannot be stopped. The F-117a Nighthawk, or Stealth night-fighter, has already been superseded by the triangular-shaped B-2 Spirit bomber, designed and built for the Pentagon by Northrop. While most aspects of the B-2 remain secret, it is reportedly the world's most expensive aircraft and no less than *900* new materials and processes were developed to build it. Because of its 3-D computer-aided design and manufacture (CAD/CAM), it is the first aircraft in history to go from the drawing board to manufacture without the need for a prototype. The exact nature of its coating is still classified, but it is known to have been largely made from lightweight composites that render it invisible to radar and equally hard to detect with infrared, acoustic, electromagnetic and visual sensors. Requiring only a two-man crew, the B-2 is capable of flying for 6000 miles without refueling, at an altitude of 50,000 feet, with a top speed described by the Pentagon as 'high subsonic'. This makes it seem remarkably similar to the man-made flying saucers described in this book.

Perhaps the most legendary of them all is the Aurora, rumored to be another successor to the B-2. Though the existence of the Aurora has always been denied by the relevant authorities (and was categorically denied by

Donald Rice, Secretary of the Air Force, in December 1992), it has been the focus of intense interest since its name first appeared in a US P-1, or procurement budget document, in 1985, listed directly below the SR-71 Blackbird and the U-2. Interest increased dramatically when the budget for Aurora for 1987 jumped abruptly from $8 million to 2.3 *billion.* Yet the following year the Aurora vanished entirely from the P-1, never to return again. Naturally this gave rise to even more speculation about the supposed aircraft's importance in the world of deep black technology.

Numerous reports in the aviation press and national newspapers claimed that the Aurora, approximately 115 feet long, 65 feet wide, 19 feet high, with short, swept-back wings, had a bat-like, or wedge-shaped, appearance when viewed from one angle, a saucer-shape when viewed from another. It was believed to have one of four possible propulsion systems: Pulse Detonation Wave Engine, Ramjet, Scramjet, or regular Pulsejet. It could fly as fast as Mach 8, reaching anywhere on Earth in three hours.

In 1989, an oil-drilling engineer, Chris Gibson, also a member of the Royal Observer Corps, when working on an oil rig in the North Sea, saw what he believed might have been the Aurora refueling with a KC-135 Stratotanker and two F-111s. Certainly the drawing he did of the unusual airplane fitted the bill. During the same period, as reported in the first edition of *Projekt UFO*, there were numerous sightings of an unknown delta-shaped, supersonic aircraft flying in and out of RAF Machrihanish, located at the tip of the Mull of Kintyre, Scotland, jointly owned by the United States, and one of the most secret NATO air bases in

Europe.

Belief in the existence of the Aurora increased when, in March 1990, despite having smashed the official air speed record from Los Angeles to Washington's Dulles Airport, the SR-71 Blackbird was inexplicably dropped by the Air Force. This instantly led to a widespread belief that the still top secret Aurora was taking its place.

That same year, a series of unusual sonic booms, resembling what the locals referred to as 'skyquakes', were recorded by at least twenty-five US Geological Survey sensors over Los Angeles and central California. To at least one seismologist, Jim Mori, the low rumbling sounds of the skyquakes suggested the sonic booms of an aircraft returning from an altitude of about 10,000 feet, or even from space. The general direction of the rumbling indicated that such an aircraft would be heading towards the test ranges in Nevada, where the top-secret Groom Lake (Area 51) test site is located.

During the period covered by the skyquakes, there were many sightings of a wedge-shaped, or triangular, seemingly supersonic airplane with short, sweptback wings, over California and Nevada, including Groom Lake. Nevertheless, while the sightings continued for many years, the authorities continued to categorically deny the existence of the Aurora. And though there were rumors to the affect that the plane had been canceled in 1986, there are many who believe that it still exists and is still operational, possibly as an unmanned, robotic craft. 'Aurora', some say, is an acronym for 'Automatic Retrieval Of Remotely Piloted Aircraft'.

So the Aurora at least exists as the most legendary

UFO, or flying saucer, of them all.

Definitely in operation is Northrop-Grumman's X-47 Pegasus UAV (unmanned aerial vehicle). This was rolled out on 1 July 2001 and flown for the first time in February 2003. A scaled-down version (27.9 feet long, 27.8 feet wing-span) of the B-2 Spirit, it looks remarkably like a flying saucer even when stationary, preparing for take-off from its aircraft carrier. Its successor, the X-47B, is expected to take its initial flight this year (2007).

Another man-made flying saucer look-alike is the LoFlyte, the product of joint research by NASA and the US Air Force. Described as triangular, wedge-shaped or resembling a 'flying manta ray', the LoFlyte has a 'waverider' design (first proposed by a British scientist, Terrence Nonweiler, in the early 1950s) that prevents air building up in front of it and slowing it down; instead, using flight-control software, it 'surfs' on a stream of air by wrapping the shock-wave generated by the high speed around the fuselage while trapping a cushion of air below it; thus, while in flight, it meets with no resistance and can attain speculative speeds of up to 3000mph. This seems very much like an extension of the 'boundary layer' theories proposed twelve years ago in *Projekt UFO*.

Beginning in 1990, there was a whole spate of unexplained reports of flat, wedge-shaped objects seen by pilots near air force bases in California and even as far afield as Belgium. Indeed, in Belgium there were over 2,000 sightings in a single year. In at least one instance, when two F-16 aircraft from the Belgian Air Force were sent to intercept a UFO; the resultant radar tapes showed a triangular shape descending from 10,000 feet to 500 feet in five seconds, indicating a speed of 2000mph. More dangerously, in 1995 a British Boeing 737 flying from Milan to Manchester was involved in a near-collision with a triangular UFO over the Pennines. The UFO was going so fast that the air crew ducked as it passed within feet of their aircraft - yet radar operators on the ground were unable to track it. When the crew of the 737, Captain Roger Willis and First Officer Mark Stuart, filed an official 'air near miss' report, the sketches they made of the mystery aircraft looked just like a wedge-shaped waverider. Regarding the remarkably high speed of the UFO, the waverider design of the Loflyte is said to be so fast that computer software (designed by the Accurate Automation Corporation of Chatanooga) is needed to *teach the aircraft to fly itself*, after basic instruction from a pilot.

Given the nature of black technology (by the time an aircraft has been shown to the public, it has already been superseded behind closed doors) the public showings of the B-2 Spirit and the LoFlyte, which took place in the mid-1990s, are sure indications that even more advanced aircraft are already on the way. Said John Pike, director of space policy at the Washington-based Federation of American Scientists: 'The public showing of the LoFlyte vehicle is very odd. It leads me to the conclusion that there may well be classified work going on.'

Yes, there certainly was. Another flying-saucer-shaped prototype of the UAV variety was the DarkStar, America's latest spy plane. Fifteen feet long, sixty-nine feet wide, a mere five feet high, it was designed to carry the most advanced infrared and electro-optical spy cameras available, capable of taking pictures down to a resolution of one square foot, night or day. Again, that new prototype was constructed from 'lightweight, radar-absorbent materials' that would render it virtually 'invisible'. The second DarkStar, which looks even more like a flying saucer, completed its first test flight on 29 June 1998, taking off from the US Air Force Test Flight Center at Edwards AFB, California.

Not dissimilar is Lockheed Martin's unmanned, preprogrammed Venture Star, planned as a hypersonic reusable launch vehicle (RLV) and, again, shaped like a wingless 'wedge' or a 'flying manta ray'. The prototype was being built in 1996 at Lockheed Martin's legendary Skunk Works in California, for decades the birthplace of advanced and often highly secret aircraft; also an area renowned for its many UFO sightings.

Finally, in a 2003 report submitted to the President of the US by the Commission on the Future of the United States Aerospace Industry, it was stated: 'In the nearer term, nuclear fission and plasma sources should be actively pursued for space applications. In the longer-term, breakthroughs that *go beyond our current understanding of physical laws* [author's emphasis] such as nuclear fusion and antimatter, should be investigated in order for us to practically pursue human exploration of the solar system and beyond.' Clearly, therefore, this is where black technology is presently headed.

Further to such research, experimental work on a wide variety of special lightweight and radar-absorbent materials has certainly been going on and is related frequently to saucer-shaped designs. On 17 February 1996, *New Scientist* ran an article with the subheading: 'Hypersonic flying saucers driven by microwaves; not science fantasy but the goal of serious researchers in the US.' The article ('Rider on the Shock Wave', by freelance writer Mike Ross) described experiments taking place in the engineering laboratories of the Rensselaer Polytechnic Institute in Troy, New York State. The experiments required the use of 'one of the few wind tunnels in the world that can produce shock waves at more than twenty-five times the speed of sound' and were designed to test an 'air spike': a device that would control the airflow around an aircraft, reduce drag to a bare minimum, and enable it to travel at many times the speed of sound while greatly reducing the temperature of its skin to the degree where it would require no thermal protection. The men behind the air spike were Leik Myrabo, an aerospace engineer at Rensselaer, and Yuri Raizer, a plasma physicist at the Moscow-based Institute for Problems in Mechanics, both working on funding from the Space Studies Institute in Princetown, New Jersey. Myrabo and Raizer were keen on 'saucer shaped' prototypes. By 1996 they were planning to make detailed measurements of the pressure and heat transfer around 'a disk' protected by an air spike as it sat in a flow of air traveling at up to twenty-five times the speed of sound. Myrabo's stated belief was that if the air spike could be made to work at that velocity, it could lead to 'a revolutionary new generation of lightweight, reusable launch vehicles that would resemble flying saucers and get their power from beams of microwaves or lasers.' In pursuit of this dream, he had already designed a new type of vehicle that was called a 'lightcraft' and 'shaped like a flying saucer'. He had also envisaged 'a system in which constellations of orbiting satellites would convert solar power into microwaves and beam them downwards to a lightcraft below. The lightcraft must have a large surface area to gather as much microwave power as possible, so a flying saucer shape is ideal.'

Other innovations relating to the kind of technology first mentioned in *Projekt UFO* (brain implants, thought transference, human and animal mutations, the 'invisibility' of advanced aircraft, magical metals such as *Luftschwamm*, or aero-sponge, and Nitinol, a 'metal with a memory') have been progressing at a rapid clip. There isn't enough space here to cover all the new innovations in detail, but here are a few random samples.

Regarding the 'magic metals' and 'invisible' metal surfaces, according to *Der Spiegel*, by 2002 a ceramic research laboratory in Dresden, Germany, had developed aluminum that was three times tougher than hardened steel of the same thickness – and *transparent*. In the same vein, 'cold plasma' research presently being undertaken by research groups at Stanford, Princeton, Ohio State, Wisconsin and New York Polytechnic has the aim of shielding satellites and 'other spacecraft' by making them invisible to radar. Cold plasmas – analogs to the sophisticated defensive grids, or deflector shields, on the fictional *Star Trek*'s USS *Voyager* spacecraft – are ambient-temperature, ionized gases related to those found deep within the sun's core. Such plasmas could not only make spacecraft invisible to radar, but could also prevent the frying of electronics or the melting of metal at above-supersonic speeds. Since in theory a plasma could deflect a particle-beam or laser attack, the US Air Force has allocated millions of dollars to low-temperature plasma studies with a view to protecting their space satellites.

As recently as 19 August 2007, journalist Peter Stothard was writing in the *Sunday Times* about 'a miracle material for the 21st century'. The new material is Aerogel. Though described as 'one of the world's lightest solids' (so light, indeed, that it is nicknamed 'frozen smoke'), Aerogel can withstand dynamite blasts and protect against heat of more than 1,300C. No surprise, then, that it is already being tested for bomb-proof housing and armour for military vehicles. No surprise, either, that NASA is already using it in the development of insulated space suits for the first manned mission to Mars (scheduled for 2018), where hopefully it will protect astronauts from temperatures as low as -130C. As Aerogel has also been described by scientists as 'the ultimate sponge', with millions of tiny pores on its surface, its resemblance to *Luftschwamm* would make it even more valuable as a material for future black-technology aircraft.

Regarding thought transference, by the late 1990's the Institute of Medical Psychology in Tubingen, near Stuttgart in Germany, was engaged in experiments that proved that human beings could *think* images on a screen into moving in any direction they chose. The experiments were part of a program aimed at giving humans, possibly aided with microchip implantation, the power to control machines through thought alone. Military and commercial applications included, for instance, giving pilots the ability to fly aircraft and fire missiles by 'electronic telepathy', thus obviating the need for manual controls. The theoretical work on which the 'chip grafting' was being based was conducted by a group led by Greg Kovacs, professor of electrical engineering at Stanford University, California. It was mainly concerned with 'creating an interface between micro-electronics and the nervous system'. By 1995, the team had 'learned how to fuse the device [the microchip] with nerve endings'. Among those reported to be keen on developing the technology was the Defence Research Agency in Farnborough, Hampshire, formerly part of the Ministry of Defence. The agency's main interest was in 'the operation of machines by mental control'.

Even as far back as 1995, the British Medical Association (BMA) was expressing concern at 'how far the field has advanced'. A BMA ethics committee, set up to discuss the issue, was particularly concerned with the potential uses of microchip technology implanted in humans. Said Simon Davies, a legal expert and consultant to the BMA: 'Big Brother is here and we never saw him coming.' Who knows where such experiments, undertaken behind closed doors, have led since then?

Regarding human and animal mutations, the horrors mentioned in *Projekt UFO* have by now become almost routine. The Brave New Science of transgenics (taking sequences of DNA and either altering them and putting them back into the same species or, more controversially, introducing them into a different species) has in recent years moved away from purely animal experimentation into the human arena, with the planning of mutated and cloned human beings well on the way. Meanwhile, the scientific and commercial trade in human body parts, which played such a large role in my 'Projekt Saucer' fiction series and this non-fiction addition to it, has now become a major, legal industry, with the Chinese routinely exporting human fetuses for use in 'traditional remedies and health foods' and an American 'supermarket', the International Institute for the Advancement of Medicine (IIAM), selling human body parts, including brains, hearts, spines, liver, appendixes, testicles, knees, elbows (at least seventy-five body parts in all) for so-called 'research' purposes.

It is clear, then, that much of the speculative and documented information given in my bestseller, *Genesis*, published twenty-seven years ago and then expanded in the first edition of *Projekt UFO*, published twelve years ago, has stepped out of the world of fiction and into the realm of hard facts.

Nevertheless, despite these hard facts, the 'extraterrestrial' hypothesis regarding UFOs continues to dominate the media in general and the publishing world in particular. During the 1990s, in a desperate attempt to replace the lurid sensationalism of the early UFO writers (Adamski, Däniken, Palmer, et al), publishers turned to a new breed of writers who could be accepted as 'serious' by lieu of their backgrounds, and who would, therefore, be automatically accorded more respect by a gullible public and media.

Leading the pack was Timothy Good, warmly embraced as a 'serious' UFOlogist because, as every press release reminds us, he was educated at The King's School, Canterbury and was, further, a professional violinist who 'gained a scholarship to the Royal Academy of Music, where he won prizes for solo, chamber and orchestral playing'. While it is difficult to imagine how a career as a professional violinist can lend credibility to the normally suspect study of UFOs, we are constantly reminded by Mr Good's publicity machine that he began his musical career with the Royal Philharmonic Orchestra, remained for fourteen years with the London Symphony Orchestra, played with the likes of Leonard Bernstein, Benjamin Britten, Igor Stravinsky, William Walton, and has been a session player for such pop luminaries as Paul McCartney, Elton John, Rod Stewart and the late George Harrison.

This distinguished musical background never fails to impress those interviewing Mr Good about UFOs and extraterrestrials. For this reason, he became an instant critical and commercial success with his first book, *Above Top Secret: The Worldwide UFO Cover-up* (1987). He then went on to write more UFO books and to be invited to lecture at 'universities, schools and... many organizations', including the Royal Canadian Military Institute, the Royal Naval Air Reserve Branch, the House of Lords All-Party UFO Study Group, and the Oxford and Cambridge Union societies. He was also invited for discussions at the Pentagon, lectured at the headquarters of the French Air Force, and even acted as a consultant for 'several US Congress investigations'.

Doubtless it was a combination of Good's 'respectable' middle-class background, good education, musical talent and undeniable skill as a public speaker that led to his early UFO books being accorded an unusual degree of respect, being praised in particular for the breadth of their research and the level-headed manner in which he was treating a notoriously controversial subject. Alas, as with most of those who make a full-time career out of UFO writing, Mr Good became ever more desperate to retain his readership and gradually drifted away from cool-headed reporting into the old Whitley Streiber *Communion*-styled claims of UFO abductions and extraterrestrial or 'alien' presences right here on Earth, as the titles of subsequent books clearly indicate: *Alien Bases: Earth's Encounter with Extraterrestrials* (1998) and *Unearthly Disclosure: Conflicting Interests in the Control of Extraterrestrials* (2000). Mr Good, once highly touted as a 'serious' UFO researcher, has by now been reduced to hinting broadly during his lectures and in his more recent books that he, personally, might have been abducted by aliens. He is also selling the idea that the US Government has shrouded the UFO subject in secrecy to protect its 'privileged contact' with the extraterrestrials in our midst. Good's main source of information for this dramatic hypothesis appears to come from accounts passed on by human 'contactees' who have, in turn, received their information from friendly humanoid aliens. No attribution required.

A more recent addition to the 'serious' pack is Nick Pope, whose main claim as a credible UFO researcher and writer is that he spent twenty-one years with the MoD (Britain's Ministry of Defence) and, more importantly, worked for three of those years (1991-94) as the MoD's UFO Desk officer. During that particular period, he researched and investigated: 'UFO sightings, alien abductions, crop circles, animal mutilations and any other weird and wonderful reports that came my way'. Given this supposed wealth of 'official' UFO information, not normally available to the common man, Pope was able to produce his first 'serious' UFO book, *Open Skies, Closed Minds* (1995). Sold with the shout line, 'For the first time a government UFO expert speaks out!', the book successfully launched Pope's career as another UFO writer with a 'credible' background., leading to a secondary 'Timothy Good' styled career as lecturer, documentary film producer, and general UFO pundit on a wide variety of radio and television programs. His writing career continued with a second nonfiction book, *The Uninvited: An Expose of the Alien Abduction Phenomenon* (1997) and two UFO/alien abduction novels. Finally, when the media began comparing Pope's MoD UFO revelations with 'The X-Files', he became widely known as 'the British Fox Mulder'.

In November 2006, emboldened by his success as a writer, lecturer, 'UFO authority' and 'the British Fox Mulder', Pope resigned from the MoD and went on to star in a DVD movie entitled *NICK POPE: The Man who Left the MOD*. In the documentary, he discusses, amongst other things, Russian and Black Technology, the Rendlesham Forest Incident, Quantum Physics, Psychology, and Government reports and sightings by insiders. According to the Reality Films press release, 'Nick Pope is probably one of the best known UFO investigators on the planet. And yet, he is the only official UFO investigator employed by the British Government to ever go on record.'

Alas, as early as 1999, grave doubts were being cast on Pope's actual position within the MoD and on how much of his work at that establishment had actually been related to UFO researches. Starting to suspect that Pope's supposed MoD UFO reports were 'fiction disguised as reality', James Easton, Editor of *Voyager On-line*, wrote to the MoD for clarification regarding the work Pope actually did there.

According to Easton, he received a reply from the Ministry, stating: 'Mr Pope was employed as an Executive Officer in Secretariat (Air Staff) 2… The main duties of the post concern non-operational RAF activities overseas and diplomatic clearance for military flights abroad… A small percentage of time is spent dealing with reports from the public about alleged "UFO" sightings and associated press correspondence… The Ministry of Defence has not investigated a case of alien abduction, crop circle formations or animal mutilation.'

Of course, the fact that the MoD has categorically refuted Mr Pope's high claims regarding his position there does not necessarily mean that the MoD is telling the truth; nevertheless, their clear indication that Mr Pope had not been involved as extensively with UFO sightings as he had claimed caused ripples of discontent in many a UFO circle. Nevertheless, Pope continued to sell himself as the 'British Fox Mulder' of 'serious' UFO investigators and writers. However, just like Timothy Good, he swiftly moved from a position of healthy skepticism about extraterrestrial UFOs to a declared belief in the reality of alien intervention on Earth. And, like Good, he even began hinting, by way of half-hearted denial of 'leaks' to the media, that he had, himself, once been taken aboard a UFO.

According to journalist Mark Macaskill, writing in the *Sunday Times* of 16 February 1999, Pope, during his tenure as the MoD's UFO Desk officer, had gone from skepticism to belief not only because of what he had learned there, but also because he was 'holding back part of the reason for his personal convictions'. The reason, apparently, was that in *The Uninvited*, Pope's second UFO book, his story about the UFO abduction of a couple named 'Peter and Jenny' was actually about himself and his girlfriend of the time. Reportedly, 'Peter and Jenny', while driving along a road in Florida, some time prior to 1992, suddenly found themselves several miles away on a different road. Not being able to account for this seemingly impossible jump from one place to the next, a disturbed Pope later underwent hypnosis and recalled, in the hypnotic state, that he and his girlfriend had been 'lifted into the air' and then taken aboard an alien spacecraft. 'He remembered wandering along its metallic corridors, though he says he doesn't recall meeting any aliens. He now says it was the strangest event of his life.'

While Macaskill didn't say precisely how he knew Pope was actually writing about himself, disguised as 'Peter', and while he made it clear that Pope had neither confirmed nor denied the bizarre story, he *did* state that Pope had fictionalized his real-life experience because he was 'worried about implicating the woman called "Jenny" in the book; a woman who was then, but is no longer, his girlfriend.'

Whether true or false, whether or not Pope had actually given this story to Macaskill, the story offered a platform for Pope's move from skepticism to his apparent belief in the reality of extraterrestrial UFOs and alien abductions. Always a good man with a denial that hints at its opposite, Pope continued to keep his lips sealed about the story of his own abduction by a UFO while frequently implying that the MoD, which had failed to support his claims about the importance of his position with them, was now denying any interest in UFOs or alien abduction reports in order to conceal their own dealings with aliens operating on, or threatening, Earth.

By 2007, though Pope had produced no more UFO books of his own (he only wrote a couple of introductory texts for other UFO authors), he was appearing regularly on television, taking part in numerous radio programs, and lecturing at a wide variety of UFO conventions. By this time, he not only appeared to have moved completely from skepticism to belief, but was even complaining that the MoD UFO project had been 'virtually closed down', leaving the country 'wide open' to the possibility of an alien invasion.

'There has got to be the potential for that,' he was quoted as saying in the *Daily Mail* of 10 November 2006, 'and one is left with the uneasy feeling that if it turned out to be so, there is very little we could do about it.'

Yet despite what Pope and Good say to the contrary, there has not been the slightest hard evidence for extraterrestrial craft landing on Earth or for alien beings interacting with humans. It should be noted, however, that the most astounding and perplexing science of the past decade – quantum physics – may have produced the nearest we have come to an explanation for the many seemingly real experiences that thousands of perfectly sane people insist that they have had with UFOs and/or extraterrestrials.

We are reminded by Phil Patton, in his marvelous book, *Dreamland* (Villard, New York, 1998) that some of the world's most respected physicists, in discussing the paradoxes of quantum theory, have raised the possibility of parallel or multiple universes and space-time 'wormholes' that make time-travel a theoretical possibility. Says Patton:

"According to quantum theory, subatomic particles could apparently be in several places at once...Or, more to the point, a subatomic particle that is *here* in one universe might be *there* in its neighbor." Given this scenario, it is not beyond the bounds of probability that the more extreme or 'dreamlike' UFO sightings and extraterrestrial 'contactee' experiences could be, in the words of UFO photographer Kathleen Ford, confrontations with 'interdimensional entities', or, in Patton's words, 'creatures from other realms of space-time'. If this idea seems far-fetched, it has, as Patton says, 'roots in mainstream physics' and it certainly has, indeed, been presented as a viable proposition by the reputable physicists David Deutsch and Fred Alan Wolf. In *The Fabric of Reality: The Science of Parallel Universes – And Its Implications*, (Allen Lane/Penguin, 1997), Deutsch speculates that all of twentieth-century physics points to parallel universes. In *Parallel Universes* (Touchtone/Simon & Schuster, 1988), Wolf speculates that parallel universes could be the source of dreams, visions, schizophrenia, and... UFO sightings.

So the countless cases of normal people recollecting UFO/extraterrestrial experiences could be explainable within the scientifically possible, albeit bizarre, parameters of quantum physics, rather than proving that flying saucers, piloted by aliens, have landed on Earth.

Interestingly enough, the most recent attempt to make UFO writing 'serious' and 'respectable' came in the form of the only book, apart from my own, to suggest that UFO sightings might be related to experimental man-made craft. *The Hunt for Zero Point* (2002) received a lot of publicity because it was written by Nick Cook, Aviation Editor for the 'esteemed' *Jane's Defense Weekly*, the bible of the defense establishment and highly respected for its 'no-nonsense, nuts-and-bolts' reporting. Subtitled, 'Inside the Classified World of Antigravity Technology' Cook's book treats as a totally new concept the possibility that the US Government confiscated secret Nazi anti-gravity technology at the end of World War II and later may have tested it in experimental aircraft. Some of that technology, Cook claims, probably made its way into the B-2 Stealth bomber and may account for the rash of post-war UFO sightings.

I have to confess that I took great personal offense at this book, particularly when one reviewer wrote: 'So even if Nazi flying saucers sound nutty on the face of it, there's nothing crazy about Cook asking the questions he does. You might even call it courageous.'

Courageous? In fact, the spinal column of Cook's book was almost certainly formed from information to be found in my bestselling novel, *Genesis*, first published way back in 1980, in my World War II 'Nazi UFO' novel, *Inception*, published in 1991, and in the first edition of my nonfiction work, *Projekt UFO*, first published in 1995. Certain of Mr Cook's supposedly original ideas can also be found scattered throughout my five-volume 'Projekt Saucer' fictional series, published between 1991 and 1999. (*Inception*, *Phoenix*, *Genesis*, *Millennium*, *Resurrection*.) As for SS General Hans Kammler's involvement with Nazi flying-saucer construction projects and the US Navy's involvement with their own flying saucer research programs – both of which Mr Cook breathlessly claims to be his own discovery – they were in fact first brought to public attention through two of the above mentioned books, namely *Genesis* and *Inception*.

Even more offensive to me was the way in which Mr Cook, while selling his book as a serious technical study of the dubious evolution of workable anti-gravity programs based on Nazi technology, writes not in the cool, objective tone of a former *Jane's Defense Weekly* Aviation Editor, but in the breathless style of a second-rate thriller writer. Thus, when his 'research' first leads him to the knowledge that the SS was in charge of the most secret Nazi technology (as first revealed by this author nearly thirty years ago), Cook feels 'a constriction in my throat. I was so keyed, my breath was coming in short, sharp gasps.'

More likely he was simply breathless from reading my novels and factual book, none of which were credited in the main text of his supposedly original tome, though the original edition of *Projekt UFO* was at least listed in his bibliography.

However, personal gripes aside, *The Hunt for Zero Point* can be credited with bringing the possibility of man-made UFOs and other secrets of black research programs back to public attention after all these years, particularly with regard to the still problematical anti-gravity programs.

Rereading *Projekt UFO* twelve years on, I find myself still harboring doubts about certain aspects of it, notably the speculative underground colonies in the Antarctic (though they were certainly *physically* possible and anything *is* possible); but in the main I am struck by how accurate, not to say prophetic, most of the factual material, though considered speculative at the time, has turned out to be.

While the possibility of underground Antarctic UFO research facilities remains problematical, there can be no doubt that similar facilities, many of them vast, all of them highly secretive and dedicated to black technology, including the creation of bizarrely-shaped experimental aircraft, exist in a wide variety of known or rumored locations. Such top-secret facilities are to be found in Dulce and White Sands, both in New Mexico, in Tehachapi (known as 'the Anthill') and Helendale, both in California, and even in Bascombe Down, in the UK. While the American sites, in particular, have been widely credited with harboring aliens, or 'humanoid aliens', engaged in highly advanced technological experiments, including the surgical mutation of abducted human beings, the most famous site of all, Area 51, is more realistically recognized as the very hub of America's black technology.

Also known as Groom Lake, Dreamland, Paradise Ranch, and Home Base, Area 51 consists of approximately 4,742 square miles of restricted airspace and nearly four million acres of bomb range located in the Emigrant Valley of southern Nevada, close to Las Vegas, hemmed in by the Nellis Air Force Range and the Nevada Test Site, in an area of parched, windblown desert and lunar-like dry lakes. For years its very existence was denied by the US Government, but it came to the attention of the public in 1962, when the first Soviet spy satellite began orbiting Earth. Shortly after this momentous, threatening event, the existence of the fabled supersonic AF-12 Blackbird fighter, frequently observed flying over Area 51, was officially acknowledged as a desperately needed US propaganda exercise.

Nevertheless, Area 51 remains an area so secret that

unwanted visitors are warned off with signs stating, '*Deadly force authorized and photography prohibited.*' Helicopters routinely sweep its borders to either sandblast intruders with the downwash from their rotors or pick them up and arrest them. Indeed, it is an area so secret that even the fighter pilots flying in and out of nearby Nellis Air Force Base are forbidden to enter its airspace. Because of this extraordinary security, the area is one of particular fascination for those interested in black or 'stealth' technology. That interest grew phenomenally when one Bob Lazer, a man with a seriously checkered background, known to some as a professional con artist, claimed that he had seen and worked on flying saucers in an area known as S-4, at Papoose Lake, south of Groom Lake. However, even as the hordes of sky-watchers who then swarmed to the area were seeing 'mysterious lights' and UFOs, it became clear that Area 51 was in fact the top-secret, black technology site where the SR-71 Blackbird, and, most famously, the triangular F-117 Stealth fighter plane (both of which were often mistaken for flying saucers or, at least, triangular-shaped UFOs) were first constructed and flown. It was also the site most often mentioned in regard to the highly speculative Aurora and Black Manta prototypes. At the very least, it was, in the words of one sky-watcher, the place where 'we are testing vehicles that defy description, things so far beyond comprehension as to be really alien to our way of thinking.'

'UFO' is an acronym for Unidentified Flying Object(s) and many of the experimental craft observed over Area 51 were definitely of unusual, even bizarre, configuration, including shapes that resembled flying saucers. The bat-shaped F-117 Stealth fighter was certainly such a craft and its rumored successor, the Aurora, had, as we have noted above, a similarly unorthodox appearance. Thus, while its existence was being officially denied, the Aurora, when sighted by sky-watchers during a test flight, would have justifiably been described as a UFO.

And it has to be repeated that despite the 'extraterrestrial' or 'alien' theories put about by writers such as those mentioned above, the UFO sightings of the period covered by *Projekt UFO* were almost certainly caused, not by alien spacecraft, but by the experimental aircraft that preceded the supersonic, 'radar invisible' Stealth fighters, the 'otherworldly'-shaped UAVs (no cockpits, no windows, no wings or fins; bat-shaped, saucer-shaped or doughnut-shaped), and the even more contemporary prototypes mentioned at the beginning of this introduction: the secret products of an ongoing black technology.

Even the Roswell Incident of fifty years ago, which could reasonably be said to have started the UFO age (along with the Kenneth Arnold sightings of the previous month), can now be attributed to the early days of black technology. While that particular incident has spawned more than three dozen books, hundreds of television documentaries or program segments, thousands of pages of press speculation, serious accusations of a massive and far-reaching government conspiracy, at least one complex hoax (the Ray Santilli 'alien autopsy' film) and a made-for-TV movie, no definite confirmation for what crashed in Roswell, New Mexico, on 7 July 1947, has so far come to light. Yet an increasing body of evidence supports the theory that it was some kind of man-made flying device.

Over the years, various kinds of balloons have been suggested, with the official explanation changing at least two times. First, as recounted in *Projekt UFO*, the military claimed that what crashed was a Rawin weather balloon – but a simple weather balloon could not account for the kind of debris reportedly found at the crash site. Next, on 8 September 1994, following pressure from Congressman Steven Schiff of New Mexico, the US Air Force issued an official statement that laid the blame on a 'high altitude' balloon of the kind used in a secret program known as Project Mogul. This may, indeed, have been the case.

Project Mogul's task was to detect Soviet nuclear tests by using sensitive instruments carried aloft by high-altitude balloons. Some of those balloons were launched from the Roswell Army Air Field.

According to Professor Charles B. Moore, then working at the Langmuir Laboratory for Atmospheric Research in Socorro, New Mexico, and the man in charge of balloon launches in the Roswell area, the Mogul balloons carried a new kind of monitoring instrument, designated the ML-306. The device utilized aluminum foil and wax paper, with balsa-wood beams and reinforcement tapes that were painted with various markings. Those markings, probably scientific symbols, were described by Air Force Major Jesse A. Marcel, placed in charge of the crash debris, as 'hieroglyphics'. (Marcel's unfortunate use of that word, so suggestive of mysterious races – as well as his growing conviction that what had crashed was not of this world – was almost certainly influenced by Kenneth Arnold's sensational UFO sightings of the previous month. Thus, the 'hieroglyphics' were soon taken up by cultists as the letters of 'extraterrestrial' or 'alien' writing.) Also, Professor Moore insists that the Mogul balloons used for that particular project were made from neoprene, instead of the customary polyethylene. When the cluster of balloons expanded at high altitude and then burst, falling back to earth, Mac Brazel, the rancher who found the wreckage, described the debris as being 'smoky-gray in color'. This, says Professor Moore, is exactly how he personally would have described the color of neoprene balloons that had been stretched, as they would have been at high altitudes.

So the Mogul balloons *might* have been what crashed at Roswell, New Mexico.

However, a more intriguing possibility was raised in the November 2000 issue of *Popular Mechanics*. In an article entitled 'America's Nuclear Flying Saucer', author Jim Wilson recounts that among America's various top-secret projects of the time was an unmanned 40-ft 'flying saucer' designed to rain nuclear destruction on the Soviet Union (now Russia) from 300 miles up in space. Designated the Lenticular Reentry Vehicle (LRV), designed for the US Air Force by engineers at the Los Angeles Division of North American Aviation, and managed by Wright-Patterson Air Force Base in Dayton, Ohio (where German engineers who had worked on Nazi rocket and flying disk projects had been resettled, and over which, at the time, many UFO sightings were made), the LRV could have been powered by one of the nuclear rockets then under development by the Air Force and the Atomic Energy Commission or, as an alternative, lifted into the stratosphere by a 'heavy-lift balloon'. According to the Air Force, such balloons were capable of lifting 15,000-pound payloads to 170,000 feet.

In 1997 the Air Force revealed details of several heavy-lift balloon research projects and stated that during the Cold War it had routinely used them to lift 'unusual airframes' for aerodynamic tests. It should therefore be borne in mind that the test flight of an LRV could, as Jim Wilson reminds us, 'certainly match the classic UFO reports of a silvery disc hovering motionless in the sky, then silently shooting upwards'.

So an LRV of the kind described above could be another explanation for what crashed that fateful day in Roswell, New Mexico.

Either way, if what crashed at Roswell was related to a top-secret aeronautical or defense project, the official response would have been to ensure that the general public did not learn about it. The best way to do that would be the spreading of carefully plotted disinformation. This may explain why, fifty years after the event, the many questions raised by the Roswell crash have never been fully answered.

What we can, however, say with conviction, is that what crashed at Roswell in 1947 was, like most of the other sightings classed as UFOs, almost certainly man-made.

There the case rests.

W.A.Harbinson
West Cork, 2007

Sources

Chariots of the Gods? (Souvenir Press, London, 1969; Corgi, London, 1971) by Erich von Däniken and *The Spaceships of Ezekiel* (Corgi, London, 1974, Bantam, New York, 1979) by J.F. Blumrich, are the two major books on the 'ancient astronaut' hypothesis. A healthy antidote to von Däniken's view of the intelligence of the technocrats of the ancient world is to be found in *Ancient Engineers* (Souvenir Press, London, 1963; Tandem, London, 1977) by L. Sprague de Camp. The most detailed criticisms of von Däniken in particular and the 'ancient astronauts' hypothesis in general are to be found in *Crash Go The Chariots* (Lancer Books, New York, 1972) by Clifford Wilson and *The Space Gods Revealed* (New English Library, London, 1978) by Ronald Story.

The earliest article about the German 'foo fighter' was published in the *South Wales Argus* of December 13, 1944. An Associated Press release by Marshall Yarrow (Reuters special correspondent at Supreme Headquarters, Paris, France) was published in the New York *Herald Tribune* of January 2, 1945. Another article was published in the London *Daily Telegraph*, also on January 2, 1945.

Information about Nazi Germany's 'Projekt Saucer' and related flying saucer projects, including the Flying Flapjack and the Avrocar, or Omega, was found in the following newspaper and magazine articles: 'Untertassen - Flieger Kombination', *Der Spiegel*, March 30, 1950. 'Flying Saucers - The Real Story', *US News & World Report*, Volume XXVIII - No. 14, April 7, 1950. 'Fliegende

Untertasse in Deutschland erfunden', *Sonderbericht der Deutschen Illustrierte*, S.1350, 1951. 'Fliegende Untertassen -eine Deutsche Erfindung', *Die sieben Tage*, No. 26, June 27, 1952. 'Die Deutsche Fliegende Untertasse', *Das Ufer - die Farb-Illustrierte*, No. 18, September 1, 1952. 'Erste Flugscheibe flog 1945 in Prag', *Welt am Sonntag*, April 25, 1953. 'Man Made Flying Saucer', *Royal Air Force Flying Review*, April, 1953. 'The Air Force and the Saucers', an extended article by Dr Leon Davidson, published in two parts in *Saucer News*, New Jersey, February-March and April-May 1956. 'Wunderwaffen 45', *Bild am Sonntag*, February 17, 1957. 'Die UFOs - eine Deutsche Erfindung', *Das neue Zeitalter*, October 5, 1957. 'Flugkreisel, irdisch', *Heim und Welt*, No. 14, April 2, 1959. 'Deutsche UFOs schon 1947/48 einwandfrei beobachtet', *Das neue Zeitalter*, February 6, 1965. 'Deutsche Flugkreisel', *Luftfahrt International*, No. 9, May-June, 1975. 'Mit UFOs zu neuer Gravitationstheorie', *Kurier*, November 20, 1976. 'Biotechnische Schriftenreihe', *Implosion*, 'Biotechnische Schriftenreihe', Vol.No. 25. 'Fliegende Teller statt Hubschrauber', *Hobby*, December 14, 1977. 'The Question Mark Above Our Heads', *Out of This World*, (Editor Perrott Phillips; Gravitic propulsion system designed and drawn by John Batchelor), a Phoebus partwork, Vol 1, 1978. 'Fliegende Scheiben und Viktor Schauberger', *Kosmische Evolution*, No. 4, 1979. 'Prototypen der Kreisflügler AS 6 V 1', *Luftfahrt International*, No. 4/ 1979. 'Nitinol, the Magic Metal', is an uncredited article published in *Science Now*, a Marshall Cavendish partwork, Vol 1, Part 2, 1982. The views of the German physicist Dr Eduard Ludwig were extracted from an undated, declassified Central Intelligence Agency document SO DB 27143, entitled 'The Mystery of the Flying Disks: A Contribution to its possible explanation'.

UFO-related articles by W.A. Harbinson on the 'hollow Earth' theory and Captain Richard E. Byrd's Antarctic expeditions were published in *The Unexplained*, an Orbis partwork, Vol. 2, issues 27 and 28, 1981. Articles by W.A. Harbinson about the man-made UFO were published in *The Unexplained*, Vol. 4, Issues 37 and 38, 1981.

Books on rocket and aircraft development include: *Soviet Rocketry* (David & Charles, Newton Abbot, 1971) by Michael Stoiko. *Robert H. Goddard: Pioneer of Space Research* (De Capo Press, New York, 1988) by Milton Lehman. *The Papers of Robert H. Goddard* (McGraw-Hill, New York, 1970), edited by E.C. Goddard. *The Birth of the Missile: The Secrets of Peenemünde* (Harrap, London, 1965) by E. Klee and O. Merk. *German Guided Missiles* (Ian Allan, London, 1966) by R. F. Pocock. *V2* (Hurst and Blackett, London, 1954) by Walter Dornberger. *Hitler's Last Weapons: The Underground War Against the V1 and V2* (Julian Friedmann, London, 1978) by Jozef Garlinksi. *Hitler's Rocket Sites* (Robert Hale, London, 1985) by Philip Henshall. *Raketon-Flugtechnik* (Edwards Press, Ann Arbor, Michigan 1945; reprint of 1933 edition, published by Oldenbourg of München) by E. Sanger. *Alsos* (Schuman, New York, 1947) by Samuel A. Goudsmit. *From Hiroshima to the Moon* (Simon and Schuster, New York, 1959) by Daniel Lang. *Rockets, Missiles, and Spacecraft of the National Air And Space Museum* (Smithsonian Institution, Washington D.C., 1976/1983) compiled by Gregory P. Kennedy.

The indispensable book on the development of disc-shaped aircraft is *Intercettateli Senza Sparare* (E. Mursia & Co., Milan, Italy, 1968) by Renato Vesco. This was later published in an English translation by Grove Press, New York (1971) under the title *Intercept - But Don't Shoot*, then reissued in 1974 by Zebra Publications, New York, as *Intercept UFO*. Unfortunately it has been out of print for years. *German Jet Genesis* (Janes Information Group, Surrey, 1982) by David Master, contains a section of Projekt Saucer. A short but decent article on Projekt Saucer and related projects is *German Secret Weapons of World War II* (Neville Spearman, London, 1959; the Philosophical Library, New York, 1959) by Major Rudolph Lusar. Most of Lusar's article is reproduced with other German flying-saucer material and considerable wishful thinking in *UFOs: Nazi Secret Weapons?* (Samisdat, Toronto, Canada, undated) by Mattern Friedrich, aka Ernst Zundl.

The most comprehensive studies of the UFO phenomenon as a whole are *The UFO Controversy in America* (Signet, New American Library, New York 1975) by David Michael Jacobs; and *UFO Exist!* (Ballantine, New York, 1976) by Paris Flammonde. Both of these books include detailed accounts of the Great Airship Scare of 1896-97. *The UFO Encyclopaedia* (Corgi, London, 1981) by Margaret Sachs, is exactly what it claims to be, and this book could not have been written without it. *The Report on Unidentified Flying Objects* (Doubleday, New York, 1956) by former Project Blue Book head, Captain Edward J. Ruppelt, is the classic book of its period; and its natural companion is *Project Blue Book* (Ballantine, New York,

1976), edited by Brad Steiger. For purely scientific, or pragmatic, examinations of the phenomenon, one can do no better than Dr J. Allen Hynek's authoritative works, *The UFO Experience: A Scientific Inquiry* (Abelard-Schuman, New York, 1972; Corgi, London, 1974) and *The Hynek UFO Report* (Dell, New York, 1977; Sphere, London, 1978). Also recommended in this category are *Phenomenon* (Futura, London, 1986), which is a collection of articles from the files of BUFORA (the British Unidentified Flying Object Research Association) edited by John Spencer and Hilary Evans. BUFORA's director of field operations is Jenny Randles, an admirably objective writer on the subject (though she did not agree with the premise behind *Genesis*), whose *UFO Study* (Robert Hale, London, 1981) is the best guide in print for DIY (Do It Yourself) UFO researchers.

Other UFO books relevant to this subject are: *UFOs: A Scientific Debate* (Norton Library, New York, 1974), edited by Carl Sagan and Thornton Page. *The Crack in the Universe* (Neville Spearman, Jersey, 1975) by Jean-Claude Bourret. *UFOs From Behind the Iron Curtain* (Souvenir Press, London, 1974) by Ion Hobana and Julien Weverbergh. *The Interrupted Journey* (Berkley Medallion, New York, 1974) by John G. Fuller. *Beyond Earth: Man's Contact with UFOs* (Corgi, London, 1974) by Ralph Blum with Judy Blum. *The Humanoids* (Neville Spearman, London, 1969; Futura, London, 1974/77), which is a compilation of articles from *Flying Saucer Review*, edited by Charles Bowen. *Celestial Passengers: UFOs & Space Travel* (Penguin, London, 1977) by Margaret Sachs and Ernest Jahn. *Socorro Saucer* (Fontana, London, 1976) by

Ray Stanford. *The Roswell Incident* (Granada, London, 1980) by Charles Berlitz and William Moore. *Above Top Secret* (Sidgwick & Jackson, London, 1987) by Timothy Good. *Out There* (Simon & Schuster, London, 1990) by Howard Blum. Finally, I am indebted to Phil Patton's *Dreamland* (Villard, New York, 1998) for the essential details of Area 51 and its place in the mythology of UFO and 'stealth' sightings.

Useful private press publications were: *UFO Landings Near Kirtland AFB* (William Moore Publications & Research, Burbank, California, 1985) by Bruce Maccabbe, with comments by William Moore. *The Riddle of Hangar 18* (Global Communications, New York, 1981) by Timothy Green Beckley. *Crashed UFOs: Evidence in the Search for Proof* (Publication No. F-258) by William Moore.

The indispensable book on UFO technology is *UFOlogy* (Celestial Arts, California, 1976) by physicist James M. McCampbell. Articles on the subject, and related articles, are to be found in the excellent *Worlds Beyond* (An/Or Press, the New Dimensions Foundation, Berkeley, California, 1978), edited by Larry Geis and Fabrice Florin, with Peter Beren and Aidan Kelly. Technical terms were clarified with the help of *The Dictionary of Space Technology* (Frederick Muller, London, 1982) by Joseph A. Angelo, Jr. Information on CAMS, cyborgs, other man-machine interactions, and general bio-engineering and various nightmarish experiments was found in: *As Man Becomes Machine* (Abacus, London, by David Rorvik. *Man Modified* (Paladin, London, 1969) by David Fishlock. *The People Shapers* (Futura, London, 1978) by Vance Packard. *Manipulation* (Fontana, London, 1975) by Erwin

Lausch. *The Immortalist* (Panther, London, 1973) by Alan Harrington. *PSI: Physic Discoveries Behind the Iron Curtain* (Abacus, 1977) by Sheila Ostrander & Lynn Schroeder. *Future Science* (Anchor Books, Doubleday, New York, 1977), edited by John White and Stanley Krippner. *Robots: Fact, Fiction and Prediction* (Thames and Hudson, London, 1978) by Jasia Reichardt. *The Science in Science Fiction* (Michael Joseph, London, 1982) by Peter Nicholls. *The Modern Frankenstein* (Blandford Press, Dorset, 1986) by Ray Hammond.

For many crossover subjects relating to scientific and paranormal matters, I used that indispensable and fascinating desk companion, *The Directory of Possibilities* (Webb & Bower, Devon, 1981), edited by Colin Wilson and John Grant.

U-Boat 977 (William Kimber, London, 1952) by Heinz Schaeffer includes that submarine commander's personal account of his final voyage to Argentina. The Hollow Earth (Citadel Press, New Jersey, 1969), by Dr Raymond Bernard is the standard, but hardly credible, book on this bizarre theory. Another book, *This Hollow Earth* (Sphere, London, 1972) by Warren Smith, is even less credible. *Secret Nazi Polar Expeditions* (Samisdat, Toronto, undated) by Christof Friedrich, alias Ernst Zundl, is a neo-Nazi view of this subject which, combined with the aforementioned *UFOs: Nazi Secret Weapons*, by the same author writing under a different pseudonym, is almost certainly responsible for the articles published in the neo-Nazi magazine, *Brisant*, in May 1978. The literary sources for the many Nazi-Antarctic-UFO theories are well covered in *Arktos: The Polar Myth in Science, Symbolism, and Nazi*

Survival (Thames & Hudson, 1993) by Joscelyn Godwin.

Information on United States knowledge of, and concern about, man-made UFO was found in declassified US Air Force and other intelligence documents made available through the Freedom of Information Act. These included: 'German Flying Wings Designed by Horten Brothers' by Captain N. LeBlanc, Air Corps, Headquarters Air Materiel Command, Wright Field, Dayton, Ohio, Report No F-5U-1110 NF, dated 5 July 1946. 'Ten Years Development of the Flying-Wing High Speed Fighter' by Horten Brothers, Bonn, Flying Wing Seminar, April 14, 1943, Chance Vought Aircraft (Division of United Aircraft Corporation) Report No. GTR 33, dated 18 July 1946. 'Unconventional Aircraft' by Colonel R.F. Ennis, GSC Chief, Intelligence Group, Department of the Army, Memorandum No. 7, dated 21 January 1948. 'The Mystery of the Flying Disks: A Contribution to its Possible Explanation' by Dr Eduard Ludwig, originally published in *Condor*, a German-language magazine published in Chile; 'CIA Information Report No SO DB-271/3', dated 31 July 1950, a US Air Force Memorandum For Record to justify a request for temporary (UFO related) duty for Lt. Col Sterling, Chief, Special Study Group and Dr Possony, Air Intelligence Specialist, CS-15, in Europe for a period of approximately five weeks commencing 15 May 1952; Memorandum number obscured, dated 29 April 1952. 'Military - Unconventional Aircraft', CIA Report, number obscured, dated 18 August 1953. 'Flying Saucers: Theories and Experiments', CIA Report No. 00-W-30367, dated May 27, 1954. 'Request for Intelligence Information', Headquarters Strategic Command, Offutt Air Force Base,

Omaha, Nebraska, Reference SAC D/I Control No.417, dated 28 August 1954. Air Intelligence Information Report, 'Flying Saucers', prepared by USAF 1st Lieutenant Joseph A. Calhoon, ATI Specialist, Aircraft; Report Number obscured, dated 13 September 1954.

W.A.Harbinson
London, 1991

Index

Revelation

W.A.Harbinson

Without warning, after a night of terrifying disturbance, an event of unparalleled significance occurred to shake the foundations of civilisation.
It was an event so magnificent, so extraordinary, that it would alter forever the political structure and the spiritual beliefs of Western society.
Bringing, ultimately,
the peace that passes all understanding…

'An extraordinary combination of love story, occult, horror and science fiction… an electrifying read.'
-*Bookbuyer*

'It's a great idea and Harbinson makes it work wonderfully. A book with a difference that teases the imagination with its ingenuity.'
-*Sunday Tribune*

'It has the lot – love, horror, science fiction, political and religious intrigue involving the major religions and world powers, and an extraordinary story of the resurrection of a man hailed by those religions as the saviour of the world.'
-*Bookseller*

All at Sea on the Ghost Ship

W.A.Harbinson

In the year 2001 the son of bestselling novelist and biographer W.A.Harbinson offered his father a free trip as the sole passenger on a container ship that would sail from Shanghai to Haifa, with many other ports in between. Once on board the ship, Harbinson found that he was the only white face in a crew composed solely of Indian officers and Chinese seamen. He also realised that while he had previously sailed on passenger liners, he was 'all at sea' when it came to a working ship.

All at Sea on the Ghost Ship is Harbinson's account of his unpredictable, always fascinating voyage. Rich in feeling, acute in observation, and often very funny, *All at Sea on the Ghost Ship* is a book to give us hope and make us smile. It is also an intriguing, rare glimpse into the mind of a writer.

The Writing Game

Recollections of an Occasional Bestselling Author

W.A.Harbinson

The Writing Game is an autobiographical account of the life and times of a professional writer who has managed to survive the minefield of publishing for over thirty years.

Unlike most books on the subject, ***The Writing Game*** does not try to tell you how to write, or even how to get published. Instead, it focuses with gimlet-eyed clarity on the ups and downs of a unique, always unpredictable business.

On the one hand, a compelling look at a life lived on the edge, under the constant threat of failure, both artistic and financial, on the other, an unusually frank self-portrait enlivened with colourful snapshots of editors, fellow authors and show business celebrities, ***The Writing Game*** succeeds, as few other books have done, in showing how one professional, uncelebrated writer has managed to stay afloat in the stormy waters of conglomerate publishing.

Here, for the first time, a working author tells it like it really is.

More information on books by W.A.Harbinson can be found at:

www.waharbinson.eu.com